39 WAYS
TO NOT KILL YOUR BEST FRIEND

Tales of Caution for Dogs Lovers

39 WAYS

TO NOT KILL YOUR BEST FRIEND

Tales of Caution for Dogs Lovers

Dr Judith Samson-French

Published by Meerkat Media 2013

No reproduction of any part of this book may take place without the written permission of Meerkat Media, except in the case of brief quotations.

39 Ways To Not Kill Your Best Friend – Tales of Caution For Dog Lovers may be purchased at special discount for bulk purchases and fundraising through www.dogswithnonames.com or Meerkat Media, Box 1040, Bragg Creek, AB, T0L 0K0, Canada.

First Printing 2013

Library and Archives Canada Cataloguing in Publication

Samson, Judith, 1960-, author
39 ways not to kill your best friend / Dr Judith Samson-French.

ISBN 978-0-9917240-2-4 (pbk.)

1. Dogs--Health. I. Title. II. Title: Thirty-nine ways not to kill your best friend.

SF427.S24 2013 636.7'083 C2013-903068-9

Cover and text design by Sue Impey, By Design Desktop Publishing Inc.

Contents

Prologue

It is with great love that I perform the act of killing. This is an act I have committed hundreds of time, out of necessity and always with compassion. You see, I have a license to kill; indeed, I get paid to commit the act. As a doctor of veterinary medicine, I was taught many years ago how to perform this act, and it has become a regular part of my practice. Yet it is never easy. Even though each incident unfolds differently from the previous one, putting another being to death – watching the last breath exhaled – is always, and will always be, painful. People come to me knowing it will be done gently and with dignity. I do not like to be known for this. It is not a skill I possess; rather, it is a state of mind, one in which the brain comes into unison with the heart. If the two do not instinctively and rationally come together, I will decline to commit the act of killing, as I feel it would be done for the wrong reasons. Legally, as long as the other being is not human, I can exercise this privilege of decision-making as I see fit.

Our modern society, fast-paced and burdened with so many pursuits, prefers not to dwell on end-of-life issues. In accordance with that preference, I never refer to the act of terminating a life as "killing." Euthanasia is the euphemism that must be used to soften the impact of our deadly actions. Euthanasia is defined as "an act of painlessly killing, especially at the patient's request, a person or animal suffering from an incurable condition." However, the term is often wrongly used. Early in my career, I worked at a municipal animal shelter where, thankfully, I performed spays and neuters on animals to be adopted. Unfortunately, many animals at the shelter had not captured the hearts of people coming in for adoptions, and were ultimately euthanized by the resident veterinarian to make room for others. Abandonment was the reason they were put to death. Abandonment, to satisfy the definition of euthanasia, had become "an incurable condition." The term "euthanasia" seemed to make the weekly killing and disposal of healthy dogs more bearable for all concerned.

Just like their human counterparts, companion animals suffer from natural causes of death. The act of euthanasia is much more socially acceptable when a being is faced with advanced age and its inevitable debilitating conditions. As in humans, aging in animals will bring forth three major categories of serious health conditions that take them another step closer to natural death: degeneration and failure of organs, such as hearts and kidneys; the very broad category of cancer; and the debilitating conditions of the mind, such as dementia and Alzheimer's disease, referred to as cognitive dysfunction in animals.

In the case of humans, hospitalization, specialized medical home care, and palliative care provide respite for both the affected persons and their loved ones. For several reasons, these options become rapidly exhausted for aging pets. Financial limitations on the owner's part, for example, may limit end-of-life options. In other cases, the intractable character of some animals during the required confinement for advanced medical care, such as a perpetual intravenous drip, severely restricts end-of-life care.

At some point, an aging pet afflicted with a debilitating disease will invariably suffer from a decrease in quality of life, but when does living become unbearable for the animal? When should we decide to humanely end the life of a companion animal because there is too much suffering that cannot be attenuated? But I am clearly getting ahead of myself here, since this a very emotionally charged topic, rife with countless cultural barriers. Together, in this book, we will explore the reasons why so many of our canine companions meet an untimely death. It is often due to simple ignorance, negligence, naïve good intentions or flagrant abuse that our best friends suffer a painful or abrupt ending. In some cases, death arrives as deliverance, naturally and miserably. In other cases, it becomes our moral responsibility to take action and clean up the mess that fellow human beings have created for animals. Euthanasia is then performed, without rancor but always with sadness.

Although identifying details have been altered to protect the anonymity of all involved, *39 Ways To Not Kill Your Best Friend* is not a work of fiction. The stories you will find on these pages, about more than 39 real-life canine companions, are all true. These events should not have happened, but they did, and our challenge now is to learn from them. By reading about these dogs – what went wrong for them and how it could have been prevented – you may be able to protect your own pet from a similar fate.

A kilogram of dog food will be donated to dogs with no names roaming unclaimed on First Nations lands with the purchase of this book.

Judith Samson–French DVM

This book is dedicated to all the countless loving companion dogs who lost their lives too early.

CHAPTER 1

BDLD (Big Dog Little Dog): deadly encounters

The first entry in Photon's file was BDLD, the veterinary abbreviation for "big dog little dog". By the time he arrived at our clinic, Photon, a middle-aged, mixed-breed dog with predominant Spaniel traits, was at death's door. As the little dog lay on the table, his worried owner reviewed the radiographs with us: as a radiologist in human medicine, he was quite capable of understanding the gravity of Photon's situation.

In truth, Photon's owner could not quite believe what had befallen his pet. Not for a moment had Dr. Corbett ever thought there was anything wrong with the "let them fight it out – they will sort it out" approach to dogfights. While at the dog park earlier that day, Photon had met a German Shepherd cross and, as expected, the ritual canine greeting soon occurred: both dogs became intensely engaged in sniffing each other's private parts. They quickly discovered that both were missing their testicles, as both had been neutered. Suddenly, for no apparent reason that either owner could fathom, the hackles of the Shepherd cross went up and, in a flash, the dogs were embroiled in a frenzied, snarling struggle. Watching, Dr. Corbett thought the brawl would be over in seconds; once both dogs figured who was "top dog," they'd ease up, and then get along fine on subsequent encounters.

Dr. Corbett was right on only one point: the skirmish was over in seconds. Photon yelped sharply as he went down, and he stayed down as the other dog was pulled away. Panting heavily, the small Spaniel mix lay where he'd fallen, unable to stand up. At that point, his owner scooped him up and rushed him to our clinic, where we immediately began working on him.

The injured dog was clearly in distress, and not a pretty sight. Besides a couple of perforating bite wounds to Photon's neck, severe skin hemorrhages were evident over his entire abdomen. As is common in dog bite incidents, strong pressure from the larger dog's biting teeth had caused trauma and bleeding of the inner layers of the little dog's skin, causing mottled discoloration but no actual perforations of the skin. If only the skin is traumatized, such a wound will likely heal over a few days to weeks, with or without sloughing, and with the help of antibiotics and anti-inflammatory meds, depending on the extent of the damage. In Photon's case, unfortunately, the damage was also internal: either his spleen or liver had sustained a tear. The little fellow was bleeding internally into his abdomen.

In the end, the physical damage he'd sustained was simply too much for the small Spaniel mix. Before a blood transfusion could be initiated, Photon passed away from his injuries before the eyes of his distraught owner. As shocked as he was by the rapid set of events, Dr. Corbett was equally distressed by his own role in his pet's death: he knew he could have prevented it.

Dogfights do not happen only at dog parks and off-leash areas, nor do they occur only between dogs unfamiliar with each other. Sometimes they occur in the same household, as in the case of Dell and Pixel. These two sisters are Great Pyrenees-Collie crosses, each weighing around forty kilograms and fully grown by two years of age.

Mr. Nicks, a computer programmer, initially intended to adopt only one dog, but when the time came to pick up Pixel, Dell was the last remaining puppy of a litter of eleven, and no one was coming for her. So Mr. Nicks, being a compassionate guy and unaware of potential future difficulties that could arise during interactions between two dogs of the same sex, took both puppies home with him.

Until all the trouble began, Dell and Pixel had been getting along well. They shared a large outside enclosure, and a ten-by-twelve-foot pen inside in a double-door garage, where they played nicely with each other. They went for daily walks on their leashes, and behaved well with other dogs and people they met along the way.

While they were home alone one day, one of the sisters decided to break the peace treaty. When Mr. Nicks arrived home from work that day, he found both dogs covered in blood and limping badly. At first glance, it looked like a horror show gone wild: Dell and Pixel had had a fight in his absence and, judging by the injuries to both dogs, there had not been a clear winner. Roughly the same number of stitches was required to mend the lacerations on each dog's front legs and neck: about forty per dog. During their stay in the veterinary hospital, neither dog seemed bothered by the other's presence, but then again they were heavily sedated following their wound repairs.

Over the following month, Dell and Pixel returned to our emergency services twice more for bite wound repairs. Obviously, the aggression level between them was rapidly escalating, as the injuries were more severe each time. Mr. Nicks faced a tough question: could Dell and Pixel continue to share the same home without literally killing each other?

To understand aggression in dogs, we must travel back in time and look at their closest living ancestors and relatives: wolves, wild dogs, and dingoes. All share similar social behavior, typical of life within a pack. Without a doubt, dogs are pack animals and, like all pack animals, they must have a social order to maintain harmony and avoid infighting. Feral dogs, which live their daily lives together just like wolves do, must work out a permanent pack structure. However, companion dogs that work or play together but do not live together need only to agree on workable rules for the interaction time, not on a permanent pack structure. Therein lies an important distinction: successful interactive co-existence dictates that dogs living together, such as Dell and Pixel, must establish a permanent pack order, while dogs meeting on occasion, such as Photon and the German Shepherd cross at the park, must establish workable rules only for their few specific encounters.

So why do dogs fight? The answer is often unknown to us, and frequently depends on whether dogs are trying to establish a permanent pack order or workable rules. In the wild, a canine misfit within a pack would usually leave the pack in search of another one where it would be better accepted. For obvious reasons, this escape mechanism is not available to most dogs living in the same household, and it thus becomes the responsibility of their owners to keep them safe.

Among dogs, there appear to be established rules or guidelines for maintaining good social order. Growing up together and sharing the same home since puppyhood, as Dell and Pixel did, offers no guarantee of harmony when dogs reach maturity. Dominance is often fully expressed at maturity, which for canines is two years of age. So when a dog owner raves about how cute and cuddly his Rottweiler puppy is, and how well he sleeps on the couch, I can't help but think to myself, "You ain't seen nothin' yet!" In reality, this is the same Rottweiler that, at two years of age, will growl menacingly at its owner when the latter attempts to heave his full-grown Rottie off the couch.

Some people fear that dogs that develop aggression toward other dogs are at risk of developing aggression toward humans as well. Not necessarily so; dog-directed aggression is a poor prognostic indicator of whether a dog will develop aggression towards humans. These are usually two distinct and unrelated traits. Remember, dog-directed aggression often relates to establishing working rules or a pack order among dogs; humans are left out of this arrangement entirely.

For this reason, humans should establish themselves as clear pack leaders, not alpha dogs. Our clever canine friends can't be fooled into thinking we are dogs, and therefore we are best left out of the pack structure altogether. At the same time, dogs need to develop confidence in their owners as trustworthy leaders, who will protect them and keep them safe in situations involving other dogs. Remember, unlike wolves, socially inept or "misfit" dogs at the park cannot run away and find another pack; they are stuck dealing with whatever dogs are present at that moment, on or off leash. The key factor here is *at that moment*. Many dog groups will work out rules, or a hierarchy, that will shift according to the activity they are involved in at the time, or at the moment. So the alpha role is a fluid one that can change as events or influencing factors change in the group. This is precisely why it can be so difficult to determine which is the alpha dog when breaking up a dogfight. If an individual must intervene, s/he should focus solely on stopping the fight, and avoid dispensing punishment or making accusatory eye contact. Whether we like it or not, dogs are social animals that will ultimately work through establishing a pack order. And some may get seriously hurt in the process. The frustrating part for us humans is that pack formation is like a secret society – and let's face it, we are not privy to the special handshake that is the price of admission.

Although the premise is not yet fully understood or definitively established, the pairing of dogs of different sexes in the same house is often easier on the owner and promises greater harmony. Nature will favor the formation of a pack in such an instance: the male dog will naturally become the top male dog, and the female dog will assume the role of the top female dog. This would be much the same dynamic as between a reigning king and a queen, each having their own throne, as opposed to two princes or two princesses vying for a single throne.

When living together in a household, female dogs such as Dell and Pixel are more likely to fight to the death than males, because females apparently have a harder time working out a stable pack order. We do not know for sure whether spaying females and neutering males can help in this regard, or to what extent it might; but we do know that there are plenty of dogfights involving spayed or neutered dogs.

Aggression between dogs may occur at all ages, regardless of sex, and usually develops around a guarding obsession for certain resources – toys, food, water bowls, even a certain person or a certain place in the house or yard. Dogs will fight to gain or retain the right to a certain resource, and for this reason the obvious must be stated: in multiple-dog households, dogs should be fed apart from each other, and toys and chews should be given to individual dogs in their own personal space. You – yes, you reading this book – may be an "object of possession" for your dogs. How you dispense your words, your greetings, your eye contact, and your affection may interfere with the stabilization of a pack order. Again, not knowing the secret handshake to the secret society of dogs, we must be very observant and remain neutral in all aspects until clues become evident.

A word of caution: one of the most disheartening scenarios is for an owner to drop off his BDLD-injured dog at a veterinary hospital, then have to drive himself to a human hospital to get stitches on a bitten hand or wrist, along with a tetanus injection. Invariably, Health Services then get involved to establish whether the dog that did the biting is properly vaccinated against rabies. If not, an owner must be prepared for the ordeal that will surely follow and all the headaches that go with it. Therefore, the *last* resort for breaking up a dogfight is to grab a dog by the neck where all the biting is happening. If you do so, dear dog lover, you will undoubtedly become an accidental victim. If you simply *must* intervene to separate fighting dogs, say, "No!" repeatedly in a firm voice, and grab the dogs by their tails – but be willing to let go fast if a dog turns on you. Better yet, if you have access to a garden hose, aim a blast of water at the dogs' faces. Or if you have access to a handy object like a folding chair or a large piece of wood, use it to pry apart the dogs' jaws instead of using your hands to pull the animals apart.

So what happened to Dell and Pixel, the warring sisters? Three years after their frequent fighting episodes, both are still living in the same house, aggression free. Mr. Nicks took a chance by keeping both dogs, as one could easily have killed the other. Once he had made that decision, he managed the problem as well as he could. Dell and Pixel slept in separate crates at night, and were provided plenty of time apart during the day. Often, one stayed in the house while the other enjoyed the outside enclosure. And when they were together, Mr. Nicks deliberately became very indifferent and neutral in his attention toward both dogs. When he arrived home, he avoided creating a high level of excitement by not playing and talking enthusiastically to his dogs. Instead, he pretended they did not exist. As soon as they both calmed down, he greeted them with furtive eye contact and a quick pat on the neck.

Plenty of time apart, long walks, and a more neutral demeanor from their owner have allowed Dell and Pixel to harmoniously share a home together. But, as Mr. Nicks knows, a lapse into old habits could spell disaster for his beloved Great Pyrenees-Collie girls. And so he remains ever vigilant.

As a dog lover, you can...

- Play the role of pack leader – not alpha dog – if you have multiple dogs.

- Feed your dogs separately, and dispense toys and treats in the same manner.

- Avoid grabbing dogs by the neck to break up a dogfight; rely instead on safer methods that do not put you in harm's way.

CHAPTER 2

Choked to Death:
training collars for dogs

L illy had presence. Each time she came to see us, she would strut into the veterinary hospital as though she owned it, with great confidence. On a leash, she was well behaved, but she did have an insatiable yen for crotches – especially those of unsuspecting two-legged beings – and would seek them out for an exuberant muzzle nuzzle. She saved her favors for humans, scornfully ignoring all other four-legged animals, as though they were beneath her.

This was surprising, considering that Lilly was nothing like the dainty princess she thought she was. At eleven months of age, the sturdy little Boxer was still a puppy and not particularly regal-looking; she had neither ears cropped nor tail docked. Mrs. Henley frequently received credit for this, as she had gone out of her way to find a purebred dog that had not been "mutilated" (her words). She wanted a companion dog, not a show dog. As dog owners often do, Mrs. Henley chose a breed of dog she was familiar with, with nostalgic connections to her childhood. And that was precisely the reason that Mrs. Henley had selected a Boxer when she adopted Lilly. Given her strong stance against cosmetic surgeries, however,

Mrs. Henley was sending rather mixed signals regarding the care of her puppy, as you will see here.

When Lilly came into our office one day recently, she displayed neither her proud strut nor her usual crotch-sniffing habit. Something was clearly amiss: she was unusually subdued and had a hoarse, hacking cough. Her eyes, usually bright and filled with mischief, had changed in appearance: the rims looked swollen and edematous (fluid-filled), and the inner eyelids were an angry cherry red rather than a healthy pale pink. To my surprise, Lilly was wearing a choke collar.

"Mrs. Henley," I said, frowning, "Since when does Lilly wear a choke collar?"

"She's just started obedience classes," Mrs. Henley responded, "And the trainer recommended a choke collar for Lilly, to prevent her from pulling on her walks – you know how she always goes for people's crotches!"

So now the issue was becoming clearer. The night before had been the first class for both Mrs. Henley and Lilly, and obviously Mrs. Henley had been too forceful with the choke collar. Like so many other owners, she was simply too inexperienced to handle this type of training tool which, according to some vocal opponents, belongs in the archives of a dog museum.

The choke collar is problematic in dog training for a couple of reasons: firstly, it is based on the principle of pain infliction to achieve compliance; and secondly, it is next to impossible for the average dog owner to understand and use properly. Choke collars were popular in the 1970s, but it was time for Mrs. Henley to fast-forward to the twenty-first century and learn newer – and more humane – training techniques. Because choke collars work on the principle of hurting a dog if it does not behave as its owner wishes, the timing of well-placed punishment is all too important. Unfortunately, Mrs. Henley, with only one obedience class under her belt, had not yet developed any expertise with this tool.

Mrs. Henley was not alone in this predicament: the vast majority of dog owners who try a choke collar are neither willing to use it correctly nor capable of doing so. First of all, it must be fitted properly to a dog's neck. Second, if the punishment (yanking upward on the chain, assuming the chain is indeed properly fitted to the dog's neck) is not dispensed properly, the collar becomes ineffective and cruel. The only reason a choked dog will eventually stop pulling is because it hurts if he does not stop pulling.

This was precisely what had happened to Lilly. Lilly kept pulling on her choke chain, not understanding what was asked of her because of the erratic timing and inconsistent strength of corrections, until a frustrated Mrs. Henley finally yanked too hard on the choke in a backward motion to bring Lilly back to a heeling position by her owner's side. The pressure of the choke chain on Lilly's neck had been too strong and, as a result, likely damaged or irritated the cartilage rings of her trachea. This was what caused her frequent and intermittent hacking and coughing. As well, the inner eyelids of both eyes appeared severely hemorrhaged.

Any time a clinician sees evidence of hemorrhage anywhere on the body, a list of differentials should be drawn up; possibilities include rat poison ingestion, hypertension, drug-induced platelet dysfunction, and autoimmune diseases such as hemolytic anemia. However, a clinician must remember this basic principle: when we hear hoof beats, we should think horses, not zebras – unless of course we live in Africa. In Lilly's case, what was the horse? Obviously the choke chain! Without a doubt, the most common cause of subconjunctival (inner eyelids) redness or hemorrhage in a young dog is a strong correction via a neck collar, and choke chains are frequently implicated. As a result of excessive pressure on the neck area, the jugular veins become obstructed, causing an increase in blood pressure in the head whereby the blood vessels in the conjunctiva (eyelids) rupture, giving the eyeballs a scary, swollen, red appearance.

Since Lilly's eyes were likely to get better on their own, professional neglect was appropriate in this case. Most often, the hemorrhage and swelling associated with the eyes subside naturally within a few days. As far as her tracheal irritation, we were hopeful that the cartilage rings had not been permanently damaged, but a short course of anti-inflammatory medication was prescribed to decrease the inflammation associated with Lilly's coughing. In the meantime, we advised Mrs. Henley to avoid the use of any neck collars, and resort to either a body harness or a head halter for a while. The use of a choke collar as a training tool is controversial and, considering her inexperience, Mrs. Henley was ill advised by her trainer to employ it.

There are many ways to train a dog to walk on a leash in a civilized manner. The training goals should always be as follows: to achieve the desired response, such as heeling, effortlessly; to reinforce the behavior positively; and then to have the dog repeat the desired behavior on cue. For practical purposes, dog owners should select whatever method or technique is the most effective and most humane in soliciting the desired response. This is why choke collars remain controversial: they do not fulfill these two criteria.

Prong collars also arouse their fair share of discontent in the dog world, but if used correctly (and properly fitted), they at least should not result in the dog pulling persistently, since they produce an unpleasant and uncomfortable sensation. Dear dog lover, remember that the opposition reflex is a normal reflex, and present in all mammals: an animal will naturally pull away from restraint. This certainly helps explain why dogs pull ahead when pulled back on their leash.

In Lilly's case, the spunky little Boxer had no lingering ill effects from the choke collar episode, but this is not true of all dogs. Choke collar misuse can have tragic outcomes, as it did for a dog named Blue Dog, who met a fatal end because he was wearing one. A tricolour Border Collie, Blue Dog was mildly hyperactive when he was not working, which was five days a week. But Blue Dog was a true weekend warrior, and his personality blossomed whenever he was out herding sheep on the 160 acres of land that his owner, Mr. Leaky, kept for weekend getaways. A shy but successful oil executive, Mr. Leaky enjoyed country living away from the office, raising Romney sheep for meat and wool. A true gentleman farmer in every sense, Mr. Leaky admittedly did not know much about sheep rearing: he relied on Walter, his ranch hand, to assist in all practical aspects of farming. Unfortunately, Walter had little affinity for Blue Dog, and usually kept him enclosed in his chain-link pen.

One frosty morning, much to his horror, Walter made a grisly discovery when he went out to feed the dog: Blue Dog was hanging by his neck from the top of the chain-link fence. The dog had tried to escape his pen by climbing over the fence, and the ring of his choke collar had snagged on the top spike. He had already maneuvered his body over the fence, and had not been able to free himself by pulling upward on the ring. By the time Walter discovered him, Blue Dog was hanging limp, his eyeballs protruding and reddened. Sadly, it was too late for anyone to save him: Blue Dog was stiff and dead. A necropsy (the equivalent of an autopsy in humans) was not requested, as the cause of death was known: strangulation and perhaps cervical (neck) dislocation. Had a necropsy been performed, Blue's lungs would probably have exhibited some changes compatible with respiratory impairment, depending on how long the hapless animal had struggled to free himself.

Would Blue Dog have survived if he had worn a regular fabric or leather collar? Possibly so: he may have had more time to free himself than with the choke collar, which had instantaneously tightened its grip. For that reason, a choke collar should *never* be worn as an everyday collar with tags but rather only while a dog is in training and closely supervised.

Woodruff's brush with death serves as another powerful reminder of the potential dangers of choke collars. Woodruff did the alligator roll with his choke collar on, and likely saw the white light at the end of the tunnel when he nearly choked himself to death. A Retriever cross, Woodruff was wearing a choke collar with his metals tags attached to it on the day of his close call. This was, in fact, his everyday outfit: the collar was never removed from his neck, and over time had rubbed his fur grey.

Woodruff was having a lazy dog day afternoon, napping in the sun on the wooden deck out back when, unbeknown to him, his tags slipped down between two of the wooden planks. When the Retriever woke up, he tried to lift his head but was unable to do so. His metal tags, now wedged at perpendicular angles beneath the wooden planks, fastened his neck firmly to the deck. In a panic, Woodruff repeatedly yanked his neck away from the deck, and as he did, his choke collar grew tighter and tighter. Fear-stricken, Woodruff finally started to roll over on himself like an alligator.

Thankfully, his owner was at home. Alarmed by all the commotion outside, he rushed to Woodruff's rescue, in time to prevent the dog's death but too late to prevent physical damage. In his struggle, Woodruff had nearly strangled himself, and within an hour had developed dyspnea (abnormal breathing) and audible lung sounds. At the veterinary hospital, the frightened animal was treated for pulmonary edema and, within a day, was ready to go home. Would Woodruff have experienced the same trauma and near-death ending had he worn a regular collar instead of the ever-tightening choke collar? Perhaps not.

As these cases so vividly illustrate, choker chains do not work very well for the average dog owner, and may not be worth the risk to your pet. Other training tools, such as no-pull harnesses and head halters, are effective alternatives and should be considered.

As a dog lover, you can…

- Avoid the use of choke collars with your dog, if at all possible.

- Be aware if you do use a choke collar for training purposes, do so only under the guidance of a qualified dog trainer.

- Remove the dog's choke collar whenever you are not there to supervise.

- Rely on safer dog training tools if possible, such as no-pull harnesses or head halters.

CHAPTER 3

Leaving a Deadly Mess: antifreeze spills

Capone lived and worked on the land, and loved it. His job was not to keep predators away, but rather to keep sheep together, day in day out. He excelled at herding; in fact, he thrived on it. This was hardly surprising, since Capone's lineage of red Border Collies is known for their tremendous work instincts, not their conformation. His drive to work was so strong that Capone often did not take the time to eat his food, however exhausted or hungry he might be.

At a mere sixteen kilograms, however, this Border Collie was a lightweight among members of his breed. Since puppyhood, Capone had been encouraged to learn and obey one more command: eat! So the distressed dog was thoroughly bewildered when he was admitted to our emergency ward after a dietary indiscretion. As we soon discovered, antifreeze poisoning was the cause of his deteriorating condition. In animals, antifreeze is known as a classic killer, due to its sweet taste and scary fast mode of action.

Had Capone really slurped up antifreeze, when he usually did not even take the time to eat his food? Indeed he had – but it took the investigative talents of Allan, Capone's owner, to figure out the details of what had happened. That day, Allan had all of his farm vehicles in the workshop for re-hauling, which included changing and refilling antifreeze. Although the antifreeze had been diluted, we calculated that Capone would have had to lick only seven to fourteen teaspoons of the liquid spilled on the workshop floor from the three trucks, to show the clinical signs he was now exhibiting. In retrospect, Allan thought this was very possible, especially since Capone's water bowl outside had frozen over and the dog was probably thirsty.

Was it too late to save Capone's life? A little math and a bit of insight into the chemical composition of antifreeze and its mode of action will give you some clues. Currently, there are three commonly used antifreeze solutions on the market: methanol, ethylene glycol and propylene glycol. Of these, ethylene glycol is the most dangerous and is highly toxic to pets. Although toxicities can occur with the other substances, they are generally less severe and more easily managed. Most commercial antifreeze products contain 95 to 97 percent ethylene glycol. As we had calculated earlier, the minimum lethal dose of undiluted ethylene glycol antifreeze for Capone was seven teaspoons. When ingested by animals, ethylene glycol causes profound metabolic acidosis and acute renal failure (death of the kidneys). In most cases of ethylene glycol poisoning, vomiting occurs within the first few hours. Then, within one to six hours, signs of depression, ataxia (wobbly gait), weakness, panting, drinking and urinating excessively become apparent. Somewhere between eighteen and thirty-six hours, the kidneys will fail, and survival becomes very unlikely.

In the liver, ethylene glycol is metabolized into glycoaldehyde (even more toxic than ethylene glycol), which will metabolize into glyoxylic acid. The presence of these metabolites in the body causes the damage to the kidneys and central nervous system. Clearly, time is of the essence: the goal of treatment for ethylene glycol ingestion is to slow down this breakdown of its metabolites, so they can be absorbed and eliminated with minimal harm to the animal.

Since peak levels of ethylene glycol are reached within one to four hours after ingestion, induction of emesis (vomiting) is only helpful with recent exposures (within one hour). Similarly, both stomach lavage (cleansing) and the addition of activated charcoal to slow down absorption of toxins are helpful, but are considered effective only within an hour or so of ingestion and before the manifestation of clinical signs. The antidote, which goes by many names, works by competitively inhibiting the breakdown of ethylene glycol. One vial of the antidote, at a cost of several hundreds of dollars, is administered to dogs intravenously over a thirty-six hour period, along with aggressive intravenous fluid therapy. If the dog is already beyond the phase of excessive urination (polyuric) and into the phase of too little urination (anuric), the prognosis becomes extremely grave: this is a sure indication that the kidneys are shutting down, likely irreversibly.

If the antidote is not available, vodka (ethanol) IV at a specific concentration can serve as a substitute to compete with the breakdown of ethylene glycol; however, vodka has several unfavorable side effects, such as depression. Until recently, vodka was a mainstay of all medicine cabinets in emergency veterinary hospitals, specifically for this form of toxicity.

In Capone's case, it was already 9:15 in the evening when he was admitted to Emergency with symptoms of vomiting, walking erratically, and having difficulty standing up properly. Allan had worked on his vehicles until 1:30 that afternoon, and Capone was at his side the entire time. Since Allan had tidied up his tools but not cleaned up the liquid mess on the floor, he thought it likely that Capone had licked the small pool of fluid under his black truck, where significant spillage of antifreeze (ethylene glycol) had occurred. The spillage there was very likely around one to two cups in volume. Both Allan and Capone had exited the workshop around 2:00 that afternoon. The workshop was locked behind them, so there was no chance that Capone had returned to it later in the day.

That meant that the antifreeze ingestion had occurred over seven hours ago, and Capone had likely ingested a fatal amount, given his extreme thirst from not having fresh, unfrozen water to drink. The math was anything but encouraging: too much ethylene glycol in the body, and more than seven hours to absorb it in the alimentary tract. This could have dire consequences for the ailing Border Collie.

But Allan was not ready to give up on his companion: he elected to treat Capone with the antidote even though the prognosis was poor. Within two hours of aggressive intravenous therapy and with a proper dose of the antidote on board (only half a vial was used, based on Capone's size), the dog passed some crystals in his urine, which confirmed his toxicosis. In the early hours of the morning, Capone fell into a coma and stopped producing urine completely. The next step in Capone's treatment protocol was to move on to peritoneal dialysis, which unfortunately was not available at the time in the ward. To have access to this form of treatment, Capone would need to be transported to the Veterinary University Hospital, six hours away by car. With a heavy heart, Allan decided against pursuing this medical option, as his dog's prognosis was very grave.

Only one option remained, and that was to deliver a faithful and loyal pet from any further suffering. So while Capone was still deep in the slumber of his coma, he was given a euthanizing solution in his IV drip. Watching, and no doubt torn by feelings of guilt, Allan held back tears and remained at his beloved friend's side as Capone slipped away, at the tender age of five years, due to kidney failure.

Antifreeze poisoning is avoidable. First of all, we can use safer products that do not contain ethylene glycol. Since ethylene glycol is so toxic to our companion animals, we should search for antifreeze that contains propylene glycol as the main ingredient, as it is approximately three times less toxic to dogs than ethylene glycol. Automotive antifreezes that contain 50 percent or more propylene glycol are safer and will not cause the serious kidney damage observed with ethylene glycol poisoning. (Note the use of the word "safer" and not "safe."). Finally, propylene glycol antifreeze is less likely to result in fatal ingestion as it does not have the characteristic sweet taste of ethylene glycol.

We can also prevent our dogs from wandering into areas of risk (for example, a neighbor's garage where there is an antifreeze spill). If ingestion has already occurred, or is suspected, immediate medical attention is the key to survival. Depending on the amount swallowed, death can occur within a mere eight hours of ingestion in dogs; for cats, the time is even shorter.

Capone did not deserve such a heartbreaking ending, inadvertent as it was. This energetic little Border Collie had many years of living left to do, and much love left to share... as do all of our pets. Let's keep them safe.

As a dog lover, you can...

- Avoid using ethylene alcohol antifreeze products; instead, choose products that contain propylene glycol, which is less toxic for dogs, bio-degradable and recyclable.

- Keep your dog away from areas where he could ingest antifreeze.

- Seek immediate veterinary attention for your dog if you suspect antifreeze ingestion.

CHAPTER 4

Home Alone:
separation anxiety

Lord Underfoot came to us as an abandoned dog at the age of three years. He was very sweet, but somehow we could sense that all was not right with this dog. For one thing, Lord Underfoot was always underfoot, never claiming his own space. And his eyes darted anywhere and everywhere, seemingly without focus. He was intensely restless, as if always looking for something – but what?

Although I had my suspicions, it was not until later that I discovered all the answers to the puzzle that was Lord Underfoot. All we knew for sure when he arrived at our clinic was that he had no one – and nowhere to go. On the eve of his family's departure for another continent, Lord Underfoot had been casually dropped off at a neighbor's house.

"We're off to Australia in the morning," his owner announced, "And we're not taking Lord Underfoot with us. Can you please take him to the SPCA for us, or whatever....? We've already dropped off our other dog, a little Boston Terrier, with another neighbor. G'day mate!" And off they went, without a backward glance – out of Lord Underfoot's sight and out of his life.

The little Boston Terrier found a home very quickly. But Lord Underfoot presented a challenge: although very gentle, he was not well mannered at all. Worse yet, the same night he was dropped off at the neighbor's house, he'd had what seemed to be a small seizure. He apparently fell to his side, and feebly flailed about with his front legs. He did not involuntarily urinate or defecate, as is often the case with full-blown seizures, but he seemed unresponsive when his name was called. Afraid that the local shelter would euthanize the orphan dog, another sympathetic neighbor decided to take matters in her own hands: she decided to bring Lord Underfoot to our veterinary hospital for an assessment and an appeal to our sense of humanity.

As soon as I laid eyes on Lord Underfoot, memories from my genetics classes came flooding back to me. Initially I saw the whole dog, but with a nagging sense of unease that I could not explain. Then I began systematically peeling away the layers, one at a time, just like an onion, to get at the truth about this intriguing fellow. Here's what I saw: Lord Underfoot was a mostly white Border Collie; he had blue eyes; he had some merle coloring (a recognized and distinguishable grey mottled color); and oddly, he did not seem to focus at all.

Was it not obvious? I clapped my hands: no response. I blew a whistle: nothing. I threw some car keys around: still nothing. I stomped my feet and, finally, Lord Underfoot turned toward me. Did he actually hear that, or was it the vibration of the floor? Later tests confirmed that he was attuned to vibrations and visual clues, but missed all the auditory ones. No question, Lord Underfoot was deaf. And he had not been trained in the appropriate manner for deaf dogs, so he behaved a bit on the wild side. He had likely become dependent on his little Boston Terrier mate to help him navigate through daily living, but now they had been permanently separated.

Lord Underfoot was on his own in an unfamiliar world, and understandably wary of his new surroundings. Within his first twenty-four hours with us, he served us three more challenges: he suffered another mild seizure; he marked everywhere with small dribbles of urine, as unneutered males often do; and when we kenneled him overnight, he kept himself very busy biting and destroying his kennel door.

"God does not love a coward," is a favorite quote from an older client of mine who established a homestead in the area sixty-five years ago. In this case, the coward's way to deal with Lord Underfoot would be to take him to the local shelter and hope that, miraculously, their low-kill policy would vaporize overnight and be replaced with a no-kill policy instead. Despite everything, that was just not an option for us. No, the humane way to deal with Lord Underfoot was to treat him as a dog with special needs, and there was the ultimate challenge. This dog had a whole list of special needs that demanded to be addressed: deafness, territorial marking, separation anxiety, and possibly idiopathic (i.e., cause unknown to the medical community) epilepsy.

Fortunately, the territorial marking was promptly cured with proper anesthesia, pain management, and a couple cuts with a scalpel blade to remove his testicles. For the time being, we simply ignored the seizures; we would address that problem later when we had further evidence of them. Managing his emotional stress was a priority, but we dealt with it by establishing a strict routine of activities for him. Really, the main problems that would make adoption difficult were his deafness and his separation anxiety.

Was his deafness permanent? Very likely. Since Lord Underfoot did not show any signs of current or previous ear infections, we determined that he had probably been born deaf by looking at his phenotype (physical expression of his genes, his physical characteristics).

How common is deafness in dogs? The answer depends on the breed. There are several breeds at risk for congenital deafness. They include Dalmatians, English Setters, English Cocker Spaniels, Bull Terriers, Border Collies, Australian Cattle Dogs, Whippets, Catahoula (listen to how this word rolls off the tongue with such joy!) Leopard Dogs, and Jack Russell Terriers. Overall, there are over thirty-five breeds of dogs reported to have hereditary deafness. Ethically, dogs found to have inherited deafness in one or both ears should definitely be removed from breeding programs. Interestingly enough, certain markings on a dog will increase the odds of deafness. For instance, a predominance of white color, the presence of merle color, and blue eyes often tag along with the deafness gene. Lord Underfoot displayed all of these characteristics.

Also, a study from the UK (Prevalence of unilateral and bilateral deafness in border collies and association with phenotype. *Journal of Veterinary Internal Medicine,* November/December 2006; *20(6):* 1355–62.) described that the odds of deafness were increased by a factor of fourteen for Border Collies with deaf dams, relative to the odds for dogs with normal dams, after adjustment for phenotypic attributes. This means that when you are acquiring a puppy from a breed at risk for deafness, and that animal displays some of the above physical characteristics, you should really investigate the hearing acuity of the dam. For Lord Underfoot, however, it was too late. Technically, he could be tested with the Brainstem Auditory Evoked Response Test (BAER), a standard test also used with premature babies to evaluate their hearing, but this would be merely an academic exercise, as he was now neutered and could not pass his hearing defect on to offspring.

Lord Underfoot's separation anxiety problem now required all of our attention. If he were destructive in an adoptive home, he would be surrendered again, guaranteed. Coping with his deafness, and not having his little Boston Terrier friend nearby to alert him to events in his environment, no doubt made his adjustment to new surroundings difficult. For example, when anyone enters our boarding facility, all the dogs will start barking, wagging tails and generally getting excited at the prospect of some positive interactions. Not our dear Lord: lying on his side, deep in sleep, he would not even stir. As we were dealing with a deaf dog, we needed to always alert him to our presence in a consistent manner. So any time Lord Underfoot had to be awakened, it was always with a gentle touch over his rump area. That way he never became startled, as he came to associate a soft touch on the rump with a friendly human interaction. We made sure that Lord Underfoot received more playtime and walks than any other stray dogs we had ever dealt with. In fact, the name of the game was "Get the Lord tired!" The more worn out he was, the better he slept – and the less destructive he became when left alone at night.

Given his physical handicap and our difficulty in communicating with him, we decided to try a DAP diffuser, with successful results. A DAP (Dog Appeasement Pheromone) diffuser is a plug-in, scent-releasing device much like the ones we use in our homes to create a clean, pleasant aroma. The material released by a DAP, however, is odorless to humans; it is a genetically engineered pheromone normally secreted by mother dogs to their puppies as a message telling them to relax, that everything is all right. The diffuser continuously releases its message to keep anxious dogs calm. It does not always work, but thankfully it did for our dear Lord. Noteworthy is that DAP diffusers are now available as a collar which the dog can wear 24 hours a day for consistent calming effects.

The final step was to find a suitable owner for Lord Underfoot, preferably one without very young children who would inconsistently startle him. Before too long, Ms. Hammond, a single woman in her forties, came forward to adopt him. Although she did not have another dog at home that could serve as Lord Underfoot's ears, Ms. Hammond had two tremendous assets: she had suffered a tragic personal loss, and needed someone to fill the huge void in her heart; and she was a marathon runner! Lord Underfoot, at eighteen kilograms, was the perfect jogging companion for her, and the two have since become inseparable running mates. Lord Underfoot has not suffered another seizure since his adoption almost a year ago. His separation anxiety, which manifested through his scratching and biting the door, completely disappeared once he was adopted, likely in part due to the great amount of exercise he received daily. Unfortunately, most owners cannot indulge their anxious dogs and themselves with such a vigorous physical routine to alleviate a behavioral problem such as this.

For a dog, being home alone can be very stressful. Remember, dogs are by nature pack animals. Let's now take a closer look at this very common behavioral problem that, if not resolved, often results in the abandonment or surrender of a companion dog.

Gunner, a four-year old Weimaraner, was an incredibly handsome fellow, but if we could classify a dog as a Type A, Gunner was a *triple* A. Everything he did, he did with extreme intensity and drive. He knew nothing of the joyful nature of a Golden Retriever, the light gait of a Poodle, the quizzical look of a Cocker Spaniel or the affectionate face lick of a just-groomed Bichon with a snazzy blue bow on her head! He knew only to keep a sharp, focused eye on his owners at all times, and move accordingly. Constantly panting, constantly jittery – that's pretty much who Gunner was. Not surprisingly, Gunner exhibited a high level of stress whenever he was left alone, and his people suffered the fallout. Each time Gunner's owners arrived home after work, they'd find a different part of the house destroyed: the door and its frame would be scratched up beyond recognition, the couch cushions would be shredded, or the linoleum tiles would be ripped from the floor and chewed into small pieces. At some point, I started to wonder who was suffering most from all the stress: a lonely Gunner, feeling isolated and abandoned? Or his exasperated owners, who would peek warily through the door after an absence, scanning for damages, expecting the worst?

What exactly was going on here? Was Gunner just having fun tearing the house apart? Or was he truly frustrated by loneliness, not knowing when it would end? That was the puzzle: was he acting out due to his fear of being alone, or was he being just plain spiteful?

In Gunner's case, he was undoubtedly having episodes of separation anxiety, which is a behavior that occurs only when a dog is left alone, or *anticipates* being alone. Often the dog is much too bonded to his owners, to the point where he will follow them everywhere in the house. It certainly can be an ego booster for the owners, to have a one-dog admiration committee tagging along, much like a groupie, but the dog really has to learn some independence. In most instances, this fear of separation, and the ensuing destructive behavior – with or without vocalization – starts within the first thirty minutes after the separation.

Here was a typical scenario for Gunner and his owners. As most people do, his owners followed the same routine every morning: alarm goes off, wake up, shower, have coffee and breakfast, get dressed, grab the keys, and head for the door.

Here was Gunner's interpretation of their morning routine: "Oh, oh…was that the alarm I just heard? Oh, oh… the coffee is on! Oh, oh… they're getting dressed in their work clothes! Oh, oh… this is madness! They've just reached for the keys…time to start panting! Disaster! They're heading for the door without me, after giving me lots of love and petting! Time to explode, and run to the window to see them off…my heart is pounding with fear! Quick… I need to get to them… time to start chewing through the door!

Needless to say, this became an ongoing nightmare for both the owners and Gunner. If only we could have given the high-strung Weimaraner a "chill pill" so his people could have returned to an intact home at the end of the day, with Gunner greeting them with a self-assured wag of the tail, and intact, non-chewed slippers in his mouth. How wonderful that would have been! Unfortunately, this was but an impossible dream. In reality, training is always the primary focus for solving this aberrant behavior, and medication is only an adjunct.

Training often involves lessons for both the owners and the anxious dog. Let me explain: to treat separation anxiety in dogs, some important steps must be achieved, requiring the owners' full cooperation. First of all, excessive bonding is discouraged: owners must resist the temptation of always petting the dog, or having the dog at their feet at all times. The dog needs to learn that he has an identity separate from that of his owners – and this can be a tough lesson for him.

Second, the dog needs to learn how to attain a certain "Zen" state on his own. A tool such as the DAP mentioned above may help, or a certain irresistible toy/chew given only at times of impending separation. Leaving the radio on so the dog can hear human voices may also help.

Third, a dog needs to be desensitized to his owners' departure. This was where Gunner's owners needed to start mixing up the clues by altering their usual habits. Ideally, Gunner's perspective would then also be altered: "How come the coffee's not on…but they've reached for the keys already? Huh? Now they're having a shower *after* breakfast? What's going on? Perhaps they're not leaving…okay, no need to start fretting yet. Let's see what else my owners are going to do now…." By mixing several clues, his owners were able to set the stage so that Gunner did not start getting anxious the moment he heard the alarm go off.

Though not intended as a long-term fix, the use of medication to treat separation anxiety can really help a dog like Gunner learn to mellow while he and his owners are in training. But such meds must be used cautiously, lest the dog becomes dependent on them for life.

How did Gunner fare on tricyclic anti-anxiety medication accompanied by some reassuring training? He was off to a terrific start, and settling into a routine where destruction of the house was fast becoming only a memory for him and his owners, when tragedy struck his family. The husband was diagnosed with advanced pancreatic cancer, and passed away quickly. As you can imagine, his grief-stricken widow went through a difficult time adjusting to her new life, and Gunner absorbed a lot of her stress.

When caring for him finally became too much for his widowed owner, Gunner was given to a relative living in the next county. Gunner started his "country living" lifestyle on a large acreage shared with two other dogs. Since his move, we have not seen the handsome Weimaraner, though we still think of him with affection. I sincerely hope that Gunner was able to find lasting peace in his ever-racing mind, and a kind-hearted caregiver in his new life away from the home he had known for so long.

As a dog lover, you can…

- Encourage independence in your dog to reduce the likelihood of separation anxiety.

- Seek professional guidance on appropriate training methods if your dog exhibits signs of separation anxiety.

- Supplement your dog's training with anxiety-reducing medication only if advised to do so by your veterinarian.

CHAPTER 5

In Your Will, In Your Dreams: what will happen to your pet?

Mrs. Galan called recently to make an appointment for Louise's checkup. Oddly enough, five-year-old Louise, a miniature Dachshund, had already had her yearly wellness exam just two months ago. So why was she being booked for her annual exam *again*?

We would find out soon enough. Upon her arrival, Mrs. Galan strode into the exam room with a firm step, a large garbage bag in her arms, and little Louise trotting at her heel. Skipping all her usual friendly greetings, Mrs. Galan got straight to the point, blurting out the words as fast as she could in a non-stop monotone: her husband had just been diagnosed with a terminal illness, and he was going to be admitted to a palliative care unit any day. Due to a paucity of financial resources, Mrs. Galan would be selling their home and moving into a small apartment. Bluntly put, Louise could not go with her.

At the end of her shocking spiel, Mrs. Galan handed me the large garbage bag and said curtly, "Louise is all yours – you can do with her whatever you wish." Without even a glance at Louise, she thrust the little dog's pink leash onto the exam table and walked out of the room, closing the door behind her so that Louise could not follow her back to the car.

As the Dachshund looked on in confusion, I opened the garbage bag; inside were a plastic container filled with dog food, Louise's bed with her name hand-stitched in one corner, a couple of squeaky toys that appeared unused, and a very small choke collar. Staring at the door through which Mrs. Galan had disappeared, Louise finally seemed to realize she'd been abandoned, and began barking with such intensity that her little head jerked backward and lifted her front legs off the ground with each yip.

I was stunned – Mrs. Galan had been in the exam room for less than two minutes. What was that all about? Was this a cowardly pet abandonment, or a trusting surrender? Was I the best – or simply the easiest – option for Louise? Was Mrs. Galan gracefully bowing out, or acting out of sheer desperation?

Louise's persistent bark brought me back to the matter at "foot": a little dog that needed attention. I checked with our front desk receptionist, who told me that Mrs. Galan had hurried out the door with tears streaming down her cheeks. Most likely, she'd spoken so rapidly and left so quickly for fear she would break down before her desperate mission was fully accomplished.

For now, Louise needed to get settled in until a new owner could be found. Unbeknownst to all of us, there must have been a little guardian angel hiding in the garbage bag that arrived with Louise: an elderly couple who had lost their beloved Dachshund came forward and adopted Louise the very next day after she was surrendered. At first sight of her still-grieving new owners, Louise immediately trotted over to them with her tail erect and wagging, delighted to see them. Had they met before? Louise was so spontaneously comfortable with them! Despite Mrs. Galan's very difficult decision, this little Dachshund had already won over two new hearts and clearly found her forever home. She proudly departed with her new people that day.

Other cases – like Kirby's – are more complicated. A rugged senior wildlife biologist, Kirby owned two old Chesapeake Bay Retrievers that he had just retired from bird hunting, so we were surprised to see him come in one day with a Bichonesque type of dog. Lollipop was nine years old, bright and alert, with very matted white curly hair. Other than her disheveled appearance and severe halitosis – that had both Kirby and me holding our breath – Lollipop was in good health and of happy demeanor. But what was Kirby doing with a small fluffy dog that he would normally consider cougar bait? An extreme outdoor enthusiast, Kirby wore nothing but jeans and plaid flannel shirts even in the heat of the summer, and spent all his waking hours hiking and flying over the Rocky Mountains, studying big game animal migration patterns. This little white companion dog was totally out of character for him. So what was he doing with Lollipop, a lovely dog but definitely not a match for his unique, rough-and-tough lifestyle?

Fortunately, Kirby had read my mind, so I didn't even need to ask the question. As soon as he settled into the exam room, with Lollipop at his feet, he explained everything.

"My mother passed away last month, at age eighty-nine, and Lollipop was her only lifeline to this world," Kirby told me, "Her arthritic hands wouldn't let her brush Lollipop without causing much pain in her old joints, hence Lollipop's matted coat. But Mom loved her dearly, and they spent countless hours together sitting in the rocking chair, looking out the garden window. And that's exactly how my mother was found after her passing – stiff and cold in her rocker, with Lollipop sitting calmly at her side."

But, as Kirby reluctantly confessed, there was more grief to come. His mother, unbeknownst to her son, had written in her will that she wanted Lollipop euthanized and cremated, so that she and her pet could be buried together for their "eternal afterlife." Kirby was clearly dreading this moment.

"Kirby," I inquired gently, "Are you asking to have a perfectly healthy dog, with a dynamite personality, euthanized because it's been requested in a will?"

"Yes," he answered meekly.

That made no sense. "Kirby," I pressed on, "Am I the only one feeling uncomfortable with this situation that others would call 'convenience' euthanasia?"

"Yes," he said again, without conviction. But Kirby did admit he was feeling relieved that his mother's request was not being carried out without some reflection. Dear dog lover, as you know, anyone can request the humane euthanasia of a companion animal. However, the request can also be vetoed by those who have been granted a license to kill – like me.

Why would such a request be turned down? Truthfully, because agreeing to this request would prevent the doer of such a deed to sleep peacefully at night! The primary objective for veterinary professionals is for an animal to be better off at the end of the day as a result of our decisions and actions. Would Kirby – and I, as a veterinary practitioner – sleep better that night knowing that we had conspired to terminate an animal's life needlessly, because of the wishes of a lonely, elderly lady, who was most likely unaware of her choices for Lollipop due to her reclusive nature and mild dementia? Absolutely not!

Luckily for the little dog, Kirby was on the same page as I was, although still uncertain about what to do next. "What are my options?" he asked.

I had an idea. "Is there a deadline stipulated in the will for Lollipop's death?"

"No," Kirby answered, apparently seeing the silver lining in his dilemma.

So Kirby and I collaborated on the following plan. First matters first: Lollipop was in dire need of a grooming, as the matted hair in her inguinal (groin) area was prompting her to lick excessively as she tried to dismantle the irritating mats; this was causing a mild pustular dermatitis (skin inflammation with pustules). Once the little dog was groomed and shaved, the skin condition was likely to resolve without further treatment, other than application of a simple antibiotic and anti-inflammatory ointment for a week or so. Her halitosis was caused by moderate grade II periodontal disease, which could have significant health repercussions for Lollipop if not rectified. Kirby agreed to have Lollipop undergo a full ultrasonic teeth cleaning, and gave his permission for any needed extractions. As it turned out, two of her molars were abscessed, causing the rotting smell in Lollipop's mouth and likely much discomfort, and were consequently extracted.

The next step was the emotionally difficult one: the search for a new owner for Lollipop, preferably someone that either Kirby or I knew well. We needed to be familiar with the prospective owner so that one or the other of us could keep tabs on Lollipop in her new life. The reason for this? So that when Lollipop passed away, her adoptive owner would (we hoped) relinquish her ashes to be buried at Kirby's mother's gravesite, according to her wishes.

Again, a guardian angel flew in with the westerly winds, when an acquaintance of Kirby's – who was already a regular client at our veterinary hospital – stepped forward a week later to adopt the small dog. With much enthusiasm, this kind soul endeavored to energize Lollipop's life with love for the next four years. At the age of twelve, in the arms of her beloved second owner, Lollipop was euthanized due to heart failure caused by a defective mitral valve.

Together, Kirby and Lollipop's second owner ceremoniously buried Lollipop's ashes at the gravesite of Kirby's mother, facing the setting sun over the Rocky Mountains. There, forevermore, these two feminine spirits could watch Kirby roam his favorite hillsides and mountain peaks.

Unfortunately for many companion animals, the people who own them pass away without having made proper provision for their pet's care after their departure. Similarly, but just as sadly for their dogs, some owners make the same provision as Kirby's mother did. This makes for a very unhappy ending: a call for an end to a pet's life when the owner's life ends, even though the companion animal is often still in good health. This provision may alleviate anguish and emotional suffering for the dying person, but it disregards the key point about euthanasia – that the procedure should be performed exclusively to alleviate suffering for the pet. Many are of the opinion that the only circumstance in which healthy pets should be considered for euthanasia is when they are a danger to humans, and that "convenience euthanasia" should not be considered an option otherwise.

If no provisions are made in a will for the care of companion animals, and no one steps forward to adopt them, the "orphaned" pets are likely to end up at an animal shelter, or face a privately requested euthanasia. Some forward-thinking owners have opted for simple strategies to ease the transition of their orphaned pets to another loving home upon their death, as in the following stipulations. An ideal scenario involves the establishment of a trust fund in the will, to provide financial assistance for the daily and preventive health care of a beloved companion dog in its new home. This way, the adoption of an elderly pet, or one with a medical problem, is not financially prohibitive for the prospective new owner. Some caring owners make provision for continued pet insurance to cover future health care costs, thereby easing any unforeseen financial burden should their dog become severely ill in a future that does not include them. Other owners make arrangements with friends and family ahead of time, designating a guardian for their companion dog and including such information in the will. Still others have taken a personal life insurance policy on themselves to provide a small trust fund for the care of their beloved dog, so that they do not inconvenience anyone financially with the animal's future care. Some people have considered public agencies, such as shelters, that have programs set up for continued living support of "orphaned pets" of deceased owners in return for a charitable donation to cover the costs of such service. These programs can be beneficial for some pets, but are perhaps unsuitable for those that have special physical or emotional needs. In the same vein, some veterinary colleges provide fantastic legacy/bequest services that are worth investigating, but again these are not suitable for all.

The loss of companionship experienced by some dogs after the death of their owners is truly heartbreaking to witness. Some dogs try to carry on parts of previous routines that were magical to them, such as waiting for a special treat at a specific time of the day, a unique morning or evening ritual, or seeking to interact with a particular human or animal friend that has also gone.

However, when these orphaned dogs are placed in new homes for which they have some affinity, and where they have some physical or emotional issues in common with their new owners, they generally regain enormous vitality in their new surroundings and relationships. Encouragingly, more pet owners are investigating options and taking responsibility for the future care of their companion animals in the advent of their own death. For loving and loyal pets that have shared our homes and our lives over the years, this is perhaps the most important gift we will ever give them.

As a dog lover, you can…

- Create a plan for your dog's care in the event of your death, and share it with friends and family.

- Incorporate specific information and instructions for your pet's care into your will.

- Set up a trust fund for your pet's care, if necessary.

CHAPTER 6

Do Smart Dogs Bury Their Bones?
the bane of bony treats

Maude was a memorable dog. An amiable German Shepherd living on a well-reputed Hanoverian horse-breeding farm, she was initially acquired as a guard dog, to deter any unwanted two-legged visitors lurking around the farm at night or, at the very least, to put on an impressive display of barking and growling to prove that the facility was under decent canine protection. Unfortunately, Maude had never met a stranger she didn't like, and failed miserably at guard duty. She was quickly reassigned to another job that matched her personality better: she became the jovial farm "greeter" for the many well-to-do prospective horse buyers. Maude's other duty – a self-appointed one – consisted of accompanying horse handlers and trainers everywhere, thoroughly sniffing all the tack and all the blankets, and helping herself to any horse feed that fell on the floor. And so the "fierce guard dog" morphed into a beloved greeter, with little effort and plenty of enthusiasm. She excelled as a companion dog, and everyone rewarded her for her exceptional service with soft praises, gentle strokes on the head or the chin, and plenty of the horse treats she relished.

Maude was brought in to our veterinary hospital after she suddenly became inappetent (lacking in appetite) and moderately lethargic for two consecutive days. She had stopped taking treats from the horse handlers, and frequently refused to get up to escort horses to the field, which was most surprising, as she loved to frolic with the weaned foals. Because this was so out of character for Maude, everyone worried about her: was she depressed or ill? To make matters worse, her owner was unable to answer routine questions about Maude's health, since the dog usually wandered all over the farm by day, and interacted with so many people besides her owner. Indeed, anyone would think she was the "extrovert extraordinaire" of the canine world.

Our initial exchange at the clinic went something like this:

Me: "What are her bowel movements like? Firm, soft, or runny?"

Maude's owner, with a shrug: "Don't know. I don't follow her around outside."

Me: "Is she drinking normally, or has she shown a decrease or increase in thirst?"

Her owner: "Don't know. There are water buckets all over for the horses, so it's kind of hard to monitor."

Me: "Have you noticed her vomiting at all?"

Her owner, trying hard to be helpful: "Well, I haven't seen anything like that, but there's a whole quarter section of land where she can wander, so I don't really know."

Taking an accurate history of Maude's health status was rapidly proving to be a futile exercise. But at least her owner was honest in revealing his ignorance about Maude's condition, and for that I was grateful. Some owners, embarrassed at not knowing the answers, just make them up, which complicates the process of reaching a proper diagnosis.

In the veterinary world, a SOAP system, or a modified version of it, is utilized by most clinicians to work up medical cases. SOAP stands for Subjective Objective Assessment Plan. In Maude's case, the subjective part took no time at all, since the owner knew so little about Maude's health; this is often the case with companion animals that live on large farms. They are generally well cared for, but unlike their urban counterparts whose owners meticulously scoop every one of their bowel movements off the sidewalk, farm dogs are given more freedom and have a variety of caregivers. In other words, much more is left to the imagination with the rural crowd. So Maude's subjective assessment did not reveal any particular direction or any clues to take into account for her physical exam, the objective part.

Every clinician has a very precise and routine way of conducting a physical exam. For many, it is as simple as starting the exam with the tip of the nose, and finishing with the tip of the tail. Other clinicians prefer to work by systems, i.e., check the cardio-respiratory system first, then the digestive system, then the urinary system, and so on. Whatever routine a clinician uses, it is useful to repeat the same sequence over and over. Why? The answer is simple: if s/he conducts a physical exam the same way thousands of times, the brain automatically starts to pick up anomalies, with no in-depth analysis and hardly any processing. This is a huge evolutionary adaptation, as it allows a human being to conduct many tasks at once without really trying. During a physical exam, then, a clinician can talk about the weather with the owner, listen to the owner's children tell stories about their dog, make visual note of numbers on the electronic stethoscope, and smell odd and unusual flatulence. Even with all five senses occupied in these many and diverse ways, a practitioner can still perceive small and subtle changes in how an animal feels or responds to the touch of her hands.

The physical exam on Maude had barely begun when she gave us an important clue about her discomfort. Just petting Maude and running my hands over her side made her immediately tuck in her abdomen. With gentle palpation of the dog's abdomen, an experienced clinician would normally be able to feel the edge of the liver lobes, portions of the spleen, the consistency of the stomach, and fluid movements of the soft intestines. This was impossible with Maude: she kept tensing all her abdominal muscles as tightly as she could, so no distinct tissues or organs could be palpated in her abdomen. She was definitely experiencing some abdominal discomfort, but nothing else significant was found on her physical exam.

Maude was more cooperative in the X-ray room, and her abdomen was radiographed without any difficulty. Based on the radiograph, her diagnosis was obvious and simple. Maude was not only constipated, she was clearly and painfully obstipated – as evidenced by the large amount of compacted material, including bone chips TNTC (Too Numerous To Count), throughout at least two-thirds of a meter of colon. Obstipation refers to an extreme case of constipation. This was easily confirmed by insertion of a lubricated, gloved finger into Maude's anus: a compacted, crumbling, cement-like material was retrieved with great difficulty. When this little cement-like ball was dissected, we found pieces of bone chips intertwined with green grass, straw, and oat flakes from the feed trough. Other digested pieces were not recognizable. On radiographic images, we could see that Maude's stomach was clearly full of bone chips. The danger? If Maude were severely impacted, a bone chip could penetrate the lining of her digestive tract. Since later blood work confirmed that all of her blood cell lines were within normal ranges, and Maude did not suffer from a fever, we surmised that Maude's stomach and intestines had not suffered any breach of integrity. This was both a blessing and a curse for Maude. No exploratory surgery was necessary (the blessing), but the warm water was already running to prepare for the first of many enemas (the curse).

Maude was hospitalized for two days, during which time she received six successful enemas. Through the entire process, the afflicted Shepherd remained connected to an IV line to alleviate any signs of mild dehydration, since she refused to drink. With the completion of every enema, ridding her body of ten to twenty centimeters of cement-like fecal balls each time, Maude's gait became lighter and perkier. But the ordeal was not easy on the poor dog. By the time we were done, the sight of a clear, lubricated plastic tube had likely been permanently and adversely imprinted on every one of Maude's brain cells.

Should dogs be allowed to chew on bones? This question is a difficult one to answer, since any responses are based solely on opinions and anecdotes. If Maude's owner were asked that question now, his answer would be an unequivocal "No way!" You can understand why.

So before getting into a lively discussion on whether dogs should chew bones or rawhides, whether the bones should be raw or cooked, chicken backs or pig knuckles, large or small, allowed or not, let's all agree on one fact: there is no thorough, evidenced-based science behind either the benefits or the drawbacks of bone chewing. Everyone has a story to tell, just like Maude's owner, but keep in mind, a story or an anecdote is just that – not fact and not proof.

Why should anyone have concerns about giving a dog a bone to chew on? For a start, there are four common medical problems associated with bone chewing: teeth fractures, gastrointestinal (stomach and intestines) upset, constipation, and choking.

A bone is harder than a tooth, so when too much pressure is applied between the two surfaces, a piece of tooth enamel ends up being the casualty. The chewing activity in a carnivore's mouth – such as that of a dog – occurs near the rear of the mouth, where the large premolars and molars are positioned. Because that is where most of the bone chewing occurs, that is also where many slab fractures of teeth happen, often unbeknownst to the owner. Depending on the severity of the tooth fracture, and involvement of the pulp, close observation of the mouth will reveal the dog's sensitivity on the side of the fractured tooth. Minimal chewing on that side, due to the animal's pain, will lead to greater plaque accumulation around the injured tooth. The affected dog will also show a preference for eating on one side of the mouth, or chewing his bones on the side opposite the injured tooth.

Gastrointestinal upset is the most significant and life-threatening consequence of bone chewing. This is likely also the most divisive and contentious issue among dog owners when it comes to whether or not bone chewing should be allowed for their pets.

"Wolves in the wild eat bones all the time – so why shouldn't my dog?" is a common defence. There are two main arguments against this, however, which can be summarized as follows: dogs were domesticated over 10,000 years ago, and in that time have developed several anatomical features that differ from those of their ancestors, such as length of intestines and dentition. Obviously, the length and diameter of the small intestines of a Teacup Poodle are significantly reduced in comparison with those of a wolf; unfortunately, this allows for easier obstruction and perforation when the little dog ingests bones of any size. Perhaps more importantly, when wolves in the wild eat an animal carcass, including the bones, they also ingest the hide and the fur, which effectively cushion the sharp edges of bones. These two additional supplements, low in nutrition, are not usually incorporated into a dog's diet when he is given bones to chew on. To close the "wolf in the wild" argument, anecdotal evidence tells us that wolves in the wild rarely live as long as companion dogs, and often suffer from intestinal injuries due to their raw carcass diet.

Here Maude has exemplified the bone-chewing problem of constipation. In her case, she was fortunate that all her obstructions were located in the intestines and moved through with help, and without negative consequences. In some dogs, constipation or intestinal obstruction has no chance to occur because a bone fragment gets lodged in the roof of the mouth, straddling the soft or hard palate sideways. If the dog does not become frantically obsessed with this foreign object in its mouth, it can remain there to rot away the soft tissues of the mouth, creating ulceration, abscesses, and necrosis (death of tissue). The putrefied odor exuding from the dog's mouth, and the animal's inability to chew on food due to pain will finally alert the owner to the problem. But by then it may be too late.

In some instances, a bone can get stuck right at the exit point of the large intestine, blocking the rectum or anus. The affected dog will be unable to push stools past bone fragments lodged across the rectum or anus, again creating infection and a foul odor – and a bum-licking, obsessed dog. As you might suspect, digital retrieval of such bone fragments invariably elicits major pain and growling in the suffering animal.

When a dog is fed cooked bones, such as pieces of barbequed T-bones or ribs, there is a very real danger of the bones splintering, and the splinters then penetrating the lining of the digestive tract. In the best-case scenario, the unlucky dog is diagnosed early, has its abdomen surgically opened and explored, and has its digestive tract operated on to retrieve bone fragments. Necrotic sections of the intestines are then resected, and the dog recovers with the help of intensive pain management and infection control. In the worst-case scenario, the dog is diagnosed too late and major complications – with or without surgery – lead to a painful and avoidable death. Some dog owners, fully aware of the danger of feeding cooked bones, opt to feed raw bones instead, such as knucklebones. True, there is less chance of splintering, but obstruction made of cartilage flaps from the ends of the bone, pancreatitis triggered by the ingestion of fatty marrow, and gastroenteritis from raw food pathogens are considerable risk factors.

A final and very real danger of bone chewing, especially with small, round cross-sections of humerus and tibia bones, is that some dogs swallow these bones whole, which causes obstruction in either the larynx or esophagus, and choking. For safety reasons, any bone-chewing dogs should be supervised by adults, ready to assist in case of choking.

Giving bony treats to dogs remains a highly contentious issue among owners, as we'll see in the case of Spot the Dalmatian. Spot had just turned three years old when his owners threw him a birthday bash at the local park, where his favorite dog friends gathered to play and celebrate the occasion. A dozen dogs of all sizes and colors romped around together while their owners socialized and blew out candles on a bone-shaped cake. At departure time, all the guests received a doggy "goodie bag." And what was inside? Wow! There was a lovely bandanna imprinted with paw prints, along with a heart-shaped dog tag, a stuffed fake sheepskin squeaky toy, and a couple cross-sections of a smoked bison femur to chew on. Lucky dogs!

As with any gift, we know it's the thought that counts. And true enough, most of the dog owners were happy with the contents of the doggy goodie bag. But comments on the bison bones were varied. Some owners discarded the bones, based on their bad experiences related to canine medical problems. Others were delighted, as they felt bone chewing was a great "recreational" activity for their dogs that contributed to their mental and physical wellness. Some owners had noticed that bone chewing seemed to help in maintaining their pet's good oral health, while yet others simply saw it as part of a behavioral enrichment program for their dogs. A number of owners reported that their dogs suffered from food allergies, so they had withdrawn all dairy, beef and chicken ingredients from their dog's diet; they were reluctant to try bison, since it was closely related to beef. Some owners expressed relief that the bones were smoked, thus avoiding the potential bacterial contamination of raw bones, while others saw the smoking process as too much like cooking, which can cause bones to dry up and splinter. These owners considered splintering a definite health hazard to their dog's mouth and digestive tract.

Spot had always been allowed to eat bison bones, and clearly relished his chewing sessions. To prevent him from getting sick, as he had occasionally been in the past, his watchful owners always ensured that very little marrow was present in the bones. So Spot never suffered from a fractured tooth or any major gastrointestinal upsets. If you were to ask Spot's owners if bone chewing is good for dogs, they would definitely answer, "Why not? We've done so for years, Spot loves it, and he's got great teeth!"

Bone chewing is usually perceived as a safe practice by owners whose dogs have never experienced problems with it. To draw a comparison, giving bones to dogs is much like jumping out of an airplane and hoping that the parachute is functional. Or diving off a bridge and hoping that the bungee cord is strong enough. Or picking up hitchhikers late at night and keeping your fingers crossed that they're nice people. All is well as long as all is well. But when the parachute fails to open, or the bungee cord breaks, or the hitchhikers turn out to be not so nice after all, we might wonder why we went ahead with the activity in the first place, when it was neither essential nor proven to be safe.

Some dog owners stand perplexed at the sight of their dog burying a fresh bone, never again to retrieve it. What a waste of a juicy bone! But think about it: perhaps smart dogs bury their bones for very good reasons.

A final note: clients always ask me whether I give my own dogs bones to chew. The answer is no. As in the sport of parachuting, too many bone-chewing dogs have come and gone because their parachutes failed to open. Are you prepared to take that risk with your dog?

As a dog lover, you can…

- Do thorough research to educate yourself on the potential problems of bone chewing for your dog.

- Weigh all the risks carefully before deciding whether or not to give bones to your dog.

- Always supervise your dog when he is chewing on a bone, in case of choking.

CHAPTER 7

A Breed to Suit Your Need: how to choose

C hoose a dog breed suited to your needs – or not! Why does it matter?

Archer's story may shed some light on the "whys" of the issue. Young Archer was born into luck, destined for a life of luxury. At eight weeks of age, Archer had no idea that, at the other end of the country, an oil executive and his wife had already boarded their private jet to fly to his birthplace and choose him from among a litter of ten pups. What was so special about this little guy to prompt such a trip? To be sure, he was cute, he was playful, and he was blond. But most importantly, he was a Golden Doodle.

A few years back, this new breed of dogs was making headlines as a "designer" breed, the result of cross breeding a Standard Poodle with a Golden Retriever. Indeed, Golden Doodles were all the rage (and still are), widely heralded as the new hypoallergenic dog. Rather sensational for a dog that, less than a decade ago, would have been called a mutt!

I could not wait to meet Archer, as he would be the first of many happy and exuberant Golden Doodles under my care. They all had friendly manners, and all were high-energy dogs, but there the similarity ended. Some had straight hair, others very curly, and most were quite large in size (one was named "King" for this reason), but they all looked very different from one another.

Oh, but wait a minute, dear dog lover, I owe you an apology: I believe I may have misled you, as I was misled myself. Did I mention the word "breed"? Allow me to correct myself: a cross between a Standard Poodle and a Golden Retriever is a crossbred mix, or more bluntly, a mutt. Even if a dog owner pays $1500 to $2000 for a Golden Doodle, it is still a mutt, not a purebred – albeit one of the most expensive mutts around.

Is there anything wrong with a Golden Doodle? I think not; however, this so-called "breed," with its newfound notoriety, has created much confusion about dog breeds and their inherent purpose, performance and conformation. Before we take a closer look at these issues, dog lovers, please note that any implied biases during the following discussion are unintentional.

All dogs come from some "mixture" at some point. Remnants of the first domesticated dog, dating back more than 12,500 years, verify the mixed ancestry of contemporary dogs. That early canine may have weighed about twenty kilograms, and apparently did not look like any of today's breeds. By definition, a breed is a canalization (streamlining) of various genes. All dog breeds have evolved with a certain amount of selected pressure to canalize particular genes, so that different breeds are equipped to perform specific jobs, as you will see in the examples later in the chapter.

Historically, however, all dog breeds shared a common trait: socialization. In order to live in the presence of humans, they had to develop a social structure that was compatible with early human social structure. In other words, animals that cohabited with our early ancestors were selected both for a job purpose *and* their sociability around humans. Stated in today's terms, that meant they had to be "good family dogs" or "good with children." This is not a new concept but an ancient one, and definitely not exclusive to Golden Doodles. However, people of any era would do well to realize that, even though all dogs have evolved to be compatible with the human race, there is nothing foolproof about dog behavior. The genetic inheritance of behavior is still poorly understood and likely quite complex. Just ask police dog or service dog trainers: they raise many puppies before they find one that will work out to specs. Only a stuffed dog is ever guaranteed to not bite!

In contemporary terms, it would be fair to say that our ancestors selected dogs, either actively or passively, for their work performance and compatibility with humans. This paradigm has shifted tremendously over the last fifty years or so, during which looks have clearly hijacked both performance and function, and aggression toward humans has ironically become a welcome trait (think Pit Bulls and Rottweilers). This is where Archer re-enters the picture.

Will this puppy, as a representative of the new Golden Doodle society, ever become part of a breed, or is he doomed to remain a mutt for eternity? I believe the latter is true. Remember, for a breed to evolve, we have to canalize genetic variation and select for certain traits. But a Golden Doodle is the result of crossing two breeds, where only the first generation of the cross (referred to as F1 in genetic terms) seems desired and valued. Any further crosses of Golden Doodles will dilute their appeal – except apparently in Australia, where some Doodles are being bred to produce further generations. There is not, to my knowledge, any attempt so far to gain American Kennel Club (AKC) breed status or to form an official registry for these dogs in North America.

Here comes a little controversy: is a Doodle then actually a "designer" breed? If so, how do we define what is meant by "designer" breed, beyond the obvious: that it is simply a breed of dog with no work function or defined purpose, along the same lines as the Chihuahua and the Bichon Frise, which have been classified more humbly as "toy" breeds?

The perceived problem with Doodles is that Doodle breeders are not intent on creating a breed: they are simply repeating F1 crosses, with no attempt to produce a breed with consistent traits, establish standards or a registry, or exhibit the dogs in conformation or performance events that demonstrate their abilities. When Golden

Doodle breeders are asked which specific traits they are seeking in the breeding process, answers are varied and simple but can often be summarized as "a likeable dog that is good with children." In order for a breed to be recognized and acknowledged as a true breed, a breeder must breed true over five generations at least. This excludes Doodles, for which breeding stops at F1. For the sake of accuracy, should we now refer to Golden Doodles not as a breed but as a new society of dogs, in which members share some hybrid vigor and tremendous genetic variations?

If so, what are the implications of developing new societies of dogs? The primary implication is that breed reliability will be lost. Dog breeds have evolved over long periods of time, often with exceptional breeder dedication to developing breeds that always present a similar appearance, and perform in similar ways. That has long been the true dual intent of dog breeding: purpose, and physical characteristics to complement that purpose. Accordingly, many of us have acquired dogs of a certain breed, confident that they would have a certain physical appearance at maturity and a certain cluster of behaviors. If people were to choose dogs based on only one of the two traits, i.e., either purpose *or* physical appearance, disaster would likely strike: we might like the look of a Rottweiler puppy, but we must also like the strong-mindedness and aggressive tendency of the mature Rottweiler, since one does not go without the other!

In the past, many dog breeders made it a lifelong endeavor to develop premium examples of the breed with which they were so enamored. Dogs raised to perform in the show ring had to be socially affable, for instance, since dogs that growled at judges or nipped at other dogs somehow never won. Temperament was – and is – an essential component of breed standards. Equally important was the health of dogs, as verified through health clearances for many physical conditions typical of certain breeds. For example, Golden Retrievers have always needed clearance for such conditions as PRA (Progressive Retinal Atrophy), which is a gradual onset of blindness, and OFA (Orthopedic Foundation of America) certification to detect hip and elbow dysplasia or a malformation of those joints.

So what happens with a new society of dogs that are still considered mutts, and cannot compete in show rings? In all likelihood, the sires and dams have few or no health and temperament clearances, making their offspring more of a gamble in terms of how they will turn out, both physically and temperamentally, as adults. Some Doodles have wavy coats, and some have straight coats; some of them retrieve, and some of them bark incessantly. Are they truly "hypoallergenic," as is often claimed? Not a chance!

In fact, little Archer exemplified several of these misconceptions about Doodles. His owners were not at all fond of two of Archer's traits. One, his coat was wavy and he was most definitely not hypoallergenic. When his owner finally tired of the ever-increasing doses of antihistamine he was forced to take, Archer was relegated to a strictly outdoor life.

And two, as an active outdoor dog, Archer too often exercised his excessively high-pitched vocal cords, as Poodles often do at the sight of anything that moves, even a trembling leaf. As disappointed as they likely were, Archer's owners took full responsibility for what he was and what he had become, and in this regard Archer was fortunate. Less patient owners may have resorted to the hasty disposal of a dog that fell short of their expectations.

If we enjoy the new societies of dogs (the Doodles, the Woodles, the Malidors...) and care so little about breed standards, then why bother having dog breeds at all? I say we *should* bother, mostly because dog breeds are about lineage, and not just what one specimen looks like. The art of breeding is about knowing which line of dogs lives a long life, which carries a low incidence of certain diseases, and which blesses its members with exceptional temperament. The breeders able to carry a desired line through time, with care and respect for breed standards, who are committed to maintaining or improving these breed standards, are educated and caring breeders – unlike backyard breeders, who blatantly disregard all of the above.

At this point, anyone of us might be tempted to say, in a most non-argumentative way of course, that not all educated breeders are good breeders, and not all backyard breeders are bad ones – and these are indeed arguable points. Indiscriminate line breeding (which involves incestuous mating of closely related animals, entirely orchestrated by breeders) and profit motivation have ruined many lines of purebred dogs, and understandably shaken public confidence in terms of their expectations of dog ownership.

Purely for entertainment purposes, let us stroll now through the list of the ten most popular dog breeds in the USA, as defined by the AKC registration statistics, to determine what exactly people believe to be the most suitable breeds for their needs. Points of interest only are mentioned here; for more detailed information on each breed, interested readers should peruse the AKC website. You may note that most of these popular breeds have in fact been recognized as breeds by the AKC only in the past hundred years or less.

For each dog breed, I have added one or two words, or a thought, to describe the category from the perspective of a clinician. This can be a useful practice for any clinician about to enter the exam room, since it provides a quick mental snapshot of what awaits behind the door – including breed, age, sex and likely health problems. Please do not take offense, dear reader: although this simple exercise is admittedly very subjective, it is worth considering if you are in search of a dog and tempted by the breed!

In terms of popularity, the top-ranked spot is decisively held by the **Labrador Retriever,** in the USA as well as in many other countries throughout the world. This versatile breed, bent on pleasing people, hails from eastern Canada and comes in three colors – yellow, black, and chocolate. These days, however, the "red fox" and "charcoal" coat colors are most in demand, often fetching higher prices than the three traditional, approved breed colors. The trendy new colors are part of a new society of dogs: basically, they are expensive mutts without registration papers.

Originally from Newfoundland, where they worked alongside fishermen pulling nets and catching errant fish, Labrador Retrievers were initially crossed with Setters, Spaniels, and other Retrievers to produce true Retrievers. They became efficient retrievers of game, and totally devoted companion dogs. The AKC recognized the Labrador

Retriever as a breed in 1917. In terms of breed standards, the AKC will severely penalize dogs that show aggressiveness toward humans and other animals, and any evidence of shyness in adulthood.

One word: ALLERGIES. Unfortunately, this vulnerability translates into chronic ear and skin problems for the dogs, and chronic vet bills for their owners!

The second-place rank belongs to a member of the Toy group, and – being a Terrier – it is a brave and determined little dog: the **Yorkshire Terrier.** This dog, originating from the county of Yorkshire in England, was used in the nineteenth century to catch rats in clothing and weaving mills. The status of the Yorkshire Terrier was elevated when it finally left the work force and became a companion dog to high society families in Europe. The AKC recognized it as a breed in 1885.

One word: C-SECTION. These dogs often require surgical assistance when birthing their litters.

The quintessential guard dog, the **German Shepherd,** takes third place. Originating in Germany from herding and farm dogs, the Shepherd was recognized by the AKC as a herding dog in 1908. AKC disqualifications include a white coat color, cropped or drooping ears, noses that are not predominantly black and, understandably, "any dog that attempts to bite the judge."

Two words: FEARFUL AGGRESSION. Given this tendency, the breed is not always suited to a busy family life. Additionally, a degenerative nerve and muscle condition of the hind end, known as degenerative neuromyopathy, afflicts many aging German Shepherds to the point that they can no longer ambulate on their own.

Next on the list, originating from the Scottish Highlands in the late 1800s, is the **Golden Retriever,** which ranks fourth. This breed was developed through the integration of several breeds, including the Irish Setter, the Water Spaniel (now extinct), and the Bloodhound, in an effort to create a breed of dogs that would excel at hunting. The

AKC recognized this breed as a member of the sporting group in 1925. In England, dogs in the sporting group are referred to as "gundogs" and include three main categories of dogs, namely the Retrievers, the Pointers, and the Setters. They all work primarily with game birds: Retrievers find and deliver killed game to the hunter, Pointers stand in front of their prey and point out their location, and Setters "set" or crouch in front of their prey to prevent escape.

Due to their strong work ethics, Golden Retrievers have evolved beyond the scope of hunting to join the ranks of working dogs. They are commonly employed as service dogs, and have become very popular as family dogs because of their reliable good character. It is noteworthy that the AKC will penalize any Golden Retriever with a tendency toward "quarrelsomeness or hostility towards other dogs or people in normal situations, or an unwarranted show of timidity or nervousness."

Two words: HAPPINESS and CANCER.

The **Beagle** occupies fifth place in the ranking. Snoopy, from the comic strip "Peanuts," is perhaps the best-known representative of this popular breed. Although the AKC only recognized the breed in 1885, it likely originated in the 1500s as a scent hound to track rabbits. As most scent hounds worked in packs, barking and deep baying were essential for communication between dogs and hunters. For those who wish to acquire a quiet dog, this one is definitely a poor choice!

One word: NOISY

The sixth-place breed of dogs was first of all known for its fighting ability. Typically, it stood up on its hind legs and appeared to be boxing with its front paws, hence its name: the **Boxer.** This dog was imported to America soon after the First World War, but in fact originated in Germany in the 1800s. Back then, Boxers were used to chase down and restrain large prey, such as wild boar, until a hunter could arrive. The Boxer made its debut in the AKC in 1904, as a member of the working group. The only acceptable colors for

Boxers are fawn or brindle. Notably, this breed is not for the faint of heart: cardiomyopathy, a heart condition involving degeneration of the heart muscle, is relatively common in the breed, as is cancer.

One word: CANCER

In seventh place, again from Germany, is a breed totally suited for its original purpose: this fearless, long-bodied dog could dig into a badger's burrow and fight the rodent to the death. The **Dachshund** comes in two sizes: the standard, ranging from seven to fourteen kilograms; and the miniature, at five kilograms or less. The AKC admitted this breed into the hound group in 1885. The Dachshund is a dwarf breed, with all the conformation problems that go with this condition. Poor angulation of limbs and spine, typical of this breed, may engender many aches and pains for both dogs and owners.

Two words: BACK PROBLEMS. Unfortunately for Dachshund owners, surgical repair of these problems can run up to several thousands of dollars.

Ranked eighth, the **Bulldog** is now at the heart of much controversy regarding purebreds: have these dogs been bred to excess? Although the breed was originally developed for bull baiting, where ferocity and courage were important character traits, Bulldogs of today are generally very docile and sweet in personality. Recognized by the AKC in 1886 in the non-sporting group, the breed is now plagued with numerous physical disorders that preclude a long and healthy life. Potential owners should be cautious about acquiring a Bulldog if on a tight budget or averse to frequent visits to the vet.

Two words: AMIABLE and EXPENSIVE.

In ninth place, the **Poodle** comes in three sizes and solid colors only, and is known for its exceptional intelligence. Although commonly associated with France, this breed likely originated as a working dog in Germany, where it was used as a hunting retriever in water. In fact, its famous clip was initially designed to help the dog move well in water, and to protect its joints and vital organs.

The Standard Poodle, more than thirty-eight centimeters high at the shoulder, is the oldest variation of the three recognized Poodle sizes. Called "caniche" by the French, the Poodle was recognized as a breed by the AKC in 1887.

One word: INTELLIGENT.

In tenth spot is the **Shih Tzu,** an older breed that is still very popular. The Shih Tzu was registered with the AKC only in 1969, in the Toy group where all colors are allowed. Prized as house pets by Chinese royals of the Ming Dynasty, Shih Tzus were originally thought to be a cross between Lhasa Apso and Pekingese dogs. Even today, these dogs make great house pets, with their even temperament and freedom from many of the genetic conditions that plague other breeds. The acceptance of all color variations has probably allowed for a healthy amount of vigor in the breed.

One word: EASY

As you may have concluded by now, these popular breeds were the result of crossing two or more breeds of dogs over several generations. So, what is the difference between this practice and the current cross breeding trend that produces all kinds of Doodles? The primary difference is that these established breeds evolved out of repeated breeding to generate certain reliable traits. Breeders perfected lineages over countless generations, with a specific goal in mind: to unite specific traits of a breed to canalize certain genes. Today's crossbreeds, or mutts, are "invented" because people assume they can create a dog that other people will desire, without any consideration for reliability of traits, whether conformation or temperament. The vast majority of "designer" dogs are not bred for any inherent purpose, nor are they genetically cleared of dominant diseases. Worse yet, some people think it is perfectly acceptable to inbreed dogs – mothers to sons, or fathers to daughters. Aberrant couplings such as these never happen in nature, for very good reasons.

To summarize, well-established breeds come with a relatively reliable set of genetic traits. Before adopting, prospective dog owners should become well enough informed to ensure that particular breed traits would conform and adapt to their family's lifestyle. There is no point in having a Shih Tzu as a guard dog, or a Rottweiler as a family dog, as expectations will soon be dashed for both dogs and people. As for "designer" breeds, or new societies of canines like the one Archer belongs to, all bets are definitely *off*.

Please, dog lovers, do your research and take care in choosing a breed that will truly suit your needs, for both your sake and the dog's. Too often, companion dogs end up as the casualties of poor human judgment, a heartbreaking – and avoidable – outcome for all concerned.

As a dog lover, you can…

- Examine your family's needs and expectations of a dog before adopting; what qualities are you seeking?

- Research dog breeds thoroughly before deciding on a suitable match for your family's needs.

- Research breeders thoroughly to ensure you are not acquiring a dog that will later be plagued with debilitating and costly genetic diseases.

CHAPTER 8

Now Look Who Has The Headache: meds and pets

Why do dogs always ingest poison after regular business hours? This is a question that ranks right up there with the profound mysteries of the world, including "Are there really UFOs out there?"

All too often, though, dog poisoning emergencies *do* occur after hours, like the one late Friday night when Bongo's owner, Mr. Schultz, called in a panic. Bongo, a chocolate Lab, had somehow gotten into Mr. Schultz's mother-in-law's pillbox, which was filled with seven days' worth of Tylenol 3 tablets along with some other more innocuous medication.

"Is Bongo going to be all right?" Mr. Schultz asked, "Or should I bring him in to get checked out?"

Based on Bongo's weight and the amount of Tylenol he had ingested, my response was "No" to the first question and "Yes" to the second. Bongo had indeed ingested a very toxic amount of Tylenol and, unless he could be induced to vomit all that medication up, some degree of liver failure was bound to occur in the next few days.

Tylenol, or acetaminophen, is an analgesic (pain relief) drug developed for human use. Although some dogs may be able to handle acetaminophen at normal therapeutic doses, the drug has not been properly tested in canines and as such is not a drug of choice. Unlike NSAIDs (Non-Steroidal Anti-Inflammatory Drugs), such as Ibuprofen and Aspirin, acetaminophen has little anti-inflammatory effect, and its mechanism of action in canines is largely unknown.

Many veterinary clinicians believe that acetaminophen is useless for pain control in dogs unless it is coupled with codeine. A major drawback of acetaminophen use is that it can produce KCS, or keratitis sicca, also known as dry eye, a condition in which tear production drops so low that the eyes literally dry out, and the cornea (the shiny outer part of the eye globe) starts to ulcerate.

So why risk using acetaminophen as an analgesic, if its pain-killing properties have not been proven in dogs, a level of toxicity can easily be reached, and a permanent debilitating eye condition can result from its use? Those were my questions to a fellow clinician using Tylenol 3 to treat a Rottweiler with a very sore hind leg. The radiographic images of this Rottie's lower femur showed some disturbing and revealing lesions: a mixed appearance of bony changes likely compatible with a primary bone tumor osteosarcoma (OSA). This was the major "rule out" required, considering the pain that Rocco the Rottie experienced with just a light palpation over the femur. His lameness had started only the week prior, the owner reported. Money was definitely a limiting factor here: the owner had restricted financial funds available, so the priority for Rocco was to alleviate his pain for as long as possible at the lowest cost possible.

What options were available? In the Rotti's case, three choices seemed feasible: firstly, amputation at the hip joint to remove the source of the intense, fast-growing pain, assuming this lesion to be OSA if a bone biopsy could be done. The second option was chemotherapy. The most cost-efficient, single-agent drug with proven efficacy for OSA in dogs is a chemotherapeutic agent that is used in multiple cycles every two to three weeks, for a limited time.

What were the odds of survival with options one and two?

Amputation alone, which will provide some pain relief, has a median survival time of around four to five months. If chemotherapy is added, the median survival time can increase anywhere from a few months to just over a year.

Veterinary approved NSAIDs can become very expensive, especially for a dog that weighs over forty-five kilograms. This is why some owners will elect to try Tylenol as an analgesic, which is the third option. However, Tylenol must be used within the bounds of reasonable and therapeutic doses to avoid its side effects of toxicity, which range from lethargy, anorexia, abdominal pain, vomiting, anemia, elevation of liver enzymes to the point of liver failure with jaundice, weight loss, and death.

This Rottweiler, already sadly debilitated by cancer, was given Tylenol to alleviate his pain and increase his quality of life for a limited time since his owner was experiencing severe financial constraint. The side effects of toxicity were not really a concern in this case, as the dose remained within the therapeutic range, and the duration of the treatment was likely to be very short. Clearly, Rocco was in rapid decline, feeling intense pain and discomfort.

Within two weeks of the presumptive diagnosis of bone cancer, Rocco was completely lame on the affected leg, requiring another anti-inflammatory drug instead of Tylenol, which did not seem to provide the dog with any significant pain relief. The new painkiller was far more expensive, and had a different mechanism of action to suppress inflammation and thus pain.

Unfortunately, the new drug had no effect on either Rocco's lameness or his pain, and soon the ailing Rottweiler stopped eating. When trying to move finally became too painful, Rocco stopped even getting up to urinate. At the point where quality of life is so severely diminished, and suffering so evident, compassion takes over and makes the only choice left: Rocco was humanely euthanized, with his owner at his side.

While acetaminophen can be prescribed as an anti-inflammatory, most clinicians believe there are much better analgesics approved and available for dogs. So it is rather rare to see toxicity with acetaminophen, other than the odd case of wrongful ingestion, as occurred with Bongo.

"Mr. Schultz, Bongo needs to come in immediately," I told my late-night caller, "He just ingested a toxic amount of medication, and you live less than ten minutes away." Moments later, the twosome arrived – one worried owner and one irrepressibly bouncy dog. Bongo, true to his name, was jumping all over the place in the exam room, very excited to get all this attention at this late hour. It had been his first-ever car ride after midnight, so even if it brought him to Emergency, it warranted many tail wags on his part.

When we used the standard formula to calculate overdose of acetaminophen, Bongo's magic number was well in excess of the "no-worry" range. The first procedure we undertook was aggressive decontamination, which is rather unpleasant for the patient. Decontamination consists of three basic steps. First, induce vomiting: after Bongo was given emetic medication, seven mostly intact, undigested Tylenol tablets were expelled onto the hospital floor. Check. The second step is to conduct a stomach lavage, under heavy sedation, to recover any residual toxic material. And the third step is to feed the patient some activated charcoal, to bind any leftover pill residues, which we did with Bongo. Check.

The second step, the stomach lavage, was omitted in Bongo's case, as the owner was extremely confident that only seven Tylenol pills had been ingested. As well, timing was in the Lab's favor. The ingestion had happened less than twenty minutes prior to his arrival at the hospital, too little time to allow for significant gastric (stomach) emptying.

Had the time lapse since ingestion been greater, a lavage would definitely have been warranted. In that case, medication to support Bongo's liver function would have been added to the protocol, as well as an IV to support hydration, maintain electrolyte balance, and deliver drugs into his system. A blood transfusion would have been on standby in case of severe resulting anemia.

As it turned out, Bongo the Lab was very fortunate. Had his owner gone to bed that evening without noticing that his mischievous dog had vandalized the pillbox and gorged on pills, Bongo would likely have gone into liver failure, with ensuing death. As Bongo would tell you, keeping a close eye on your pet – and removing potentially dangerous temptations from reach – pays off.

As a dog lover, you can…

- Ensure that all medications are stored safely out of your dog's reach.
- Seek veterinary attention without delay if you suspect that your dog has ingested any human medication.

CHAPTER 9

The Mother of All Emergencies: bloat in dogs

B obbi was only two years old when she went under the knife for the first time – a frightening experience for any young dog, let alone one in such an excessive amount of pain. Worse yet, no one familiar was around to comfort her. Her owners had left her in a boarding kennel for six weeks, the duration of their annual winter holiday to Hawaii.

The trouble began on a routine afternoon during her second week of boarding, when a staff member noticed around 4:00 o'clock that Bobbi had refused to eat her food. As unusual as that was for Bobbi, the kennel worker was not overly worried; he let her be, and continued to attend to all the other dogs at the kennel.

At the very end of his shift, the worker came back to see if Bobbi had finally decided to eat, and was surprised at what he found. Not only had Bobbi not touched any of her food in his absence, she had vomited profusely; the floor of her pen was a slick mess of bile and partially digested food from her breakfast bowl. As Bobbi eyed the kennel worker apologetically, he noticed that she was drooling heavily, indicating that she was nauseous. But what alarmed the kennel attendant most of all was Bobbi's belly: it looked like she'd swallowed a basketball.

As a fit and healthy Great Dane, Bobbi was due to be bred at her next heat, in about one month. But now her normally slim silhouette was distorted by her oddly bulging cranial (toward the front) abdomen. It was obvious to the kennel worker that Bobbi was suffering from bloat.

Would the condition correct itself if left alone? Could her stomach become "unbloated"? Not likely – and fortunately, the kennel attendant was experienced enough to know that. Time to act! A quick phone call to the emergency hospital got Bobbi admitted within an hour of departing the kennel.

Poor Bobbi – she was feeling very ill in an unknown place, surrounded by strange people who were examining and probing her. The emergency staff immediately suspected a bloat condition, and promptly injected a combination of a sedative and analgesic into her cephalic vein to provide some relief, both from anxiety and pain. A right lateral radiograph (i.e., with Bobbi lying on her right side) of her abdomen was taken, providing us with an image of her remarkably enormous, air-filled stomach. The team quickly inserted a stomach tube, to see if some of the air would escape via the tube and provide instantaneous respite. No such luck. Bobbi's stomach was not only bloated but had already twisted on itself, preventing any air or fluid from seeping out. Surgery was required to de-rotate and re-establish blood flow to the twisted stomach, as well as to facilitate blood circulation to other organs; her circulation had become impeded by the pressure of the enlarged stomach.

Unfortunately, bloat is the number one killer of Great Danes, and Great Danes are the number one breed at risk for bloat. The St. Bernard is the number two breed at risk, while the Weimaraner follows at number three. Given the speed of its action, bloat often kills dogs in the evening or during the night, without warning and without human intervention. Not only is it an excruciatingly painful condition, bloat often becomes fatal within hours if not addressed with great medical and surgical urgency. For this reason, boarding Great Danes in a kennel carries significant risk, as most kennels do not have staff to supervise the dogs late at night when bloat often strikes.

Owners and breeders of Great Danes are not the only ones that fear this perilous condition. Breeders and owners of Akitas, Standard Poodles, Irish Wolfhounds, and Irish Setters, to name a few, are also very concerned about bloat. What do all these dogs have in common that predisposes them to bloat? A deep and narrow chest!

Before we go any further, dear reader, let us first of all make sure we are all referring to the same condition when we use the term "bloat". Bloat refers to a condition in which excessive swelling or enlargement of the stomach occurs due to either gas or fluid, or both. Encompassed within the definition are three conditions: acute (severe) gastric dilatation, torsion, and volvulus, hence the alternate term commonly used for bloat – gastric dilatation volvulus, or GDV.

A distended stomach, when dilated, may twist abruptly on its long axis. If it does, and if the twist is 180 degrees or less, we refer to the action as torsion. If the twist is *greater* than 180 degrees, we call it a volvulus. As you may deduce, the more the stomach twists on itself, the more the blood vessels will be compromised in terms of their normal diameter and blood flow, and the more likely and rapidly the dog will go into a state of physiological shock. When an animal is in shock, certain body function changes occur: the gums in the mouth become paler, the heart rate becomes irregular, and breathing becomes much shallower. At this point, a bloated dog is in extreme pain, and its abdomen will appear obviously swollen and tight as a drum. Since he is unable to swallow his saliva, the animal will likely drool from nausea, and, understandably, might vocalize his pain in desperate howls. To save the dog's life, the only possible treatment at that point is to get him to a veterinarian without delay for rapid stomach decompression, most often achieved surgically.

An excellent study was conducted some years ago by Purdue University researchers, led by veterinarian and epidemiologist Dr. Lawrence T. Glickman, and published in the peer-reviewed *Journal of the American Veterinary Medical Association* (JAVMA). The issue of November 15, 2000, contains findings that should prompt Great

Dane breeders and owners – and all others who work with breeds at risk – to step back and re-evaluate their bloat prevention information. Below is a summary of the study's significant findings.

First-degree relatives of dogs that have suffered from bloat have a 63 percent greater risk of developing bloat themselves. Older dogs are more at risk than younger dogs. Dogs that eat too quickly (and presumably ingest more air) are more likely to suffer from bloat, as are dogs that are thinner. According to the researchers' hypothesis, the presence of abdominal fat would provide less room for the stomach to dilate and twist.

Notably, dog experts have advocated for years in favor of elevating food and water bowls of Great Danes. But this study makes it clear that that action alone increases the odds of bloat by 110 percent! No question, this is too risky to even try.

According to other studies, other factors implicated in bloat include feeding only one meal a day, moistening dry foods, and restricting water before and after meals. Male dogs, especially those weighing more than forty-five kilograms, are at greater risk of bloat.

What happened to Bobbi? Well, as a Great Dane, she already had one strike against her in terms of bloat risk. But she was also young and female, and not fed from an elevated bowl. As you can see, risk factors are just that – risk factors – but they are not always predictable prognostic indicators. In this dog's case, the constellation of clinical signs and radiographic findings definitely pointed to a bloat diagnosis, which would later be confirmed in the surgery suite.

Bobbi was truly experiencing the mother of all emergencies, and if you were to look into her distressed eyes, they would tell you she was destined to exit this earthly life if help did not arrive, stat! In any bloat case, several steps must be undertaken simultaneously to save a dog's life, and therein lies the difficulty: all of these steps must be performed at the same time, with decisive speed and perfect execution. It was clear to us that Bobbi was going into a state of shock, as her enlarged stomach was severely pressing on her major blood vessels that transport blood back to the heart; in addition, we had been unable to irrigate her compromised stomach.

The only way Bobbi could escape death was for the medical team to reverse her state of shock, untwist her stomach, and allow for gas release. A stomach pump could be useful, provided the entrance to her twisted stomach was not blocked, but surgery is usually needed for full decompression. We inserted an intravenous catheter into Bobbi's saphenous vein (the one coursing over the hock of her rear leg), and quickly administered an electrolyte saline solution to combat the state of shock. In the meantime, an electrocardiograph was connected to Bobbi's body to determine whether premature ventricular contractions (PVCs), a common heart dysfunction associated with bloat, were developing.

Luckily for Bobbi, her heartbeat remained stable, but continuous monitoring over the next day would be necessary since these PVCs can occur at any time until the patient is fully stabilized. Uncontrolled PVCs increase mortality rates.

At this point, the real adventure for both the emergency team and Bobbi was about to start. Under anesthesia, Bobbi's deep-chested abdomen was sliced open to evaluate the integrity of the stomach and correct its positioning. Fortunately for our patient, there was no evidence of dying tissue in the stomach that required resection (cutting). The spleen, which occasionally joins the stomach in its twist, was also intact.

At this stage, a gastropexy was in order; without it, the recurrence of bloat can be as high as 75 percent. This simple surgery involves cutting a small piece of the outside stomach wall and tacking it internally behind the ribs, as though taping the stomach to the rib wall, to create scar tissue and prevent any future rotation of the stomach (stats tell us that, after gastropexy surgery, less than 10 percent of dogs will have their stomachs rotate again). After her gastropexy adventure, we put Bobbi on a drip of painkillers to help her in her recovery. She was closely monitored over the next twenty-four hours for post-operation surgical failure, PVCs, and possible infection.

Happily, Bobbi was young and healthy, and she determinedly clung to life. Our Great Dane patient recovered uneventfully and, within forty-eight hours, was fit to be released from the hospital. Bobbi's concerned owners had decided to come home early, since they did not want to leave her without constant supervision after her ordeal, so she was able to go home for the post-surgery care and attention she needed.

Bobbi the Great Dane died some years later, at the age of eight, from heart disease. But she never had to go under the knife again. Subsequent to her bloat episode, Bobbi was unfortunately bred twice to a purebred Great Dane that had also survived bloat. The match of these two magnificent animals no doubt produced a litter of adorable progeny with a strong predisposition to bloat.

As a veterinary clinician, I have observed, with great dismay, a recent trend among some dog owners: the increasingly popular request of a prophylactic gastropexy for breeds at risk of bloat. Prophylaxis refers to the preventive treatment of a disease, and gastropexy – which, as you will recall, was performed on Bobbi – is defined as a surgical procedure that "tacks" or attaches the stomach wall to the body wall, thus preventing it from twisting. Typically in these cases, when a puppy of a breed such as Great Dane, Irish Wolfhound, or Standard Poodle comes to our clinic, the owners will request that, at the time of spaying and neutering, we also perform a gastropexy to prevent the occurrence of bloat in the future.

The problem here is not with the surgery itself, which does seem to be effective in preventing potential episodes of bloat and is relatively lucrative to perform. No, the concern is that these owners purchase dogs from breeders whose breeding dogs have first-degree relatives that suffered and/or died of bloat, and these breeders routinely recommend the surgical procedure to any buyers and future owners of their puppies.

Then the question becomes, "Why did you decide to purchase a dog of a breed at risk, from a breeder who has puppies that are close blood-relatives of dogs that either died or suffered with GDV – and who, furthermore, warns you of the risk while blatantly encouraging you to alter the puppy's body through major surgery, at your expense, to prevent a future problem?" What drives owners to acquire a dog despite their knowledge that the animal is genetically loaded with life-threatening problems? For all of us who call ourselves dog lovers, this is perhaps a question worth pondering.

As a dog lover, you can…

- Become familiar with the health conditions common to your dog's breed, as well as their clinical signs – it may save your dog grief and pain.

CHAPTER 10

A Complex Threesome: heartworms, mosquitoes and dogs

Heartworm disease – what is it? Who gets it? Where does it strike? How is it transmitted? And, most importantly, how can it be treated? With the assistance of Toby, a feisty black Terrier cross, we'll take an in-depth look at this worrisome health issue, and uncover some of its mysteries.

Canada has ten provinces, and the USA has fifty states, for a total of sixty distinct geographical areas in North America (excluding Canada's sparsely populated three territories). Heartworm disease in dogs is present in all of these regions except two. Which two? The heartworm-free zones are Alberta and Saskatchewan in the Canadian prairies, where, until recently, Toby the Terrier lived with eighteen worms in his heart, each averaging twenty-five centimeters in length, more specifically, the worms had made their home in the right ventricle (lower heart chamber) and in his pulmonary arteries. The long, thin, creamy white worms were gently massaged and fed by the warm flow of his blood, so they had no intention of leaving the comfortable pumping station, unless they died of old age and were flushed away, or unless they killed Toby and thus perished themselves, which would certainly be a foolish and suicidal move on their part.

Within the confines of Toby's heart, unbridled sexual activity was rampant between the worms, and, as a result, many newborn babies – called microfilaria or first-stage larvae – were continually being released into Toby's bloodstream. Once circulating in the dog's body, the larvae were available to invade another warm canine body at any time over the next two years, provided they could hitch a ride to the next unsuspecting dog's body. If Toby lived in New England, or Florida, or New Orleans, or even as far north as Montreal in the summertime, Toby would share his larval load with other dogs even without direct contact with them. Free rides would be plentiful. Fortunately for the rest of the prairieland canine population, Toby lived near the Rocky Mountains in Alberta, so if he never left the area during those very crucial two years, his baby larvae would never be transmitted to any other dogs in the area.

Why is the location so important? Basically, the heartworm story is about a threesome, and so far we have only two players: Toby the dog and the heartworm invaders. The missing third player, and a very important one, is the "ride": the lowly mosquito. Not the same mosquito that transmits malaria, or Dengue fever, or yellow fever but one that specializes in heartworms, which can in turn infect up to thirty mammalian species including, most commonly, canines (dogs, coyotes, wolves, foxes). But dogs are not the only animals at risk. Cats, ferrets, and sea lions have reportedly also been infected with heartworms.

The mosquito that transmits the heartworm babies, or first-stage larvae, has a difficult time achieving its task in the colder weather typical of even the summer months in the Prairie Provinces. So for obvious reasons, the mosquitoes are totally absent in the winter months, and transmission between hosts (the dogs) is completely put on hold until warmer days return. Although present in Alberta and Saskatchewan in the summer, the mosquito does not live long enough to allow for maturation in its body of the first-stage larvae into the second and, finally, the third stage, at which point the larvae are infectious to other dogs, and easily transmitted when a loaded mosquito bites one of them.

What about arid areas such as Arizona, New Mexico, or Utah, where mosquitoes cannot survive because they need water points to lay their eggs? Can heartworm disease be transmitted in such dry regions? Obviously, wherever conditions necessary for mosquito survival are absent, such as in desert areas, there will be no heartworm disease in dogs. Even though fifty-eight geographical areas are positive for the disease, many contain only small pockets where the disease is actually prevalent. In some geographical areas, such as along the Mississippi and in Florida, where the weather is hot and humid all year round, the disease is prevalent year round.

Listen for a moment – did you hear it? That was Toby, coughing – a loose, moist sort of cough that comes in paroxysms (sudden outbursts). Poor fellow! With his neck stretched out and his mouth wide open, he was clearly struggling to get the airflow moving more easily. With all the hacking, he spat out a small amount of white foam. Can you imagine the Terrier's extreme discomfort, with eighteen worms wriggling about, feeding and reproducing in his chest and in his heart, deep inside the anguished core of his small body?

How did Toby manage to pick up this infection in the first place? After all, he was living in Alberta, where we know that heartworms are not transmitted because the average temperature is too low in the summer for first-stage larvae to mature to the infectious third stage. The answer is painfully simple: Toby was infected elsewhere. Last August, when he travelled by car with his owners to Colorado to visit relatives for two weeks, Toby's owners neglected a vital travel preparation for their pet. Even though they were traveling through Montana, Idaho, and Utah en route to Colorado, they had failed to give Toby the proper medication to prevent heartworm infection via mosquitoes.

If we travel back in time with Toby, and join him on his summertime car ride through the states, we quickly discover what happened: when Toby was let out of the car in southern Idaho, he was promptly assaulted by mosquitoes. In fact, for the entire night the family spent at the campground, the Terrier mix had mosquitoes swarming around him, snacking on his blood. And as they sucked blood out of the defenseless canine, the loaded mosquitoes dropped third-stage larvae onto Toby's skin via their saliva.

Once in his body, there was no stopping the larvae, although it took them a few months to penetrate his skin and find their way into his blood circulation while maturing to the fourth and fifth stages of their development. The fifth-stage larvae halted their migration at the canine pumping station (heart), where they became adult worms and began to reproduce. It took a full five to seven months for the third-stage larvae to become reproducing adults in the heart, so it was not until the following spring that Toby started to cough. His owners were not alarmed at first, as the cough was intermittent and did not cause any exhaustion for the dog. By the time summer arrived, however, Toby was clearly having episodes of respiratory distress, and his tolerance for exercise had dropped significantly.

At that stage, the twenty-five centimeter-long worms were not only occluding (obstructing) his pulmonary arteries and his right ventricle, they were creating the havoc that so many unwanted guests do. They were damaging the lining of the blood vessels, thereby creating a zealous but futile immune response, and also increasing the risk of small emboli (clots or plugs) to form, a situation that could become life threatening for the dog.

By then, Toby was clearly unwell; his tongue turned blue with even the slight exertion of going upstairs. To his owners' dismay and bewilderment, the little dog – usually so spunky and energetic – continued to worsen. When, finally, Toby lost consciousness, he was brought in to Emergency. Auscultation (listening to sounds) of his chest revealed a profound arrhythmia (irregular heartbeat), abnormal lung sounds, an enlarged liver that could be palpated since it was bulging past the end of his rib cage, and a generally distended abdomen that felt filled with fluid. At this point, it was clear that Toby was suffering from heart disease of some sort, but which one? A number of heart conditions were on the list of differentials, such as congestive heart failure and pulmonary embolism, which require different modes of therapy. The dog's problem needed to be characterized further: what was the trigger event that had caused his heart to malfunction? The answer would no doubt be quickly revealed through several chest radiographs. If these did not yield a definitive answer, the owner had already given approval for an ultrasound exam.

As it turned out, there was no need to go any further than the chest X-rays. All the obvious signs of pulmonary hypertension (high blood pressure in the lung field) were present, and pointed to one disease: heartworm infection. When Toby's history was taken, unfortunately, an error of neglect had occurred. Since resident dogs in Alberta never get infected with heartworm, no one had remembered to ask his owners if Toby had left the province during the last two years.

Had the Terrier mix travelled to any heartworm-infected areas without protection? (In this case, a single application of a topical product when Toby returned from Colorado would have prevented the entire ordeal.) Indeed he had! The next best move was a snap test for heartworm, performed on the spot: a drop of Toby's blood, deposited in a small incubating chamber, revealed a positive reaction within minutes. The diagnosis was certain – Toby had live worms swimming around in his heart and arteries. Each beat of his heart fed more blood to the tiny creatures, and rocked them into a happy state.

We duly informed Toby's worried owners of the difficult treatment ahead for their pet. Restoring Toby's health required killing off the mature worms in his heart, without causing a strong inflammatory response that could overwhelm the dog's small body and cause an anaphylactic reaction (an intense, exaggerated allergic reaction to a foreign substance). An equally important consideration in Toby's treatment was timing: although we needed to kill all the worms in Toby's heart, it should not be done too quickly or abruptly. Only a small number of worms should die at a time, to avoid the pileup of worm corpses that could potentially create a physical blockage in his blood vessels or heart chamber. A delicate situation indeed!

Toby the Terrier was immediately restricted from exercising and getting stressed while in the hospital, and stabilized for his heart condition and its secondary effects. We then initiated the mainstay of Toby's treatment, a painful intramuscular injection of a substance that would start killing the heartworms. Once injected, Toby was sent home for a month, after which he would receive a second treatment.

For the duration, we strongly advised Toby's owners that he should not exercise at all, nor should he undertake any activities that would exert his heart. Sadly, less than one week into the treatment, the small Terrier cross was found dead in his bed at the end of the day. His owners, grief-stricken by the loss of their pet, requested a necropsy to elucidate the cause of his death, and to determine whether it was in fact related to the presence of heartworms. Indeed it was: Toby had remnants of about eighteen worms tangled in blood clots in his chest. Their slow death had apparently caused a thromboembolus, a vital blockage to his blood flow.

Given that all dogs react differently to treatment, there was no anticipating Toby's death. Some dogs can be infected with more than fifty worms and survive, although the survival rate certainly increases with the size of the dog. Fifty worms in the heart of a Great Dane is one thing, but that same number in the heart of a dog weighing thirteen kilograms is a critical problem. Toby, who weighed less than thirteen kilograms, might have survived an infection with fewer worms, but eighteen worms, averaging twenty-five centimeters each, add up to a four-and-a-half meters of worms in a canine heart the size of a woman's fist! In the end, that was just too much for Toby's small body to tolerate.

A final note: The world of parasites is a most fascinating one. The word "parasite" itself defines an organism that lives off another organism (the host) to promote its own survival. Ideally, the parasite will not kill its host. Death of the host generally means death for the parasite – unless killing the host is necessary for the parasite's leap to the next host. In the case of heartworms, the death of a dog, as the final host, also means the demise of the adult heartworms, since they can only live in or near a beating heart. In the simple image of a coughing dog, millions of years of evolution have created a beautifully synchronized system of multicellular organisms, all interconnected given the right environmental factors. There are the dogs: the final host. There are the mosquitoes: the intermediate host, just providing a ride. And, finally, there are the dreaded heartworms: the parasites that invade two hosts to complete a life cycle that involves four larval stages and an adult stage.

Less than two decades ago, this is precisely how the story of heartworm disease and its treatment was taught and generally perceived. Today, we know better. An evolutionary system that already seemed so complex, yet harmonized to perfection, has become even more complex: the parasite is, in reality, also parasitized!

A bacterium-like organism, belonging to the genus Rickettsia and called Wolbachia, has been discovered within the cells of every adult heartworm in the hearts of afflicted dogs. Researchers now suspect that the inflammatory response to worms that occurs in dogs may actually be a response to the irritating presence of Wolbachia, hence the addition of antibiotics to the heartworm treatment protocol. The discovery of this intracellular parasite that parasitizes another parasite presents a new paradigm in our search for understanding of the pathogenesis (origin, development, and effects of a disease) of heartworms. Most of all, this discovery is another humbling reminder of the interconnectedness of life on the planet, and of our immense ignorance of the true scope of its vast and intricately complex components, including the human brain.

Now that a complex threesome has in fact been revealed as a complex foursome (dog, mosquito, heartworm, Wolbachia), how long will it be before it becomes a fivesome? Life evolves, knowledge changes, and so treatment protocols for our beloved dogs must be continually adjusted to keep pace. Our responsibility, as dog lovers and caregivers, is to educate ourselves and stay abreast of new developments in animal care – and in so doing, protect our animals from unnecessary harm.

The great tragedy of Toby's story is that his death was completely preventable. Heartworm medication is widely available to stop the disease from developing in dogs. The medication is administered as a monthly dose, either orally or topically (applied to the skin), and is very effective. Unless your canine companion never leaves "safe" zones such as Alberta or Saskatchewan, heartworm education – about its dangers, prevention and treatment – is beneficial for you, and potentially life saving for your pet.

As a dog lover, you can…

- Educate yourself about heartworm infection and its dangers, especially if you live in an area of risk.

- Have your dog on heartworm preventive medication if you live in an area of risk, or if you will be travelling to such an area with your dog.

CHAPTER 11

Salmonella:
the kiss of death

Not long ago, Mrs. Roth brought Hailey, her four-year-old black Portuguese Water Dog, in for her rabies vaccination and a certificate of health, so Hailey could continue her valuable contribution to society as a therapy dog. Several elderly patients at a local hospice await Hailey's weekly visit, looking forward to her generous loving kisses and their conversations about this and that with Mrs. Roth. To witness the immediate cheer that companion animals can elicit in lonely, elderly people, and the obvious benefit to their emotional and physical health, is truly amazing. Mrs. Roth reports that she often observes patients come out of their shell when they greet Hailey, and during the thirty minutes or so that they walk or talk with the therapy dog. They literally come alive when the dog is present. Then, upon Hailey's departure, they seem to mentally shut out the world again, often just sitting silently in bedside chairs, with sadness in their eyes.

Hailey is the perfect therapy dog, very gentle with everyone. She never leaps or bounces on frail hospice residents, and shows her exuberance only with a soft wag of her tail that would never knock over or rock a walker. Always eager to please, she has impeccable manners, listens attentively to commands, and never vocalizes her moods. Some might say Hailey is easy to get along with because she lacks any definable personality. No matter what's happening, she just goes with the flow and blends in.

The requirements for canine therapy service dogs are simple and straightforward: the dog must pass temperament evaluations, a complete physical exam, i.e., the dog must be free of diseases, especially periodontal disease considering the frequent hand-to-mouth contact between dogs and patients; and of course have a current rabies vaccination, for obvious reasons. During Hailey's physical exam, however, I noticed one outstanding feature that had nothing to do with her work requirements – her coat was magnificently luxurious.

"I'm curious, Mrs. Roth," I said, out of interest, "Do you know why Hailey's coat has become so soft and shiny?"

Mrs. Roth nodded. "Oh, yes!" she announced, with great pride, "I've just changed Hailey's diet from a commercial kibble to raw food."

Oh my! All the coffee I had just swallowed spurted right back up through my sinuses and left me sputtering.

A routine, no-brainer appointment had just turned into anything but: all my brain neurons were firing at once, exploding with warnings, and questions, and more warnings. Where to start? The main problem – the one that practically had my coffee spewing into my sinuses – was the frightening implication of "raw food" coupled with "elderly people." There are obvious benefits and risks to every decision we make, but when our decisions significantly impact others, we hope that the risks have been weighed with an extra measure of caution.

The clear benefit of feeding Hailey raw food was her shiny coat. Raw meat often contains a much higher fat content than commercial kibble and, for this reason, dogs on a raw-food diet tend to put on extra weight (desirable if the animal is a finicky eater and too thin), and develop an unusually lustrous coat.

On the adverse side, the considerable risk in having Hailey on raw food came with her weekly contact with elderly people, who may not have strong immune systems. What could Hailey, with her raw meat diet, potentially inflict on them that would challenge their immune systems? Here's what could happen: bacteria, such as Salmonella, E. coli, and Campylobacter, which have amazing ubiquitous abilities, will happily transfer from raw red meat or chicken to a dog, which becomes a silent carrier (with no signs of illness) and, finally, to susceptible people such as elderly hospice residents, who can become seriously ill as a result. All thanks to a wet, cheerful doggy kiss on the mouth that happens to be loaded with pathogens (disease-producing microorganisms)!

Depending on a person's immune system, and the virulence of the pathogen, disease may or may not become overt. However, there are certain people and animals whose immune systems should not be challenged if at all possible. They include the very young, whose immune systems are not yet fully developed; the very old, whose immune systems are worn out and tired; and the immunosuppressed group, such as individuals affected by AIDS, on chemotherapy, or suffering from chronic ailments.

Mrs. Roth had not considered the implications of Hailey's raw meat diet, so our conversation about its risks left her perplexed. Admittedly, I was disappointed and somewhat surprised that the animal league, which had recruited Hailey as a therapy dog, had not been more specific regarding that aspect of a dog's health requirements. Feeding commercially prepared raw food to dogs is a relatively new phenomenon in North America, and one that is gaining some popularity. In their defence, perhaps groups such as the animal league had not yet had time to adjust to this trend.

Would this "red alert" prompt Mrs. Roth to stop feeding raw food to Hailey? Or did she see enough benefits to the new diet that she would continue feeding it to Hailey, and abandon her weekly visits for the time being while doing more research on the issue?

"Would taking a bacterial culture of Hailey's stools be enough to prove the absence of food-borne pathogens?" Mrs. Roth inquired.

The answer, unfortunately, was no. Even when a culture is negative (showing no growth of pathogens), it does not necessarily mean the animal is negative, i.e., not carrying such pathogens. It only means that, at that point in time, the animal was not shedding pathogens. But a few hours to days later, it could very well be shedding pathogens, if the animal were indeed a carrier.

"What do you mean by a 'carrier'?" Mrs. Roth asked.

"A carrier is either an animal or person that carries a potentially harmful pathogen," I explained, "but is not showing any clinical signs of the disease."

A cow in a feedlot, for example, might have Salmonella bacteria in its gut, but produce normal stools and have a normal appetite, all the while shedding the bacteria intermittently into the environment. Other cows in the same pen, foraging on the ground, might inadvertently pick up the bacteria and become ill themselves, with overt signs such as profuse liquid diarrhea, fever, and anorexia. Unless the "carrier" is removed and possibly treated, other cows with varying states of immunity will be constantly exposed and affected.

Could Hailey become acutely sick from bacteria, such as Salmonella and E. coli, found in raw meat? Absolutely. If Hailey were to be infected with these bacteria, she could develop hemorrhagic gastroenteritis (bloody gut), and possibly die within hours to days of pathogen ingestion. During that period of time, if there was any transfer of pathogens through Hailey's enthusiastic face licks, everyone she came into contact with would also be at risk of contracting bloody gut – never mind the possible contamination from cleaning up bloody vomit and diarrhea on the floor.

The topic of feeding raw food to companion dogs is one that deeply polarizes dog lovers. Some vehemently support the practice, others vehemently oppose it – but both groups have strongly entrenched positions. It need not be an issue of polar opposites, however, as we'll see as we investigate the issue further. First, let's find out what led to Mrs. Roth's decision.

"I'm curious, Mrs. Roth," I said, "Why did you decide to switch Hailey from her regular kibble to raw food?

Very quickly, Hailey's owner presented a variety of reasons. She was concerned that dog kibble was not well balanced, considering the presence of grains such as corn on the ingredients list. She was worried that Hailey was not getting enough satisfaction out of her meals, as she ate her kibble with so little enthusiasm, compared with her display of joy whenever raw food landed in her dish. Finally, Mrs. Roth thought it would be better to provide food "closer to nature," i.e., what the dog's ancestors traditionally ate – a return to the wild and ancestral type of food.

I had a few more questions. "Are you feeding Hailey raw food from scratch, prepared in your kitchen, Mrs. Roth? Or are you buying frozen commercial meat patties made by a local dog food company?"

"A little of both," she admitted, "Depending on time availability, and space in my fridge and freezer."

The feeding of raw food to our companion animals is still a relatively new and emerging trend. In reality, the massive pet food recall of 2007, which caused the deaths of thousands of pets after they ingested melamine-contaminated canned food, very likely contributed to the public's growing distrust of commercial pet food, and with good reason. On the other hand, is the radical and indiscriminate change to raw food a wise choice? Could there be another recall waiting to happen, this time involving raw food products instead of commercial kibble pet food?

In response to the first question, I'd say let's look at this more closely. But the answer to the second question is no: there is little likelihood of a raw food recall in the foreseeable future. Such a recall is improbable not because raw food contamination never happens, but rather because there are insufficient regulatory processes in place to identify and deal with such a problem, which is in effect *much* scarier.

So, dear reader, please join me in the following pet food discussion with an open mind, as we investigate whether Mrs. Roth was prudent and judicious in her decision to change Hailey's diet – or not.

The trend toward feeding raw food to pets seems to have emerged partly out of dissatisfaction with the grain (often corn) content of commercial kibble diets. This is, of course, not the only reason, but it is an important one for some dog owners. To this day, neither proponents of commercial kibble diets nor proponents of raw meat diets can make a convincing, evidence-based case for the superiority of one diet over the other. There simply are no statistically significant studies that compare the two types of diet side by side. It all comes down to a matter of opinion. Therefore, each of these two diet types must be evaluated on its merits alone, not based on anecdotal evidence or subjective assessment.

In the real world of pet nutrition, the inquiring scientific mind most often turns to AAFCO (American Association of Feed Control Officers) and its accredited feeding trials as a source of unbiased assessment and objective evaluation. A feeding trial is by no means a perfect tool, but it is a start. Basically, an animal feeding trial is conducted to ascertain whether a tested diet has met the nutritional requirements of a certain life stage, such as puppy or adult stage, following a specifically established AAFCO protocol. The submission and accreditation process is not free to the submitting company (i.e., the food producer), nor is it mandatory.

Given that the world of nutrition is in constant evolution, these feeding trials have some obvious limitations, but we must concede that companies that submit their diets to AAFCO for evaluation have invested considerable money, time and energy into their diets to provide consumers with reliable and consistent information. Thus far, raw food diet producers seem very reluctant to submit their food to AAFCO for testing; compared to commercial kibble producers, hardly any have done so. In the obscure hallways of pet food regulations, this is certainly a missed opportunity to level the playing field, if only a little.

Should a pet food diet be chosen strictly on the basis of whether or not it passed an AAFCO feeding trial? No, but since a "pass" is akin to achieving certification that a diet is balanced and digestible within some limits, it certainly is a reasonable start. Realistically, other factors such as food palatability, resulting stool quality, and resulting coat quality should also be considered when evaluating the nutritional attributes of any diet.

As far as the grain component of some pet food products, it is true that dogs do not have strict nutritional requirements for carbohydrates (except perhaps when lactating or pregnant). Carbohydrates, such as grains, are fed to dogs as a convenient, reliable, and inexpensive source of energy in the form of protein and fat. Certainly these two nutrients can be derived from other sources, such as raw meat, but are not likely to be derived as cheaply as from grains.

On the other paw, dogs have digestive enzymes, such as pancreatic amylase, and brush border enzymes, which actively carry glucose with ATP and sodium, supporting the theory that dogs are not only facultative carnivores (preferential meat eaters) but also omnivores (plant eaters that consume plant carbohydrates in the form of starches, glucose, fructose, etc.). Both physiologically and metabolically, dogs appear to be equipped to handle carbohydrates in their diet. However, commercial grain-based food products can become contaminated with fungi, such as mycotoxins, and dogs are definitely unable to handle such contamination. Therefore, if we decide to choose grain-based commercial pet foods for our dogs, we must be careful to select foods produced by reputable companies that have extensive quality control protocols in place to prevent such a problem.

Some advocates of a raw meat diet will rely on the argument of "wolves in the wild" to support their practice of feeding raw meat, but this is a difficult argument to sustain, to say the least. Wolves, considered the dog's ancestors, are probably closer to being omnivores than exclusive or obligate carnivores (meat eaters only), as cats are. Now consider that the evolution of domestic dogs over the last 15,000 years has produced a significant genetic drift that differentiates them in very distinct ways from wolves. If we were to apply this argument to two other closely related beings, humans and great apes – such as chimpanzees – where more than 98 percent of their genetic pool has been shared for much longer, and compare their diets, we would find that very few humans would be able to sustain themselves for eight decades (the human lifespan) on an ape's diet, which consists primarily of jungle herbivorous food. We cannot assume that, just because dogs and wolves share a common ancestry, they are physically and metabolically identical, any more than humans and chimps, who differ enormously in their digestive tract capabilities despite their genetic similarity. Consider for a moment the enormous selection pressure put on dogs to develop into such varied breeds as Teacup Poodles and Chihuahuas; these breeds have drifted so far away from their ancestry to wolves that we can hardly imagine how these tiny dogs could ever survive as hunters and strict eaters of raw food.

The "wolves in the wild" argument brings us to another fault that raw meat diet proponents find with commercial kibble: the presence of byproducts, notably organs such as heart, liver, and kidneys. This issue was broached briefly in a previous chapter, but it bears repeating here that the wolf status – as something of an omnivore or, at the very least, a facultative carnivore – only weakens the argument of "wolves in the wild." Wolves do eat entrails and byproducts, where many essential amino acids (the building blocks of proteins) are found. They actually eat the entire carcasses of their prey. If organ meat is good for wolves, why is it not for dogs?

Dog lovers and truth seekers, let us round another corner on this topic. Typically, commercial kibble pet food advocates base their refusal to switch to raw meat pet food on three main arguments. The first relates to safety and food-borne pathogens. Most people are aware of the precautions needed when handling raw meat for human consumption. The CDC (Center for Disease Control) refers to raw meat, poultry, raw eggs, unpasteurized milk, and raw shellfish as potential sources of harmful pathogens. The CDC also reports that an estimated 76 million human illnesses are due to food-borne pathogens, with 325,000 hospitalizations and 5200 deaths in the USA every year. This is serious stuff! Feeding raw food to dogs means handling potentially harmful pathogens twice daily in the kitchen, the same environment where human meals are prepared. Doing so safely involves much vigilance and cleanliness in the kitchen; this is a realm of pet care that definitely should not involve children. To be fair, commercial kibble is not necessarily free of pathogens either, but occurrences of contamination seem far less frequent, and easier to trace if recalls are required.

I hear you well, raw food supporters, I hear you well indeed – and you are right. Dogs can handle a multitude of bacteria; after all, they eat their own feces, drink out of the toilet, roll on and eat road kill carcasses that have putrefied in the sun, and go through garbage cans on a regular basis. On the clinical side, however, many of them can, and do, become very, very ill as a result of indulging in such dietary indiscretions, especially if the dogs are especially young or old.

Some raw food advocates, of course, use only raw meat from their own hunting trips, or from animals raised on their farms and butchered at home. In these instances, heralding the food pathogen warning is much more difficult, as pathogens are more than likely not present. Generally, food pathogens are introduced into the food chain when animals are raised in extraordinary densities – like the crowded conditions common to battery chickens and feedlot cattle – where contamination occurs on factory farms or at slaughterhouses. Again, the "wolves in the wild" argument becomes very weak here: wolves do not eat factory farmed grain-fed animals slaughtered in mass numbers, so they face a much lower risk of contamination via food-borne pathogens.

The second argument used by commercial kibble pet food supporters is the worrisome nutritional imbalance present in raw food. This is a decidedly difficult argument to intelligently refute. Rickets, a bone-softening disease – caused by a deficiency or imbalance in vitamin D, calcium and phosphorus – that makes bones soft and prone to bending, was assumed by many to be a nutritional disease of the past, or occurring only in captive wild animals such as green iguanas that are fed an inappropriate diet and lack sunlight exposure (Vitamin D) in northern latitudes. In fact, rickets is a disease on the rise again since the recent advent of commercial raw food diets for dogs. To illustrate this point, let's look at what happened to Mister.

Mister represents a typical example of rickets now being seen in dogs. A Harlequin Great Dane puppy, Mister was purchased at two months of age. He apparently came from a reputable breeder, and Mister passed his first puppy physical exam with flying colors. When his owner, Mrs. Reid, inquired about offering Mister a raw food diet, she was given this advice: unless she worked closely with a certified nutritionist to ensure that Mister received a complete and balanced diet, it was not the best idea. Mister was likely going to weigh forty-five kilograms by the time he reached six months of age, and even a small mistake in his calcium, phosphorus, and Vitamin D intake could put Mister in danger of suffering from osteodystrophy (rickets).

Sure enough, four weeks after Mister's initial wellness exam, the dog was in bad shape: all four of his legs were facing the wrong direction, his joints were swollen, and Mister had lost all of his vitality. Mrs. Reid admitted that she had fed him nothing but raw chicken backs and buffalo meat for an entire month. Unfortunately for the poor puppy, this exclusively meat-based diet was severely deficient in the three nutrients mentioned above, all necessary for normal bone growth. Mister was immediately prescribed a commercial pet food designed for large-breed puppies, along with supplements, and within a month he grew to become the dog he was supposed to be.

Does a raw food diet provide dogs a balanced ratio of all the necessary vitamins and minerals essential for growth and maintenance? This is difficult to evaluate if the raw food producer does not provide a complete nutrient analysis, or if the product has not undergone scrutiny by AAFCO. The odds would be against it.

The third argument against raw food diets is one we have already touched on, and relates to all the bone-chewing problems that can arise. These problems, which range from fractured teeth to stomach and intestinal perforations, are very real, and clearly reflect what each dog owner views as an acceptable risk. Unlike bacterial contamination, which can affect humans, the risk factors of bone chewing are limited to individual animals.

One concern that is not often mentioned, perhaps for privacy reasons, is that some dog owners find the cost of raw pet food diets financially prohibitive. Some acknowledge the bacterial contamination link to human illness, and start cooking the raw food before feeding it to their dogs. But for many owners, this culinary practice soon becomes too laborious and is quickly abandoned.

Purists in the raw-food camp believe that cooking raw meat destroys all the "good enzymes" needed for digestion, but these "good enzymes" remain somewhat elusive, as they are not referred to in the scientific literature.

Another major concern regarding the feeding of raw food to dogs is the potential impact of such a diet on a pregnant bitch. Unless balanced to perfection, a raw food diet will often not sustain both the skeleton formation of numerous puppies and the maintenance of the bitch's own skeleton. This can mean loss of life or health, if not both. More importantly, many fetuses will simply not be carried to term because of exposure to food-borne pathogens in utero (in uterus). Sadly, when their immature immune systems become overwhelmed, the puppies die prior to birth.

Dear truth seeker, we are nearing the home stretch. In closing, let's review some far-reaching arguments that are seldom raised in the pet food debate.

With all good intentions, most dog owners are searching for the best possible diet for their four-legged companions. Since most of North American society is urban, we naturally experience a large degree of mental and emotional dislocation from our food sources, which are primarily grown in distant rural areas. For many people, food simply comes from the supermarket, fresh and cleanly wrapped. Period. However, such is not truly the case. Much of our food, for both human and animal consumption, is imported. As evidenced by the pet food recall of 2007, protein concentrate was imported from China because the USA has become a net protein importer and must rely on other countries to feed its citizens, humans or animals. Other countries have different health standards than North America, and it is increasingly difficult for our regulatory industry to keep up with vast quantities of imported food with various standards of production, processing, and packaging.

In order to keep up with domestic food demand, our own agricultural system has turned to intensive farming methods, in which livestock such as cattle, pigs, and chickens are raised in extreme densities. To maintain animal production in such high densities, the industry must adopt strategies to manage diseases that cause morbidity and mortality. For this reason, a vast array of drugs, such as antibiotics, ionophores and growth hormones, are promoted and heavily used. Though it may be hard to believe, livestock in the USA reportedly consumes eight times more antibiotics than humans do, by volume (Union of Concerned Scientists, 2001. *Hogging it! Estimates of antimicrobial abuse in livestock.* A report written by Mellon, M., Benbrook, C., & Lutz Benbrook, K.). This is an impressive figure, but in the wrong way.

When dog owners opt for a raw food pet diet, they should take into consideration that, unless they favor the very costly free-range or organic meats, they are actually feeding their canine friends drug-laced, grain-fed meat, since grass feeding of factory farmed livestock is no longer possible. Intensively raised animals are fed large quantities of grain to promote fast weight gain and greater profit.

However, such a high intake of this type of meat may not be favorable to our pets' health and, by extension, our own. According to demonstrated analysis, the physiological profile of a grass-fed cow is vastly different from that of a grain-fed cow, with significantly different degrees of cholesterol present in the animals' muscle mass, for example. (For more information, visit World Watch Institute on the web.) Another disheartening but noteworthy consideration is that factory farming is considered by many as an inherently cruel and shameless way of treating animals – never mind the slaughter process, which can be emotionally disturbing to watch. On this basis alone, the issue of feeding pets any food that is unnecessarily high in animal protein, whether raw meat or commercial kibble, perhaps needs to be revisited from a humane point of view.

Parenthetically, it is interesting to note that in North America the definition of "byproduct" or "meal" in pet food consistently excludes chicken feet or chicken beaks. In poorer countries like China, however, where the vast majority of people are raised on diets low in animal protein, humans – not dogs – commonly consume those body parts. For many, this is the only animal protein they can afford!

In the end, which is the better pet food, raw food or commercially prepared kibble? All debate aside, the *best* pet food is the one that is nutritionally adequate, and meets a specific dog's physiological nutrient requirements. Ideally, the product will have undergone AAFCO feeding trials as one measure, to attest to its digestibility and its balanced nutritional status in sustaining different life stages; it should be free of drug residues, such as antibiotics, growth hormones, pesticides and herbicides; it should be safe and convenient, affordable, available and palatable, and produced with appropriate respect given to the environment and the slaughtered animals. Sadly, such a diet does not exist. Every dog owner, therefore, must decide which pet food is best by ranking the above criteria in order of importance, and choosing the diet that is the closest match to his or her personal preferences and unique circumstances.

As for Mrs. Roth, you may be wondering whether or not she kept up with the raw food diet for Hailey. As a result of our discussion, Mrs. Roth decided to make some changes to her dog's diet that would continue to support her two priorities. Firstly, she wanted to continue with Hailey's weekly visits to the hospice, but in no way did she ever want Hailey to be responsible for any illness of the hospice pensioners she visited. Her second priority, of course, was Hailey's proper nutrition; she wanted to keep her beloved pet healthy.

So Mrs. Roth decided to do the following: she would take Hailey off raw food completely, and put her on a high-quality commercial kibble diet that had an excellent guaranteed nutrient analysis and had passed AAFCO feeding trials. Mrs. Roth chose a food brand produced by a large, reputable food company, and she felt confident in their quality control protocols. Not wanting to give up completely on unprocessed food for her dog, however, Mrs. Roth resolved to incorporate pieces of cooked free-range chicken or bison into Hailey's dinner twice weekly.

In the process of finding a workable compromise, Mrs. Roth made some very sound decisions. Hailey was able to continue her therapy work with patients who loved her. Mrs. Roth had the satisfaction of knowing that her dog was healthy and happy. And Hailey's coat remained shiny and lustrous.

As a dog lover, you can…

- Do your research, and weigh all risks carefully when making an informed choice between a raw food diet or a commercial kibble diet for your dog.

- Make a list of your priorities when choosing a food for your pet.

- If you opt for a raw food diet, ensure that: a) the raw food comes from a reliable source and is free of pathogens; b) the raw food is nutritionally balanced for your dog's health; and c) you take the appropriate steps to prevent bone-chewing problems for your dog.

CHAPTER 12

Dogs and Chocolate: a lethal mix

Unbeknownst to him, Stetson was given a chance to live and, sadly, he blew it. So did his owners. Stetson's story begins innocently enough, with the plump, happy Wheaton Terrier patiently waiting for his family to come home. When Mrs. Madder and her five-year-old twin daughters returned from grocery shopping, the girls excitedly greeted Stetson as they began unpacking the grocery bags. Hearing the phone ring, Mrs. Madder left to answer the call in the living room while her little girls finished putting the groceries away.

When a half-kilogram bag of chocolate chips, purchased to make Easter treats, slipped from a twin's grasp and dropped to the floor, Stetson pounced on it, ripped it open and began to wolf down the sweet morsels. The little girls watched, laughing at his enthusiasm, but did not try to stop him. Stetson, having eaten too quickly, immediately regurgitated the chocolate chips onto the kitchen floor. (Unlike vomiting, which occurs after digestion and some absorption has taken place in the stomach and upper small intestine, regurgitation occurs before any digestion has taken place.)

This was the crux – the point where nature gave Stetson

a chance to live. The chocolate chips had been expelled from his stomach undigested. If the little girls had immediately removed the slobbery brown chocolate mash, or if Mrs. Madder had moved quickly to get Stetson away from the regurgitated mash, the terrier would have been fine. For a fleeting moment, nature was on Stetson's side, and then it was not. With no human intervention to guide him, Stetson re-ingested the brown chocolate mash, and this time it stayed in his stomach.

Within a few hours of his feast, Stetson started to vomit brown bile, and his whole body started to tremor. This was how he was presented to Emergency. Mrs. Madder, after questioning her little girls, understood what had happened and rushed him to the clinic. Would the little guy survive? The amount of chocolate he had ingested was well beyond the toxic dose for his size. At this stage, a quick detox was Stetson's only hope. With not a moment to waste, we induced vomiting with the help of a pharmaceutical agent, and followed it with a stomach lavage. Some brown stomach content was recovered, but unfortunately most of it had already been absorbed and moved well along in the small intestines; the body tremors were clear evidence that chocolate absorption had already happened. While he was connected to the EKG machine for an electrocardiogram (a reading of the electrical conduction activity of his heart), we noted that Stetson's heart rate was increasing at an alarming rate, and arrhythmia (erratic heart rhythm) was becoming more pronounced. His body tremors soon morphed into full-blown seizures that could not be controlled with anti-seizing drugs administered intravenously. His tachycardia (fast heart rate) and arrhythmia were totally unresponsive to the use of cardiac drugs, also given intravenously. Despite receiving 100 percent oxygen via a tube inserted in his nose, Stetson began breathing inconsistently. Soon after, his electrocardiogram began to flat line, and remained so. All was silent then except for the persistent high-pitched buzz of the machine, the sadly familiar sound of a life ended too soon.

Had Stetson eaten only a handful of chocolate chips, he would likely have survived his ravenous chocolate escapade. He would most certainly have suffered a severe bellyache with vomiting and diarrhea, and felt very tired for a couple of days, but he would have recuperated without major impact on his health.

So why do some dogs seem unaffected by eating chocolate while others suffer in the throes of tremors, tachycardia and death? To answer this question, let's go back to the origins of this popular treat. Chocolate is derived from the beans of cacao trees grown in tropical areas, such as Ghana, Costa Rica and Ecuador, with the bulk of this crop concentrated in a narrow region on either side of the equator.

The fruits of the cacao tree grow from the trunk itself, and must be picked by hand so as not to damage the tree. Wildlife, including monkeys, love to feast on the fruits of the cacao tree, but all instinctively discard the bitter seeds from which chocolate is made. As a cash crop, the seeds are collected from the fruits, left to ferment under vegetation, such as banana leaves, for a week or so, and then dried and shipped to manufacturers.

The seeds are then processed – roasted, ground and pressed to remove the oil that later becomes the cacao butter used in cosmetics and white chocolate. Grinding hulled cacao beans produces the chocolate liquor; the cacao powder is the solid left over.

Dogs are particularly sensitive to theobromine, the active ingredient contained in the chocolate liquor. Unsweetened chocolate contains about 50 percent chocolate liquor whereas milk chocolate may contain less than 15 percent; vanilla, milk solids, lecithin and other ingredients make up the balance. Therefore, a small dog that eats a large amount of dark chocolate is more likely to suffer from chocolate toxicity than a large-breed dog that eats a milk chocolate Easter bunny.

Unsweetened baking chocolate may contain as much as seven times the theobromine of milk chocolate, while white chocolate contains negligible amounts. If Stetson had eaten white chocolate chipits, he would have suffered from severe gastroenteritis (vomiting and diarrhea) due to ingredients such as cacao butter, sugar, butterfat, milk solids, and flavorings; but there would be no chocolate liquor to ingest. The high fat content of the white chocolate might even cause pancreatitis (we will look at this in "Gobble, Gobble"), but not the typical toxicity signs of hyperactivity, increased heart rate and tremors.

Theobromine, along with caffeine found in chocolate, is classified as a methylxanthine. In dogs, methylxanthines inhibit cellular adenosine receptors, with the direct result of tachycardia and central nervous system stimulation. Prevention of toxicity requires prevention of chocolate ingestion; it is that simple. Most of the chocolate toxicities I have seen in practice did not result from owners feeding chocolate treats to dogs, but from dogs nosing out chocolate treats wherever they were hidden. A wrapped gift under the Christmas tree that contains chocolate, for instance, is fair game; any dog can sniff out such tasty morsels through the paper. Chocolate Easter eggs hidden around the house are also fair game, and chances are most dogs will find these treats before the children can. For a dog, even a plate of brownies left on the kitchen table for guests to enjoy is too tempting to resist...

Death by chocolate can be totally avoided simply by making sure that dogs have no access to chocolate, especially the dark variety. When receiving a wrapped present, always ask if it contains edible products; if so, store it safely out of reach of your four-legged Sherlock Holmes.

If chocolate ingestion has occurred despite your best preventive efforts, quick action is vital: induce vomiting promptly, and/or rush your dog to the closest veterinary hospital. Either action would have saved Stetson's life and spared his family the pain of losing their pet.

A quick note on inducing vomiting: it should not be done if your dog has already started to vomit, has lost consciousness or has trouble breathing or has become too weak to stand, and has also ingested another caustic substance such as bleach. Hydrogen peroxide (3%) is the product of choice to induce vomiting by a lay person.

As a dog lover, you can…

- Avoid feeding chocolate to your dog, and make sure that others do not feed chocolate to your dog.

- Ensure that any chocolate in your house is safely stored beyond your dog's reach.

- Note the type and amount of chocolate and induce vomiting based on the advice of your veterinarian, if you suspect chocolate ingestion by your dog.

CHAPTER 13

Gobble, Gobble:
the trouble with turkey

Clearly, Mrs. Amthor was very upset – but why? Was it because Hoover ruined her Thanksgiving dinner by demolishing her fresh-from-the-oven, seven-kilogram turkey roast, wolfing down meaty chunks of the bird and slobbering all over the platter before her guests even arrived? Or because, after the illicit feast, Hoover had vomited what seemed like gallons of partially digested turkey meat, skin and yellow bile all over Mrs. Amthor's plush Persian carpets? Or perhaps because Mrs. Amthor had to spend part of Thanksgiving night at the veterinary hospital with the guilty Hoover, who was by then suffering the miserable after-effects of the food binge?

In truth, Hoover's owner was distraught about every one of these dreadful events, and became even more so after we examined her pet and delivered a diagnosis. No matter how much she tried to muster up some enthusiasm to mask her distress, we could see that the grim news about Hoover was more than a little depressing for Mrs. Amthor. But there was no avoiding the reality: Hoover, a four-year-old female St. Bernard, was not likely to recover on her own. She needed medical help. And, given her size – a whopping sixty-one kilograms – the amount of medication and care needed to make Hoover feel better was going to be very expensive.

You see, Hoover was named for her greatest talent: she would hoover any type of food, anytime and anywhere. As far as she was concerned, the more, the better. Hoover also spent last Christmas hospitalized at the veterinary hospital, and I am sure, astute reader and dog lover, that you have guessed why. Yes indeed, she had chowed down on the leftover turkey that she hoovered off the counter top. But at least that time it was *after* the meal, and the guests had already had their fill. After Mrs. Amthor rushed her in to the hospital, the hefty St. Bernard had been diagnosed with pancreatitis, and spent nearly a week hospitalized before she was able to start eating on her own again without getting sick. For Hoover's exasperated owner, the dog's recurring penchant for turkey trouble was fast taking on an air of déjà vu.

The major problem this time around was that Hoover ate most of the skin, but did not get to any of the turkey bones. So the concern was not impaction or perforation from bone ingestion, but rather pancreatitis from the sudden high level of fat intake from turkey skin ingestion. Indeed, analysis of Hoover's blood chemistry, confirming her exceedingly high levels of amylase and lipase enzymes, was pointing toward another bout of pancreatitis until a more definitive diagnosis could be reached with a specific canine pancreatic lipase test sent to a reference laboratory.

Hoover's predicament raises a question worth pursuing: is fat always rightly maligned in human and animal nutrition? Before getting back to Hoover, let's divert for a brief overview of this intriguing subject.

Excess fat, or more precisely, human body fat, has become a thriving multibillion-dollar industry in North America. Take a look around: "Get Rid of Fat" businesses are booming – from liposuction and nip-and-tucks, to weight-loss programs and exercise books. And because we are such generous, good-hearted humans, we have shared our bodily excesses with our companion animals, often indulging them with treats in the same way we indulge ourselves. Out of guilt, or perhaps a lack of something better to do, we even take our dogs to canine fitness centers to keep them fit and trim.

There are significant differences, however, between human and canine bodies when it comes to fat intake. While gaining a few extra kilograms of body fat is certainly not beneficial to our health, our bodies are usually able to tolerate the occasional "pig out." But sudden ingestion of a large amount of fat can be – and often is – deadly for our dogs. And it happens all too often. Here are some examples of the most common canine "high fat intake" scenarios: dogs ingesting turkey skin at Thanksgiving or Christmas, dogs downing 500 grams of butter inadvertently left on the kitchen counter, and dogs foraging through garbage cans and snacking on leftover pork sausages that someone threw out.

Why is a dog at such risk of dying from a little extra fat intake? Simply put, the canine food-processing organs, such as the stomach, intestines, liver, and pancreas, have never evolved to handle an excess of fat. Remember, the modern dog's ancestors were predators, and they hunted prey that was primarily herbivore, such as deer, elk, moose, or their prehistoric equivalents. One characteristic that most prey animals have in common is that they are browsers and grazers, or more simply, vegetarians. Eating plants to sustain daily functions and escape predators rarely, if ever, leads to obesity in wild herbivores. For millennia, or as long as they relied exclusively on killing and eating prey animals for food, a dog's ancestors never really had access to large amounts of fat, and therefore nature saw no reason to equip them physiologically for extensive fat processing.

Over the last millennium, of course, dogs have evolved a great deal, but only in the last half century or so have a greater proportion of dogs come in contact with a significant increase of fat in their food, a change in diet that conveniently arrived with North American affluence. This represents a very short time on the evolutionary scale for such a complex physiological adaptation to take place. What exactly am I saying here? In brief: dogs that ingest a relatively large amount of fat (in comparison to their body mass) can become very ill and die of pancreatitis. A frightening reality, perhaps, but painfully true.

In medical terms, pancreatitis refers to an inflammation of the pancreas, just as laryngitis is an inflammation of the larynx or tendinitis is an inflammation of the tendon. Whenever it is applied to a body organ, the suffix "itis" simply means "inflammation".

What, then, does an inflammation of the pancreas involve? Before addressing this question, we need to first of all become familiar with what the pancreas does for a living. A relatively small organ nestled adjacent to the small intestine (duodenum), the pancreas helps secrete enzymes, such as lipase and amylase, which degrade dietary proteins and fats and prepare them for further digestion and absorption. The pancreas is also responsible for the secretion of insulin, a hormone that helps regulate blood sugar; a lack of insulin translates into the medical condition called diabetes mellitus. As you can see, the lowly pancreas leads a rather private life behind the scenes – until it becomes dysfunctional. Then it can cause major problems, like pancreatitis.

Pancreatitis results from an unfortunate cascade of events that leads the pancreas to more or less digest itself. The cause of pancreatitis is largely unknown, but it seems to often correlate with a high fat intake. Obesity is likely a strong potential risk factor. For this reason, it is always worrisome for a clinician to see an obese dog vomiting repeatedly after stealing a package of bacon off the counter and consuming its contents. Oddly enough, young female dogs belonging to such breeds as Miniature Schnauzer, Miniature Poodle, Yorkshire Terrier, and Labrador Retriever seem to be more at risk for pancreatitis than other breeds.

There is no definitive diagnosis for pancreatitis in a live dog, just a presumptive (i.e., assumed to be true) diagnosis. A dog that presents with a history of poor appetite (a rare thing in a Retriever!), severe vomiting, lethargy (little or no energy), and pain in the abdomen accompanied by a fever should raise suspicion of pancreatitis. If we also know that this dog just ingested a large amount of gravy or other high-fat food, our clinical instincts should be buzzing loudly with the word "pancreatitis". Laboratory work may strongly point toward this diagnosis, as nothing is exclusively specific to pancreatitis.

Unfortunately, no specific treatments for pancreatitis exist either. After diagnosis, therapy is aimed at preventing secretions and activation of enzymes within the pancreas, so that the ailing organ can take a rest. Once initiated, supportive care includes intravenous fluid therapy with electrolyte replacement and several doses of analgesia. The dog's vomiting and lack of appetite typically require the animal's hospitalization until these symptoms are corrected and functions return to normal. In cases where normal function does not return, and the pancreas starts to fail, an ensuing cascade of organ failures can occur in a destructive sequence that will lead to the animal's death. As obscure as this medical condition is, the main preventive factor for pancreatitis is a simple one: avoid high-fat foods.

How did Hoover fare after her most recent fatty feast? Fortunately for the wayward St. Bernard, her Thanksgiving escapade concluded with another happy ending. After Hoover's presumptive diagnosis of pancreatitis, based on blood work and supported by the fact that she had a painful right quadrant abdomen, we started her on intravenous fluid therapy along with anti-nausea drugs.

Prompt action was also a factor in Hoover's recovery. Since Mrs. Amthor was already familiar with the problem, having gone through it the previous Christmas, she did not delay in getting medical help for Hoover as soon as she noticed the dog's health starting to decline. Less than four days after the episode, lucky Hoover was back on her paws and off in search of mischief once again. Despite our affection for this big, friendly St. Bernard, we at the veterinary hospital sincerely hope *not* to see Hoover back here again anytime soon – especially not around Thanksgiving or Christmas.

As a dog lover, you can…

- Avoid feeding turkey leftovers to your dog, especially the turkey skin, fat or bones.

- Become familiar with the symptoms of pancreatitis in dogs.

- Seek immediate veterinary attention if you discover that your dog has ingested large amounts of fat-related food and starts to vomit and become restless.

CHAPTER 14

HBC (Hit By Car):
when traffic tangles end in tragedy

Whenever a dog gets hit by a car (noted as "HBC" in veterinary files), there is a sense of complete despair in the air. The owner feels awful, and the medical team – witness to severe and often fatal bodily injuries – cannot help but feel sadness too. Everyone involved is drawn into a sense of unity with the injured dog, feeling its physical pain and its bewilderment at trying to understand what happened. If the animal is not DOA (dead on arrival), the medical team rapidly sets to work on the basics of emergency care: ABC (Airway, Breathing, Circulation), TPR (Temperature, Pulse, and Respiration) measurements, intravenous fluids, pain management, X-rays, blood work, thermoregulation, and so forth.

Invariably, among those awaiting news of their pet's prognosis, the blame game takes root and grows, a mounting crescendo in the background. It begins with guilt, fueled by worry and a sense of helplessness. How could this have happened to their dog? Below are some typical owners' reactions in HBC cases.

Some blame themselves. "It's my fault – I should never have let Buddy off the leash! But he saw a squirrel across the street, and dashed after it… and he went right under the tire!" The owner is right in this case: dogs restrained by a leash never get hit by a car.

Some blame the operator of the vehicle. "I can't believe the driver didn't even try to swerve to avoid hitting Daisy!" Truth is, swerving in traffic requires excellent reflexes, and can cause far more extensive bodily harm to innocent passersby.

And sometimes, the blame carries over to the medical team. "How much is this going to cost, to fix his broken pelvis and collapsed lungs?" Then, after hearing the response: "What? You must be out of your @#*^%# mind!" Unfortunately, blaming the veterinary team when you learn the cost of emergency medical and surgical care serves no purpose: state-of-the-art medical equipment and experienced veterinary staff are not cheap. The best advice is simply to keep your dog off the street.

Some people think that dogs actively notice and monitor moving cars, as if the animals have the ability to understand vehicular traffic and its dangers. This is a very faulty assumption, as demonstrated by the number of HBCs dealt with during emergency shifts. Dogs do not seem to have a grasp of our traffic laws, oddly enough.

Even service dogs, such as guide dogs for blind people, are limited in what they can do in traffic situations under the direction of their owners. Remember, these guide dogs undergo rigorous genetic and behavioural selection, followed by intensive training, and they must concentrate solely on their actions and the environment while in working mode. Successfully crossing the street with such a finely trained dog is the consequence of precise, well-executed teamwork by the service dog and his owner: this is not a talent that comes naturally to dogs.

Indeed, such a finely trained service animal is a far cry from Ricochet, a Jack Russell Terrier trained to dig holes and ferret out rodents, then kill them with gusto. On the day of his unfortunate mishap, Ricochet had been waiting all day in his crate for his owner to come home. Full of energy and raring to go by the time Mrs. Pitt arrived, the sturdy little dog couldn't wait to race off and sniff the private parts of all of his four-legged friends already outside. Once freed from his crate, Ricochet's tireless exuberance knew no bounds;

he leapt about as though tied to an invisible bungee cord, jumping repeatedly in the air in anticipation of his long-awaited playtime. Before his owner even had a chance to put the leash on him, the excited dog bolted out the door.

By now it was 5:00 in the afternoon, and the traffic was heavy. But Ricochet knew nothing of traffic patterns; he flew down the sidewalk and toward the street, not even pausing to check for danger before crossing. A sudden screech of tires, a split-second of frantic skidding, then whomp!

The car stopped short, with Ricochet still underneath. The shocked driver scrambled out of his car, looking totally bewildered: this all happened so fast! Lying on the ground, Ricochet, panting heavily, began to whimper in pain and fear. Luckily for the dog, he had escaped being crushed by the tires, thanks to his size. Because the vehicle had been traveling slowly, the impact was relatively light; it knocked the thirteen-kilogram Jack Russell off his feet and he rolled out of harm's way.

Even so, Ricochet did not come out of his accident unscathed. He was covered in road grease, with significant road rash (ulcerated skin, with small gravel pieces embedded in oozing blood). And that was not the worst of it, as we discovered when the injured dog was brought in to Emergency. Radiographs revealed that Ricochet's femur, or thigh bone, was completely fractured at its head, where it meets the acetabulum (cup-shaped cavity) of the pelvis.

Happily for the little dog, a simple orthopaedic surgery, involving the resection (removal) of the head of the femur, had him up and running again in less than two months. That was truly a lucky break for Ricochet, no doubt about it.

So you can imagine how surprised we were to see Ricochet in Emergency again, soon after his initial recovery. "Mrs. Pitt, how did Ricochet manage to get hit by a car again?" I asked his owner, totally befuddled, "Especially since it was so traumatic the first time he got hit three months ago and we had to operate on his hip joint!"

When he came in the second time, in fact, Ricochet still had a scar over his left hip from his previous surgery. So how did this happen *again?* Primarily at fault was the dangerous and erroneous notion – held by this dog's owner as well as many others – that dogs learn from their mistakes. Since Ricochet had been hit by a car once, he would surely remember the experience and make sure to avoid getting hit a second time, wouldn't he? Not so. Unfortunately, Mrs. Pitt – like Ricochet – did not learn from her mistake either, so her energetic little Jack Russell got hurt again.

Nikita, a beautiful red Husky, was also badly hurt when hit by a car. Amazingly – in light of the circumstances – it had been her first time HBC, but unfortunately it was also the last. Like all Huskies, Nikita was full of energy, and she ran for kilometers every time she managed to escape her dog pen by jumping the fence. Knowing her love of running, her owner, Mr. Roberts, decided the only way Nikita would ever get enough exercise was by running behind his pickup truck until her tongue started to hang sideways. For months, he had followed this exercise routine with her. And as long as the faithful Nikita remained focused on catching up with the truck, she kept running and running until Mr. Roberts finally slowed down to a stop so she could hop into the passenger seat of his truck.

One recent night, however, the exercise routine did not end well. Nikita ran and ran, as usual, but as Mr. Roberts slowed down to pick her up, Nikita – for some odd reason – picked up speed, racing past the passenger door and then veering abruptly to the left, in front of the truck toward the driver's side. Just then, out of the corner of his eye, Mr. Roberts caught a glimpse of a deer on his left. In the same instant, he felt a solid thump under his front tires and gasped in horror.

By the time his truck came to a full stop, Mr. Roberts could see, in his rear view mirror, the lifeless body of Nikita sprawled on the road. Shaking uncontrollably, he exited his vehicle and raced toward Nikita's body. He thought for an instant she was alive – he could see her rib cage moving up and down slightly. Quickly, he lifted her mangled body and carried her back to his vehicle. Blood was dripping from both of her nostrils, her hanging tongue was blue and sticky with road dirt, and there were visible tire marks over her abdomen. Wiping his tears as he drove to the emergency hospital, Mr. Roberts vowed to himself that he would never exercise Nikita behind his running vehicle again.

In the end, Nikita's owner kept his promise, but not because he had any choice: Nikita was declared DOA as soon as she arrived at Emergency, so she never had a chance to exercise again – behind the truck or anywhere else. Although it brought little comfort to her distraught owner, one small blessing was apparent: she had likely been killed on impact, as most of her ribs were fractured. That night had been Nikita's last run, her last breath, and her last chance to live the joyful life that every Husky deserves.

Not surprisingly, some dogs have a particular knack for getting themselves into trouble with moving cars. Maremma Sheepdogs, large white dogs (not recognized as a breed by the AKC) that originate from Italy and are known for their livestock guardian abilities, are one example. Maremma puppies are often born in the barn among the sheep, which they learn to protect at a young age. Maremmas take great pride in safeguarding their territory from any invading threat, whether it comes with fur and a pumping heart, such as a coyote, or with metal and screeching tires, such as a car. Given their strong sense of duty, these dogs will chase moving cars with great enthusiasm and delight. The job is a rewarding one, and always well done: when a car approaches, the Maremma gets to work pronto, and chases it out of its territory. In the dog's mind, the vehicle obviously got frightened and sped away. So, for the Maremma, this guarding tactic (i.e., chasing cars away) works 100 percent of the time, and becomes a very rewarding exercise for the dog. That is why, unless there is some human intervention, the behavior intensifies over time, often with fatal consequences for the car-chasing dogs.

Another breed that works hard at chasing cars is the Border Collie, truly one of the most remarkable working breeds. Originating from the Scottish high country, where raising sheep was the backbone of the economy, Border Collies were bred for their herding instinct, which proved to be invaluable in keeping grazing flocks of sheep safe and under control. These dogs are the "workaholics extraordinaire" of the canine world, and will strongly follow their herding instinct with everything that moves – including cars.

In some cases, a Border Collie becomes so focused on chasing a car that the animal will actually get hit by an oncoming car. In other cases, the dogs will put themselves in danger by trying to get in front of the cars they are trying to "herd." Either way, the chase often ends very badly for the Border Collie.

There are many practical ways for dog owners to prevent fatal or near-fatal car crashes involving their dogs. One is to ensure that the dog understands the command "come." For a dog to willingly and consistently come to its owner when called, two important concepts must be well established in the dog's mind. First, the owner is always a "safe haven" for the dog, i.e., the dog will always be rewarded when it comes to the owner. That means no scolding, and no angry tone. As you might expect, it creates confusion for a dog if he obediently comes to the owner in response to the command "come," and then is scolded because he took too long to come, or displayed an undesirable behavior, such as eating dog feces (coprophagia) on his way back to the owner. As a basic rule here, if he comes when called, he gets a reward (i.e., happy voice, a treat, or nice petting). You are his safe place, so when he is about to run into traffic, and hears "come," you want to be confident that he will choose to turn on a dime and run to you, rather than toward an oncoming speeding truck.

The second important concept to establish in your dog's mind is that you, as his owner, will never chase him, so he need never run away from you. Yes, you heard correctly: stop chasing your dog. And make sure that any person who interacts with your dog never chases him either. This particular human behavior is unbelievably counterintuitive for dog training. Think about it: your dog's natural instinct, when chased by someone, is to run away. This holds true whether the chasing happens in serious, real-life situations or in play activities, such as racing around after your dog when he has a toy in its mouth that he just snatched from you. In either scenario, the dog only learns to run away from you. If you really want to play running games with your dog, have the dog chase you, never the other way around.

Dogs get hit by cars because they are allowed to roam free or out of control in areas where there are roads and vehicles. Sometimes human carelessness is a factor, as it was – *twice* – in Ricochet's case. And the little guy was twice lucky. Other times it comes down to an owner's poor judgment, as in Nikita's case. But Nikita, unlike Ricochet, had no second chance.

Dogs also get hit by cars when neither the dogs nor their owners have fully grasped the complex concept of the command "come." If your dog is under control on his walks, either with a leash or through voice commands, chances are excellent that your cherished canine friend will never fall victim to a collision with a three-quarter-ton mass of moving metal.

As a dog lover, you can…

- Keep your dog leashed and/or under your control whenever you are near traffic areas.

- Avoid chasing your dog, even in play.

- Train your dog to consistently respond to the command "come" by rewarding him when he does so.

CHAPTER 15

Crop, Dock, and Tuck: cosmetic surgery for dogs

What are Doberman Pinschers with floppy ears? Or Cocker Spaniels with long tails? Or Shar-Peis without wrinkles? Losers in the show ring, most likely!

A decisive cut of the scalpel blade, an artistic touch, and large doses of painkillers will produce dogs that have a chance of winning in the show ring. For a Doberman puppy, the first cosmetic surgeries are best performed in the first three days of life: docking the tail and dissecting out the dewclaws. Four months later, the third cosmetic surgery, much more painful than the first two, is the cropping of the ears. For the dog, this involves a lot of blood, plenty of stitches, and wearing a silly Styrofoam coffee cup upside down between the ears to keep them upright for two weeks. The good news? To be eligible in the show ring, our surgically altered Dobie puppy gets to keep his testicles. Whew!

Unfortunately the last Dobie puppy that I saw was just three months old. He came in for a wellness exam and puppy vaccines, but I never saw him again: he had his ears cropped by one of the few veterinarians still performing the procedure, and the poor little puppy never woke from the anesthesia after the last suture. The owner of the dead puppy then got a new Dobie puppy, from the same breeder, and the same sad sequence of events happened all over again.

Certainly, puppies are a higher anesthetic risk because their liver and kidneys, two organs essential for metabolizing and excreting drugs such as the anesthetic gas, are often immature and easily overwhelmed. The result is an anesthetic death. Neither of these puppies was intended for the show ring, only as a companion dog. So why bother? As explained to me by animal shelter workers, the main reason is that people have a mental image of what a purebred dog should look like, and they wish to nurture and comply with that image. According to a veterinarian at a local shelter, Dobermans with docked tails and cropped ears will be quickly adopted as long as their temperament is acceptable. Time and again, shelter personnel have witnessed rejection of rescue Dobermans with long tails and floppy ears, no matter how gentle they were. For animal shelters, it has been a challenge to get these dogs adopted. "No way!" potential adopters say, "That dog with floppy ears and a long whip tail is a Dobie? No way! It looks weird. No thanks!"

Not long ago, on our veterinary network, I was privy to a heated, protracted and almost vicious discussion regarding cosmetic surgery in dogs. The discussion drew a whole community of veterinarians with different concerns and allegiances to discuss the ethics of surgically altering dogs in order to meet breed standards accepted by the AKC (American Kennel Club). While the format of this discussion has been maintained, names have been changed, and many opinions condensed for the sake of brevity and diplomacy.

Dr. Emily H:

The situation: a litter of four six-week old Boston Terrier pups, one of which has great potential as a show dog. It has outstanding conformation, and a personality with "spark". His tail, though, is too long and straight, and carries "gay" when he moves. Apparently a "gay" tail is against breed specification. The breeder has heard of a little corrective surgery that involves cutting the tendon to pull in the "gay" tail, and suggested that maybe that little surgery could be performed along with a little tail docking to reach tail perfection, even though docking Boston Terriers is not allowed by AKC standards.

Can this breeder ethically demand to have this puppy's tail surgically altered so that he can compete in the show ring? And should I feel okay about it?

Seeking pearls of wisdom on this topic. Thank you in advance.

Dr. Justin T:

Here is my two cents' worth: a docked tail in a Boston Terrier is a disqualification by the AKC, period. From her statement, the breeder is obviously aware of this but is considering having it docked anyway. She is just hoping she won't get caught when she shows him [in the ring]. Dear Emily, if you agree to dock his tail to make him a more suitable show dog, knowing this is not allowed, doing so makes you an accomplice in the deception as well.

If you search the AKC site for breed standards for Boston Terriers you will find, at the very end of the "Neck, Topline and Body" heading, the section where it states the disqualification for docked tail.

IMHO [In My Humble Opinion] – just my two cents' worth!

Dr. Emily H:

Thank you for your response, and the AKC reference. I have to agree with you: docking the tail is not an option in my mind, as it would be a deception. But what about the tendon cutting to shorten the tail and give it a curve – that is still a grey area, right? Do not get me wrong – I do not wish to surgically alter this little pup, and my final answer will be: "Sorry, I am not able to help you." I just need some strong reasons to back up my answer. You see, I tend to be a wimp and not very forceful with my opinions, to avoid confrontations, and would love to have something strong and concrete to justify my opinions.

Again, thank you!

Dr. Cindy R:

In the AKC pamphlet, "Rules and Regulations" has a section on dog shows. It is quite clear: NOTHING is allowed as far as surgical alterations except ears, tails and dewclaws, as customary for the specific breed. If she gets caught, she could be fined, and/or have AKC privileges suspended for a certain amount of time. There is nothing stated about it being illegal for you to do, though. But as indicated above, it would be unethical, and I wouldn't touch it with a ten-foot scalpel!

Good luck with your client discussion.

Dr. Emily H:

I now know that there is such a document as the AKC "Rules and Regulations," and I will whip out that little pearl of knowledge when I tell her (in the nicest way, of course) that I will not be doing anything to this little guy's tail.

I hope one day that the curse I have – to always please the client, the bus driver, the neighbor next door, the garbage man, the store clerk and the barn cat – will go away!

Dr. Kim V:

It seems to be the curse of our veterinary profession: we all want to make everyone happy with everything we do, but it is just not possible! I try to make people happy, as long as it doesn't conflict with my ethical and moral obligations.

Seize the day!

Dr. Edward K:

I do not mean to be argumentative, but who do we work for? As a veterinarian, I have no social contract with the AKC, and actually, I do not agree with their position anyway on cosmetic surgeries, defining what a breed should look like. My only concern is whether a procedure is done because it is medically necessary. I certainly hope that no veterinarian would do a surgery purely for cosmetic reasons: why is it acceptable to chop perfectly good body parts? Just because the AKC says it is acceptable. If a surgery has been performed for a medically justifiable reason, but the dog is now in violation of AKC regulations, then it is none of my business if the dog gets shown. I will not track the client's activities on that!

"If you have to question whether you are doing the right thing or not, you're probably not."

Dr. Cathy S:

I respect your opinion, but at the end of the day, I still do not want to own a Rottweiler with a long tail. Do you?

Dr. Mark B:

Indeed, it seems like an odd concept; however, cosmetic surgeries are just that, cosmetic. I don't buy the argument that these dogs' tails will either self-destruct or get torn when they get out into normal working situations such as hunting or guarding. What is the point to removing two-thirds of a dog's ear, unless you want to have less for another dog fighting yours to grab hold of on the head?

As we have learned from the Prohibition, if the demand is great enough, the supply will come. So there is likely no way to move forward on this issue by cutting off the surgical service; the demand has to decrease. As with many social changes, there will come a time when all of the social forces will align, as if by magic, and together will cause a rapid shift in perceptions. Personally, I think that cosmetic surgeries for dogs will become a thing of the past, as is already the case in several European countries.

Dr. Fiona R:

My turn on the soapbox!

Veterinarians do not work for the AKC. Never did we sign a pledge to abide by their regulations, or to honor their standards. We get paid by the clients, but more importantly, we work for the patients and are advocates for them. AKC standards are often in direct contradiction with standards of health for dogs. Just look at the Bulldog: it can't breathe, can't swim, can't walk in the heat, can't walk in the cold, and can't give birth on its own.

I have no ethical problem with you going against the rules of the AKC. I do question, however, the need for this puppy to have its tail altered for cosmetic reasons. Whoops, just fell off my soapbox!

Dr. Mona G:

I'm obviously out of the breeder loop (which I am grateful for), but what the heck does a "gay" tail mean?

Dr. Emily H:

It means the tail is carried too high. Many breed standards specify that the tail should not be carried above the level of the top line (back). Some breeds can carry the tail a bit high, as long as it isn't carried up over the back like a Husky's.

I suppose the term "gay" refers to the old days when it meant "happy," and dogs that carried their tails up high were considered "too happy"?

Dr. Kate M:

May I clear up some misconceptions?

The AKC does NOT decide what dogs are supposed to look like; each parent club does that by drawing up their own standards by which they wish their breed to be judged. The AKC, however, has the choice of whether or not to allow a breed into its ranks.

If a breeder cheats in order to win (or to get stud services or sell high-priced puppies from their substandard dog), then they should be disqualified – not for having a fault, but for cheating. And if you know that fixing a fault will enable the exhibitor to cheat to win, then you are an accomplice in the deception. I happen to think that is wrong.

The people who would profit from fixing a "gay" tail would be the veterinarian who fixes it, and the breeder who then profits from high-priced puppy sales or stud fees. It is not up to either [the veterinarian or the breeder] to change the breed by conspiring to have a heritable trait introduced into the breed without challenge. A "gay" tail, by the way, is not a disqualification for a Boston Terrier, merely a fault, and the exhibitor can show the dog as is. If the dog is good enough for the judge to overlook that fault, it will win anyway, but at least prospective puppy buyers will know what they are getting. I hope I said this all in a kind way.

Dr. Kathy L:

I just finished a C-section – now waiting for the dog to wake up. I am finding this thread very interesting, especially with the moral high grounds taken by so many of my colleagues. I wish I could take a survey and find out how many male veterinarians have been circumcised. This surgical procedure, done by lay people on baby boys, is not done for cosmetic reasons but religious beliefs. Hmm... setting standards? Hmm...

And mea culpa if I've stepped on anyone's toes. One must wear steel-toed boots when discussing ethics!

Dr. Mark S:

Sorry to hijack your thoughts, but I am on the same line here. How many women are willing to have toxic pieces of silicone inserted into their breasts for cosmetic purposes? How about tummy tucks, nose reductions, facelifts...? So how can I condemn breeding clubs for their "accepted" breed standards that include cosmetic surgery, such as tail docking, when as a society we think it is perfectly acceptable, if not desirable, to mutilate our own bodies to look better according to our own cultural standards?

My opinion, FWIW [For What It's Worth]!

Dr. Judy B:

Oh my, this is why I practice emergency medicine...

Dr. Elizabeth M:

Speaking of which, I have treated too many miserable pups with rotten ears in racks or inverted Styrofoam coffee cups at the emergency clinic to EVER consider doing or recommending an ear crop. However, I don't think I could live with a Boxer with a long tail: they can whip it at everyone, and everything on coffee tables, and get injured. We had a rescue [dog], half Boxer, half Pit Bull that beat the tip of her tail bloody on the walls of her kennel prior to adoption. We tried EVERYTHING to protect it, but she'd rip off every bandage and splint, and continue to bash it incessantly (she was a little rock star and didn't really give a rip that it hurt!). We finally had to amputate the tail to stop the constant aggravation and self-inflicted injury, so that we could place her without ruining her adopter's furniture, carpet, walls, etc. You've all had happy dogs with bleeding tail tips come into your clinics, right?

If we could get more enlightened judges in the AKC rings that would award points and winning positions to dogs without cropped ears, breeders would be quick to respond. In the ring, winning is everything, and as long as the show people believe that cropped ears are more likely to win than non-cropped ones, AND as long as there are vets out there willing to do it, the mutilation will continue to happen. Soooo... educate, educate, educate. I'm planning to, some day, acquire and show a non-cropped Doberman, just to set an example. Go to the shows, TALK to the judges, encourage your breeder clients to take a risk. Oh yeah, and ban the hooligans who fight dogs... that's a BIG reason for some owners to crop ears!

P.S. I guess in Australia, they do not crop the ears of Dobermans – they think cropped Dobies are the weird ones!
End of thread.

Numerous stakeholders are involved in the world of dog breeding and showing. At the very top of the hierarchy is the AKC, which governs and coordinates all the parent breeding clubs that set standards for breeds (currently 158 breeds). Occupying the middle tier are all the dog breeders, professional handlers, trainers, and groomers. And populating the bottom tier are all the dog buyers and dog lovers. At the bottom level of this pyramid, we will also find veterinarians. What are they doing there? As we witnessed in the earlier discussion, they are either willing or non-willing participants in the "Best in Show" world. Each veterinarian has to set his/her own ethical guidelines about cosmetic surgeries regarded as "acceptable" by the AKC.

In 2008, the American Veterinary Medical Association (AVMA) published their latest revision regarding cosmetic surgeries. The statement reads as follows:

"The AVMA opposes ear cropping and tail docking of dogs done solely for cosmetic purposes. The AVMA encourages the elimination of ear cropping and tail docking from breed standards."

As expected, this statement did not win the AKC's "best friend" award, as the AKC maintains that "ear cropping, tail docking and claw removal, as described in certain breed standards, are acceptable practices integral to defining and preserving breed character and/or enhancing good health."

Currently, thirteen breeds of dogs are routinely ear cropped, while tail docking is common in forty-eight breeds registered with the AKC. Eleven breeds, however, are subject to both cosmetic surgeries (ear crop and tail dock). These "double-surgery" breeds are listed below:

- Doberman Pinscher
- Boxer
- Schnauzer (Miniature, Standard, and Giant, recognized as three distinct breeds)
- Brussels Griffon
- Miniature Pinscher
- German Pinscher
- Affenpinscher
- Pyrenean Shepherd
- Neapolitan Mastiff

Even though some breed standards mention the acceptability of unaltered ears and tails, the key word here is "some." The Boxer breed standard, for instance, allows for natural ears that meet certain qualifications; however, undocked tails will likely be penalized. Any dog can enter any competition, with or without cropped ears and a docked tail, but the reality is that unaltered dogs rarely win major championships.

Many veterinarians feel uneasy about performing cosmetic surgeries, and much worse about witnessing the morbidity (disease) and mortality associated with these surgeries. In the hands of veterinarians, at least, analgesia and infection prevention are on board (or definitely should be). Unfortunately, in many areas, breeders themselves have taken these cosmetic surgeries literally into their own hands, performing them with human restraint only, and without any pain and infection management. The unimaginable pain experienced by dogs having their ears cut off, and then stitched – all without analgesia – must surely fall somewhere in the barbaric and cruel category.

The issue of canine cosmetic surgery is a complex one, involving cultural barriers that are difficult to remove because of a general lack of will power to do so. What can you, as a dog lover, do? Whenever you purchase or adopt a dog, simply insist on a dog that has not undergone any cosmetic surgeries. If social pressure does not work, then the law of supply and demand will surely do the job!

As a dog lover, you can…

- Do your research, and seriously consider the disease/death/safety risks of any cosmetic surgery before deciding to submit your dog to such a procedure.

- Better yet, when purchasing or adopting a dog, insist on one that has not been altered through any type of cosmetic surgery.

CHAPTER 16

The Heartache of Canine Cancer: what are the choices?

"Should I tell Mandy about this?"

"Yes, Mrs. Jones," I said gently, "If you normally tell Mandy everything, then I think you should tell her that we are discussing the fact that she may have cancer. I am so sorry and I sincerely hope I am wrong in thinking it might be hemangiosarcoma, so let's proceed swiftly with some tests."

Diagnosing cancer in dogs is first and foremost a statistical exercise, and begins with a review of symptoms. Mandy, a typical friendly, affectionate Golden Retriever – as most of her breed are – was nine years old when her worried owner brought her to our clinic. She presented with pale mucous membranes (when we looked in her mouth, the gums above the canine teeth appeared abnormally pale and whitish), a fast heart rate of 144 beats per minute (normal is 80–120), shallow breathing, and an enlarged abdomen that appears to be filled with a water balloon.

"How long has Mandy's abdomen been enlarged like this?" I asked Mrs. Jones.

"I hadn't really noticed that it was enlarged," she admitted, "But now that you mention it, it does seem to be." Mrs. Jones went on to tell me that Mandy appeared to have slowed down a couple of days ago; she just hadn't been her normal exuberant self. But what alarmed Mrs. Jones most of all was that Mandy refused to eat her breakfast this morning, for the first time in her life.

The stats are straightforward when it comes to cancer in dogs. Large-breed dogs have twice the incidence of cancer when compared to small-breed dogs. Osteosarcoma, the most common bone cancer in dogs, is very common in Great Danes, Saint Bernards, Dobermans, and Labrador Retrievers. Breast or mammary cancer is most prevalent in non-spayed female dogs. Melanomas are most frequently seen in Scottish Terriers, German Shorthaired Pointers, Cocker Spaniels, Pointers, Weimaraners, Golden Retrievers, and Boxers. Dachshunds and Beagles, oddly enough, have an overall reduced incidence of cancer in comparison to other breeds. Owners of Bernese Mountain Dogs need to become familiar with a cancer called malignant histiocytosis, so prevalent and deadly is it in that breed. Chow Chows seem to be over-represented in the category of stomach cancers, while Golden Retrievers appear to have a very high incidence of lymphoma (also called lymphosarcoma), the most common cancer in both humans and dogs. In fact, some researchers wonder whether this form of cancer has a familial link in Golden Retrievers.

Did Mandy, like so many of her breed, have lymphoma? A quick look at the findings of her physical exam told me that one key abnormality was missing: the lymph nodes were not enlarged. Although this is not pathognomonic (that is, specifically distinctive of a medical condition) for lymphoma, the "normal" finding here was certainly not pushing us in that direction.

What else might it be? The stats were leading us to consider a cancer very prevalent in four breeds of dogs: Golden Retrievers, Labrador Retrievers, German Shepherds, and Standard Poodles. Along this path, we find an alarming statistic: nearly 70 percent of dogs that present with anemia and a hemoabdomen (blood collecting in the abdomen) will have hemangiosarcoma (a cancer of the lining of the blood vessels in different organs, most often spleen, heart and skin) of the spleen. Clinically, Mandy was giving us all the indications of anemia. As mentioned earlier, her gums were pale. In addition, she was short of breath because she lacked enough circulating red blood cells, a significant indicator of anemia. And as a result, she was tachycardic, a compensating mechanism in which the heart beats faster than normal to move those few red blood cells around her body.

Did Mandy have blood in her abdomen? Yes, no question there. On palpation, her bulging abdomen felt swollen like a water balloon, and when a small three-centimeter long needle was inserted, three millimeters of blood immediately spurted into the syringe. The evidence was indisputable: with that five-second procedure, called abdominocentesis, a hemoabdomen was confirmed. This was the moment of truth for Mrs. Jones, who was in the habit of discussing all of her daily living matters with Mandy. Should she share our dire thoughts of cancer with her beloved pet, who for so long had greeted her every word with doggy adoration and a wagging tail?

From a clinical standpoint, the stats were not looking good so far: we already knew that 70 percent of the time a dog presents with symptoms of anemia and a belly full of blood, a diagnosis of hemangiosarcoma is likely. The incidence is higher if the dog is over eight years of age, and the odds get uglier if the dog is a Golden Retriever.

The next crucial step, aside from getting Mrs. Jones to understand the gravity of the situation and alleviating Mandy's discomfort, was to confirm our clinical instincts. In less than thirty minutes, we executed blood work and radiographs, inserted an IV line to prevent collapse and shock, and initiated pain management via intravenous analgesic injections. Should we need to proceed with further medical treatment, blood transfusion and surgery, and if an ultrasound of the abdomen were declined, we would need to move quickly.

Before consulting with Mrs. Jones, however, we needed to thoroughly review the details of Mandy's test results. The anemia was quite profound at 19 percent; normal red blood cell levels should be around 37–54 percent, and a dog will experience difficulty in sustaining life at levels below 10 percent. At levels of 15–20 percent or lower, a blood transfusion should be contemplated. On Mandy's radiographs, we could easily delineate a large mass of nearly six inches in diameter on the spleen.

Was there evidence of metastasis (spread of cancer cells to distant sites via blood or lymph)? We already knew that the right auricle of the heart is a common site of metastasis for hemangiosarcoma. In this case, examination of the three radiographs of Mandy's chest showed no tumors in the chest. Detection of mets (metastasis or tumors that have spread to other tissues) that might have migrated to the liver, however, is always difficult when a three-dimensional dog body is compressed into two dimensions on a radiograph. An ultrasound exam, although not infallible, would have been more helpful in this regard. (As it turned out, Mrs. Jones declined an ultrasound for financial reasons.)

At this point, if you were Mandy's owner, you would likely be immersed in a gamut of emotions, your mind racing with questions and your heart heavy with sadness. The word "cancer" frightens most of us. As humans, we experience sentiments of denial, despair and hopelessness with varying intensity when confronted with such a diagnosis. Dogs, obviously, do not respond with such feelings, as they are not aware of the implications of their illnesses.

Mrs. Jones, however, was feeling all these emotions for her precious Mandy, and this meant we had to address them too. Mrs. Jones was not in denial, but hopeful that a positive outcome would emerge. Here again, the stats provided us with clues as to the possible outcome. If we said the odds were 70 percent that Mandy had cancer of the spleen, that still left a 30 percent chance that she did not. Since we had found no evidence of metastasis, we knew that we could be dealing with a spleen abscess, a hematoma (a benign tumor in which there is an accumulation of blood), or even torsion of the spleen. If it turned out to be hemangiosarcoma, and we opted for surgery to stop the bleeding and remove the tumor, there was an approximate chance of only 40 percent that Mandy would survive to be discharged after surgery. The median survival time after surgery such as this – without any further treatment such as chemotherapy – is less than ninety days. If Mandy received additional treatment such as chemotherapy, her survival time would still be less than 365 days.

It was time to speak to Mrs. Jones. "I know how difficult and overwhelming all of this information is," I said to her, "But for Mandy's sake, we need to proceed as she is bleeding in her abdomen and feeling more uncomfortable every minute her abdomen fills up with more blood."

This is where we, as clinicians, need to dissociate from emotional matters and re-enter the realm of rationality, especially when dealing with such a loving dog and a grave illness. Even though the entire medical team wanted to break into tears with Mrs. Jones over these events unfolding too rapidly to be fully absorbed, we needed to set aside our own feelings and act quickly to help our patient.

When a dog is under veterinary care, there are always three therapeutic options available. The first is "to do nothing," or "professional neglect," which implies what it means: let's wait and see how a condition develops, monitor the situation, and re-adjust our course accordingly. The second is to diagnose and treat, in which we work to get a diagnosis – or at least a presumptive one – and offer treatment accordingly. And the third is euthanasia, which signals the end of the line – no "wait and see," no diagnosis, no treatment, just an IV injection of a substance that will induce death gently and rapidly. It is worth mentioning here that a vet always has a choice: when a dog owner requests euthanasia, the veterinarian is not obligated to comply if this option seems unsuitable.

In Mandy's case, to wait and do nothing was not an acceptable option. She was likely suffering from an open bleeding lesion on her spleen, and her distended abdomen was a further source of discomfort. Both were causing some physical distress that her pain management protocol was only able to partially alleviate. As we were halfway through option number two with a presumptive diagnosis of hemangiosarcoma, the next order of business was to stop the bleeding. This called for immediate action: surgically opening Mandy's abdomen to find the source of bleeding, likely an open tumor on her spleen, and removing her spleen.

The last option, euthanasia, could be contemplated in this case if our presumptive diagnosis was correct, based solely on the odds that Mandy's survival time was limited. Some owners, because of either personal circumstances or personal experiences, prefer not to address a difficult case like Mandy's, and request a dignified and painless ending for their companion. An honest and compassionate discussion between the owner and the clinician should bring about the best possible decision.

Before proceeding any further with Mandy's situation, let's look into some facts and opinions about cancer in companion animals.

For most of us, the primary response to a cancer diagnosis, either our own or for a loved one such as a cherished companion animal, is to value everything more, including time. No energy is wasted anymore on futile life events that rob us of our valuable presence here. Why is it that we do not live our lives this way every day, instead of waiting for a life-altering event such as a cancer diagnosis to trigger this way of thinking? It is without doubt that dogs excel at living in the present moment every day of their lives, and that is what makes them such inspiring companions on our earthly journeys. They do not wait for a life-altering event to begin living life to its fullest; for them, "living in the moment" is a daily habit.

Dogs, unlike humans, do not indulge in self-pity. No matter what is happening, they live in the present moment with great enthusiasm. When pain becomes unbearable for them, it is my belief that dogs experience bewilderment, confusion, and sadness, not understanding why they are no longer able to perform their regular activities. This confusion can be more distressing than the pain itself, which they are not conditioned to label and complain about. "A dog in pain is a dog that sleeps a lot" is such a true adage. When suffering physical pain, a dog tends not to vocalize it as humans do to everyone who will listen, but rather comes quickly to the realization that being motionless will diminish the experience of pain. For this reason, if a dog seems to spend more time sleeping than usual, the cause is often not fatigue, but an ill-defined source of pain somewhere in the body. To you as a dog owner, I say simply, "Seek and ye shall find!"

When a dog gets cancer, there is a very real possibility that the animal will die *with* its cancer, but not *of* its cancer. Remember that dogs live, on average, twelve to fifteen years. Even when the odds are stacked the wrong way, there are instances of spontaneous remission, spontaneous cure, and very good quality of life with untreated cancers. Most clinicians, even after watching companion animals live with confirmed aggressive cancers, are at a loss to explain these mystifying cases of spontaneous recovery. As dogs are not aware of their cancer diagnosis and the power of positive thinking to aid healing, how and why does nature kick in and help some dogs survive, completely against all odds? There may be a clue in anecdotal evidence: a dog that has developed a healthy bond with his owner, not an excessive and obsessive one but one where the dog retains his identity and is well matched with his owner, may have a better chance at surviving cancer.

The statistics – or the lack of them – indicate that most dogs will not be cured by alternative therapy for cancer; such treatment will only make their owners poorer. Should this fact deter anyone from choosing "unproven therapy" or alternative therapy instead of "proven medicine"? Absolutely not. However, a little research is recommended before starting any course of treatment, to ensure the best decision. Most importantly, the best decision is always based on an accurate diagnosis. Please repeat after me, as this is very important: *the best decision is always based on an accurate diagnosis.*

Be a wise dog owner, and consider that a diagnosis of cancer can be an erroneous one. This is not denial; this is about human error and shortcomings. Most diagnoses are attained through a biopsy, which involves taking a small piece of affected tissue (approximately one-quarter inch in diameter) and sending it to a laboratory, where it will be chemically prepared, fixed, and cut into small slices to be read under a microscope. Gross errors can occur when someone mislabels a biopsy sample, inadvertently swaps one dog's biopsy sample for another, or reports a biopsy result in the wrong file. These, hopefully, are accidents and rare. Of greater concern are the errors occurring more frequently in some laboratories, where the interpretation of cellular changes on a biopsy sample is wrong or totally misleading. These errors do not fall within the realm of accidents; they occur due to unacknowledged incompetence on the part of pathologists.

When a pathologist reviews a biopsy sample, s/he looks for specific cell differentiation characteristics of certain disease processes. Sometimes, certain cells present themselves in such a way as to make a diagnosis with a high level of certainty possible. Other times, cells have undergone some changes, but these are either not specific or reveal nothing more than some form of inflammation, which is the reaction of a body tissue to injury or infection. For a pathologist to make accurate diagnoses, s/he requires a great deal of experience, knowledge and dedication to self-improvement of clinical skills. Unfortunately, in the field of veterinary medicine, a growing trend is that more and more part-time veterinarians populate the specialty of pathology. Without constant and repeated exposure to ambiguous cases, ongoing discussions with peers on current cases, and a strong commitment to continuing education, these part-time pathologists find it difficult to attain a high level of accuracy when interpreting biopsy samples. A healthy dose of skepticism is recommended on the part of the referring veterinarian, especially when the pathologist's opinion seems a little off base.

In animals, we use three basic modalities of treatment for cancer: chemotherapy, radiation, and surgery. Which one has the best chance of curing a cancer? Surgery results in a cure more often than any other treatment modality. The reason is simple: if the cancer is localized to one site, and the surgeon can remove all cancer cells, then the cancer is gone and the patient is cured. Thus surgical removal should always be the first mode of treatment considered, even if the dog does not feel any pain from a tumor.

Radiation, wherever available, should be the second form of treatment considered, as it kills or sterilizes specific tumor cells at a confined site. Lastly, chemotherapy, which simply means the use of drugs, is a strong consideration when there is evidence that metastasis has occurred. At this point, neither surgery nor radiation therapy would be curative. This is why an early diagnosis of cancer is so important; ideally, treatment will be initiated before it has had time to grow too big for excision, and before it has had time to microscopically invade other body tissues. The most common question regarding chemotherapy in animals is whether they will lose their hair as humans do following treatment. In most cases, the answer is no; hair loss rarely occurs in animals, due to the different stages of hair growth (think molting or shedding in dogs).

The most relevant question regarding chemotherapy in animals is who should get it. First of all, chemotherapy should not be recommended for any dogs that fear going to a veterinary hospital: it would be an unpleasant ordeal for all involved. Second, dogs undergoing injectable chemo should have very good veins, and this may preclude any senior dogs with brittle little veins. Third, the diagnosis should be well demonstrated and beyond doubt, and the patient should have many good prognostic indicators, such as still being in good health. Fourth, the patient should have a cancer proven to respond to chemotherapy, such as lymphosarcoma. With a cancer such as this, a dog is likely to die within three months of diagnosis without chemotherapy, but could live an extra year with chemotherapy. Fifth – and this one is very important – the owners of the dog should have an abundance of time, energy and money to deal with having a pet in chemotherapy. Because this therapy can be an emotional rough ride, the owners must make sure that in their hearts they are convinced they have made the best choice for their canine friend.

So, after reviewing the above information, would we say that Mandy is a good candidate for chemo? Certainly not! We do not yet have a diagnosis beyond a doubt, and she was not in good health at the time of presentation.

As we return to Mandy's case, let us note three basic rules to remember when dealing with canine patients with cancer. One, do not let them hurt: get a pain protocol in place. Two, do not let them starve: time to get cooking and find out what our finicky patient will have an appetite for. And three, do not let them "puke": there is medication to prevent vomiting and its accompanying discomfort, so let's use it!

Fortunately, Mrs. Jones, afflicted with a good dose of optimism and realism, decided to send Mandy to surgery to stop the bleeding and investigate the source of the problem in the abdomen. This was our first priority, considering Mandy's rapid deterioration. Mrs. Jones had been forewarned that if a tumor were found on the spleen, the entire spleen would need to be removed. Mrs. Jones had also requested that, if there was evidence of spread of cancer, she did not want to proceed with chemotherapy; she thought it would be best not to wake Mandy up from surgery.

In accordance with Mrs. Jones' wishes, Mandy was immediately prepared for surgery, which included a blood transfusion in anticipation of possible bleeding while in surgery. Mrs. Jones stayed at her side until an IV anesthetic solution was administered and Mandy was connected to a gas anesthetic machine. At that point, Mrs. Jones gave Mandy a big hug and a loving "au revoir", just in case.

The surgery about to be undertaken is called an exploratory laparotomy, which means an exploration of the abdomen. If the spleen needs to be removed, the next surgical step is a splenectomy. Mandy turned out to be a little rock star under anesthetic: all of her vital parameters were within normal range, and she remained very stable. Once all the free blood had been suctioned out of her abdomen, we got started on the investigative work. Indeed, there was a bleeding tumor on the spleen, but this we could deal with relatively swiftly and safely.

The main issue, however, was whether there were other tumors or mets present on adjacent organs. There was no point in removing a bleeding spleen only to find that other tumors were present elsewhere. My hands had moved quicker than my eyes; even the assisting surgical nurse could sense the pause in my movements.

"What is it?" she asked.

"It is what we feared." I replied. The liver had several large nodules, up to one inch in diameter, ready to burst if pressed. There was no longer any doubt. What we were dealing with was most certainly an aggressive cancer, likely hemangiosarcoma. And Mrs. Jones had requested that we not put Mandy through the pain of recovering from an exploratory surgery only to be euthanized later if the prognosis was grave.

Everyone in the hospital went silent as the news of Mandy's condition was released; it felt as though we'd all had the wind knocked out of us. Meanwhile, other clients still had to be dealt with by staff members, phone calls still needed answering, and other animals still needed our attention.

For Mandy, though, we all knew what needed to happen next. The assisting nurse prepared a euthanizing solution, and from the depths of her anesthetic-induced unconsciousness, Mandy slipped peacefully away.

The biopsy results, which came back four days later, confirmed the presumptive diagnosis of hemangiosarcoma. Since the cancer had spread to Mandy's liver, the prognosis for her survival, even with chemotherapy, would have been very poor. As sad as it was to lose such a loving patient that we had known since puppyhood, we knew Mandy's owner had made the right decision. Mrs. Jones left our clinic with peace in her heart but, sadly, she no longer had someone to share her daily thoughts with. It is with hope that we all wish to see her again soon, making a grand entrance with another puppy in her arms, a brimming smile, and a voice full of exuberant puppy talk.

As a dog lover, you can…

- Become familiar with the type(s) of cancer common to your dog's particular breed.

- Have your dog examined by a veterinarian without delay if cancer is suspected.

- If your dog is diagnosed with cancer, discuss all possible treatment modalities with your veterinarian before choosing the one(s) that are best for your pet.

CHAPTER 17

A Prickly Problem:
porcupines and dogs

L exus and Mercedes apparently suffer from short-term memory loss. Perhaps this affliction was passed on to them by their owner, Mrs. Torrington. What were the chances of seeing this trio in our veterinary hospital *twice* within a twenty-four-hour period? And worse yet, with the *same* prickly problem?

As unlikely as it might sound, this scenario is actually quite a common one. Lexus and Mercedes are bouncy Springer Spaniels who live for adventure and danger. In fact, they actively seek it out, every chance they get. And they find it every time they meet a porcupine on their daily walk. Lexus and Mercedes evidently love our veterinary hospital, since one or both of them have visited us here seven times in the past three years; this is definitely a personal best when it comes to porcupine encounters.

Why do dogs so often get in trouble with porcupines? Unlike other animals in northern climates, such as marmots, gophers, and bears, these large prickly rodents do not hibernate through the winter months. Instead, they are active all year round, although they spend more time in trees in the wintertime so that they are less available to predators. In the summer, they move about on the ground, foraging among the vegetation for grubs. This is where dogs find them.

Unfortunately for curious dogs, porcupines have evolved for a much longer period than their canine adversaries, and have become adept at deterring predators like bouncy Spaniels. Porcupines instinctively self-protect by rolling into a ball and letting their quills painfully penetrate the mouth and upper torso of attackers. Quills are released either by contact with an attacker's body tissues, or by simply dropping out when the porcupine shakes its body. Contrary to popular belief, porcupines cannot project their quills through the air like missiles at their attackers.

In zoology classes, as you can imagine, the subject of porcupine quills invariably takes curious students on another tangent. The typical question is always, "Then how do porcupines mate?" And the answer is always the same, "With extreme caution!"

Porcupine quills, each measuring about 75 millimeters (3.0 inches) long, are as sharp as needles, detach very easily, and will remain embedded in an attacker. Unlike needles, however, the quills of porcupines have microscopic, backward-facing scales or shingles, which act like barbs at the tip and catch in the skin. Once imbedded, they are rather difficult and painful to extract. When quills become lodged in the tissues of an animal, the shingle-like barbs pull the quill further into the tissues with the normal muscle movements of the animal, moving up to several millimeters in a single day.

Herein lies the real threat. Quills, if not extracted promptly, may travel within the dog's body to sensitive areas like eyeballs, spine, chest cavity and heart. Although the quills may take up to a year to reach one of these deadly destinations in the dog's body, once they do, they become a life-threatening foreign body. It is not uncommon for a dog to present with 300–500 quills on the muzzle, neck, and front leg area, and this is where the difficulty arises. As you can imagine, one or two quills may easily be overlooked and left behind during quill extraction, not because of gross neglect, but because the quill shaft breaks off at the skin surface. When this happens, only the barbed tip is left under the skin and cannot be detected through a dense coat of hair such as that of a Husky.

Fortunately for many dogs, the vast majority of these broken quills hidden under the skin will travel right back to the surface of the skin, create a small abscess – the body's natural defense for rejecting a foreign body – and be expelled. Why an errant quill will sometimes migrate the wrong way (i.e., inward toward internal organs) remains a mystery. When this does occur, however, the outcome depends on which body tissue or organ the errant quill meets along its internal migration, and how much damage it creates.

If only a few quills have penetrated a dog's face or torso, an owner may try to pull them out with a pair of pliers. However, "quill pullers" beware: the dog will find the extraction process painful, and repeated attempts at pulling quills will sorely test the animal's patience and pain threshold. While the "quilled" dog may need to be taken to a veterinarian to finish the job with anesthetic drugs on board, the "quill puller" may need to take a detour to a human clinic to treat a nasty dog bite to the quill-pulling hand! Take the risk at your own peril.

Folklore has it that quill removal will be easier if the quill shaft is cut to let the air out. Truthfully, I do not think so. The backward-facing scales act like barbs at the quill's tip, which is embedded in the skin. The tip is not likely to collapse from air release; if it did, the skin layers would consequently tighten around the collapsed tip anyway. As much as we would like to believe otherwise, quill removal is never easy.

As for Lexus and Mercedes, we strongly advised Mrs. Torrington to either take her adventure-loving Spaniels to another area for walks or keep them leashed. When pets are unable to make wise choices, it falls to the owner to do so. In this case, the dogs seemed to quickly forget how painful each quill encounter was, and the resident porcupine was winning all the fights!

As a dog lover, you can…

- Whenever possible, avoid walking your dogs in areas frequented by porcupines.
- If your dog gets "quilled," be aware of the extreme health risks to dogs when quills left in the body migrate to tissues and organs.

CHAPTER 18

Thunderstruck:
when a phobia turns fatal

Dakota was a sorry looking dog when he was brought to the veterinary hospital. The poor fellow was markedly underweight, his coat was mangy, and he had profuse diarrhea that was swarming with long, wiggly, white worms. He had been picked up along the highway to Banff National Park, looking haggard and lost. Judging by his scruffy condition, this dog had obviously been wandering on his own for a while. Fortunately for him, we discovered a city tattoo in his left ear that, once deciphered, led us directly to his owner.

"Oh, you have my dog?" the owner said rather casually, in response to my call, "Is he well? We let him out of the car on the side of the highway so he could have a pee, and we lost him. Can I talk to him over the phone?"

"No, you may not," I said firmly, shaking my head at his odd question. This dog was in need of much more than a phone chat! "But would you like to come and pick him up?"

Not surprisingly, the guy's answer was no. Indeed, Dakota was one of many pets dumped on the side of the highway by vacationers headed to the mountains, who could not be bothered to find decent care for their pets while they were away. At least it was summertime when he was dumped, so Dakota had a chance at survival.

Now that he was with us, he was at least safe from the perils of mountain highways. Even so, Dakota was in rough shape: he weighed only thirty-eight kilograms, very emaciated (thin) for a large dog. Upon first inspection, we had decided he must be a German Shepherd Husky cross, but apparently he was not; his so-called owner had told me he was a purebred Akita. That gave me reason for pause: previous encounters with Akitas in the course of my work had provided plenty of evidence of their aggression with other dogs. A quick Internet search revealed that Akitas are an ancient breed originating in Japan, where they were bred for hunting. Well, that would certainly explain some of their aggressive tendencies toward other animals, including dogs. Leading causes of death for this breed are cancer and bloat (see Chapter 9). Bloat would indeed be Dakota's future demise, but we are getting away from our story here.

For all of three weeks, Dakota was the sweetest dog in our veterinary care, consistently gentle and docile. But, as I was about to find out, his agreeable personality would only last for as long as he was gaining strength and getting rid of all his parasites. Dakota, at his best, weighed fifty-four kilograms and, true to the breed, showed very strong tendencies of aggression and dominance toward other dogs once he had fully recovered. Despite his pronounced dog aggression, however, he exhibited no aggression at all toward humans. Dakota's size and temperament made him a difficult candidate for adoption, so my family decided to adopt him. As we soon discovered, though, he could never be let off leash; not only would he never return when called, but most people were intimidated by the sight of a muscular fifty-four kilogram black and tan dog barrelling toward them. All of these aspects, however, could be managed with proper measures. His fear of thunderstorms, unfortunately, was another matter. This particular phobia, which we did not discover until Dakota had shared our home for a few days, is a very difficult one to handle.

Fear of thunderstorms is common to many dogs, not just Akitas. The fear tends to worsen as the animals age; for some phobic dogs, in fact, the problem was non-existent during their first few years of life. While some aspects of this problem remain a mystery – genetic inheritance, conditioning factors, and age of onset, for example – we have some reliable knowledge that can make life easier for both thunderstorm-phobic dogs and their families. Best of all, you may be able to help your dog avoid developing this fear in the first place; prevention trumps any remedy. Once acquired, the phobia is very difficult for dogs to overcome.

Why do dogs fear thunderstorms in the first place? For some afflicted pets, the origin of their fearful reaction remains murky. What we do know is that the problem is a common one for dogs, but less so for cats. Whatever its roots, the initial fear can soon develop into a phobia, which is defined as "a persistent, excessive, and irrational response to fear of an object or situation." In the case of thunderstorm phobias, dogs may also be frightened of storm-associated events, such as changes in barometric pressure, lightning, electrostatic disturbances, and even smells associated with the storm. Our rescue Akita was an excellent example of this: I was always amazed when, on a clear sunny day, without a cloud on the horizon, Dakota's behavior would change in a very predictable pattern up to two hours prior to the onset of a storm, even when all visual clues were absent. I suspect the change of air pressure was his trigger.

In many cases, however, there is no obvious trigger event that can be ascertained. In almost all instances, the dog's fear of storms escalates, worsening with each exposure. Most certainly, the owner's attitude can influence the severity of the fear. For instance, if the owner displays a comforting attitude toward the fear-struck dog, and attempts to overly reassure him, the animal interprets this behavior as confirmation that there really is something to fear. In effect, the petting or comforting of the dog becomes positive reinforcement of an undesirable behavior.

This is comparable to the influence that flight attendants have on edgy passengers – like me – during times of flight turbulence. Truthfully, I am never keen on being in an airplane: bumpy rides make me nervous. As soon as turbulence strikes, my eyes automatically shift toward the flight attendants – I find it most reassuring to see them walking up and down the aisles as usual, looking calm. However, if their behavior changed at all, for instance, if they began showing undue concern, touching people on the shoulder and comforting them, I would indeed be alarmed.

In dogs, the common indicators of phobia, thunderstorm-related or otherwise, include hiding, urinating, defecating, drooling, shaking, panting, and pacing. Some dogs will desperately seek the owner's presence, ignore commands, and bark excessively. If you look closely at your phobic dog, the hallmark of fear will be evident in his eyes: dilated pupils. It is at this stage that dogs can harm themselves, sometimes fatally.

Typically, fearful dogs, if their owners are not present, will try to escape from wherever they are enclosed. They will chew their way through a chain-link fence, for instance, in their desperate attempt to escape. Left on his own, Dakota worked his way through screen windows. Once freed, phobic dogs will start to run, like frantic fugitives with demons on their tail. This is no leisurely walk in the rain, no indeed! They run madly, mouths open and panting, presumably to reach the safety of an area without thunderstorms. They run in fear, and often get hit by vehicular traffic.

The appropriate treatment for a thunderstorm phobia depends on a number of factors, including the severity of the phobia, how long the dog has had it, and the amount of time the dog's owner is willing to invest in managing it effectively. The most important thing to remember is that you, as the phobic dog's owner, should refrain from providing any reward or punishment. This is so important that it bears repeating: *you should refrain from providing any reward or punishment.* So, if the dog looks anxious, do not go to him, do not give him a soothing cuddle, and do not shower him with sweet baby talk. Conversely, if your dog starts to pant and voids his bladder uncontrollably, this is most certainly not the time for a reprimand. Either response by the owner – whether comforting or scolding – will only increase his level of anxiety.

Phobia treatment often combines three main therapeutic options: medications to chemically handle runaway anxiety, which can include natural remedies; changing the environment, such as heading for the basement where visual and auditory aspects of the storm are lessened; and behaviour modification, such as counter conditioning and desensitization, to change the dog's response to thunderstorms.

Be aware, however, that fear of thunderstorms can be "contagious," transferring easily from one dog to another. This makes early intervention and treatment of the problem all the more important, as fears are difficult to unlearn. Two or more fearful dogs can create a lot of damage to a house while trying to escape, by chewing through drywall or otherwise expressing their fear and concern at containment. Or they may end up running frantically through a neighbourhood and into traffic, thereby putting themselves in harm's way.

Despite all the behavioral support provided to him, Dakota's fear of thunderstorms never really abated. Due to the mysteries of his uncertain past, and the severity of his phobia, we decided that Dakota should come to work with me on days that stormy weather threatened. At the clinic, he would lie under my desk and pant heavily. As long as there was a calm human presence nearby, he stopped trying to run away. He was still nervous, but he seemed to know he was safe.

Annie's case, on the other paw, was more extreme. An outdoor dog that thrived on her owner's quarter section of land (160 acres), Annie never learned to feel safe during thunderstorms. At the first rumble overhead, she typically crawled under the front deck and hid there, shivering and panting in fear. Once the storm had passed, she would emerge as though nothing had happened, though the telltale evidence of her fear was obvious in her drool-covered fur.

One day when Annie's owner, Mrs. Miller, came home after a hailstorm had flattened her hay field, she found her dog missing. Knowing Annie's fear of storms, Mrs. Miller drove late into the evening, searching for her dog in the valleys, along creek beds, and amidst the vast farm fields surrounding her land. With all her efforts to find Annie, she finally succeeded – but sadly, found her too late.

From what Mrs. Miller was later told, her dog had run frantically to escape the storm and never stopped. At the height of the hailstorm, Annie had been spotted racing like a crazed dog across the highway, where she was struck by a passing vehicle. The owner of the vehicle, perhaps unaware of what he had done, never even stopped. But the driver of the vehicle behind him, who had witnessed the accident, immediately pulled over to the shoulder. The woman quickly scrambled down into the ditch, where she found Annie gasping for air, with gurgling sounds emanating from her chest. As carefully and gently as she could, this kind passerby lifted Annie and carried her to the car. She then rushed the injured animal to an emergency hospital in the nearby city, where Annie was declared DOA (Dead On Arrival).

Since Mrs. Miller had wisely contacted all the veterinary hospitals in the county when Annie went missing, emergency personnel were able to reach her quickly with the sad news of Annie's death. Although Mrs. Miller never learned the name of the gentle woman who had provided a caring hand to Annie in her last moments of life, she lit a lampion at church every Sunday from that day on, in memory of her beloved Annie and the kindhearted soul who had tried to save her dog's life.

As a dog lover, you can…

- If your dog has a fear of thunderstorms, provide a calm presence without undue soothing or comforting of the dog.

- If possible, relocate your dog to a part of the house where the lightning flashes and thunder booms are less apparent.

- For extreme cases of phobia, seek professional help for behaviour modifications and/or calming medication (for your dog, not you!).

CHAPTER 19

Lumps and Bumps: when to worry

Bob the dog was in trouble, but no one had noticed yet. Bob, an eight-year-old Bassett Hound, had developed a small skin lesion on his left hind foot, near his ankle. The lesion was barely one-quarter inch in diameter, and seemed to involve only the skin layer.

Was Bob's owner worried? Not yet – she knew that as dogs age, they tend to naturally develop harmless lumps and bumps. The only ones that warranted her attention were those that grew really big really fast, or the ones that the dog could not leave alone and either chewed or licked excessively. Neither was true of Bob's small bump.

The odd lump, which seemed to appear out of nowhere, had been hidden in the folds of Bob's wrinkled legs, so Mrs. White may have missed it when it started to grow. Once she'd found it, she decided that this lump was definitely going on her "watch" list, but not her "worry" list. The following week, however, Bob's lump made the leap from Mrs. White's watch list to her worry list, and soon brought him into our veterinary hospital for a checkup.

Was Mrs. White worrying needlessly? Not at all. The lump, now one-half inch in diameter, had doubled in size in just one week! If the lump continued to grow at this rate, it would be difficult to excise completely, as there would be very little excess skin available to cut and stitch around the ankle.

How should a dog owner, like Mrs. White, decide whether or not to press the panic button? The best way is simply to have a smear of the lump taken (by pressing a microscope slide on the ulcerated surface of the irritated lump), a totally painless procedure for the dog. Then the clinician scans the slide under a microscope for a cellular study, which takes about five minutes. In cases where a diagnosis is not immediately apparent, a needle aspirate or a biopsy might be required.

Was luck on our side in Bob's case? Did we manage to get a diagnosis with just a smear? Yes! And it was indeed time to press the panic button: we were looking at a mast cell tumor. We promptly booked the Basset Hound for surgery the next morning. This would require a full general anesthetic, as Bob was about to lose at least two centimeters of tissue all around the fast-growing mast cell tumor, and would need a little reconstructive surgery. This is usually the rule with mast cell tumors as they are actually a lot bigger than they appear to the naked eye and therefore large margins of normal looking tissue must also be removed.

Aging dogs, like humans, are prone to developing superficial lumps and bumps. These protuberances can grow directly from the skin, or within underlying skin tissues, and when they become large enough, they can be seen or subtly felt when petting a dog. It is not uncommon for Labrador Retrievers to develop a dozen or more lumps, called lipomas (benign accumulations of fat, as organized masses), and multiple warts on their bodies. But how do we know whether we should get excited and rush a dog into surgery each time one of these lumps or bumps appear, or simply let them be and not raise a concerned eyebrow over their obvious presence?

Unfortunately, no one knows for certain whether a lump requires serious attention until a biopsy has been performed. Certainly, any lump or bump that grows rapidly, i.e., doubles in size over a very short period of time, as in Bob's case, is cause for concern. It could turn out to be as simple as an abscess, or as ugly as a mast cell tumour (MCT). The only way to ascertain the true identity of any mass is through an aspirate or a biopsy. This can often be done with a local anesthetic, insertion of a large bore needle into the mass, and a microscopic evaluation. Mast cell tumors display their trademark signature on a microscope slide: the presence of many granules. Mast cell tumors are the most common malignant skin tumors in dogs, with an incidence rate of over 20 percent. They tend to appear very quickly, in a matter of days.

Mast cell tumors are known as "the great pretenders" because of their varied appearance – they may appear as warts, lumps under the skin, or ulcerated masses on the skin. Because looks can be deceiving, these tumors cannot be definitively diagnosed through palpation or visual inspection alone. If you own a Boxer, a Bulldog, a Boston Terrier, a Retriever (either Golden or Labrador), a Basset Hound or a Pug, you should give serious attention to any sudden lump or bump that seems to appear overnight. The gender does not seem to matter but if your dog is around the age of eight years – the average age at diagnosis – make it your concern today!

Mast cell tumors tend to behave badly: they expand quickly with many little tentacle-like arms or tendrils splaying out from the mother tumor. Their excision (surgical removal) is the first step in halting their march to faraway body systems. But there is a catch. To increase the likelihood of arresting the tumor's progress, a surgeon must remove at least two centimeter margins all around the tumor to catch all the microscopic runaway tendrils, then dig into a layer of tissue beneath the tumor and excise that too. That amounts to a lot of tissue trauma! While the procedure can easily be performed by a surgeon when a MCT grows on the thorax or abdomen, it becomes problematic when a MCT occurs on the lower part of the leg, such as on the carpus (wrist) or tarsus (heel) – which is all too common. If we chose to follow the basic rules of excision in such locations, there would be no skin left for closure, and most tendons and nerves would have to be resected (cut). In truth, a full amputation would be necessary to ensure a full excision of a moderately large MCT growing on the lower leg. But would that be the best approach initially? What if we removed smaller margins, and could still be successful in stopping the MCT from spreading?

The true behaviour of a tumor is not fully known until a piece of tissue from the tumor has been submitted to a pathologist for grading. The higher the grade, the more likely the tumor will not behave in a friendly manner toward the rest of the body. Also, the higher the grade, the more likely that adjunct therapy, besides excision, will be necessary for the dog's recovery. The dismal reality is that adjunct therapy – whether chemotherapy or radiation therapy – is not your dog's best friend either, any more than amputation is. Remember, every treatment administered has potential benefits, which are usually obvious, and potential adverse side effects, which can be very harmful and are not always so obvious. The adverse side effects of surgery may include pain (which should be well controlled with today's advanced pain management techniques), loss of function, cosmetic disfigurement (which is more distressing to the owner than the dog), wound breakdown and infection, and tumor recurrence. Every dog presented for surgery should have a surgical plan tailored to its specific needs, in order to enhance the benefits of the procedure and minimize, avoid, or at least strongly justify the potential adverse effects.

What if a dog just had a MCT removed from its hind leg, and now there is a new tumor growing on its neck? Does the dog now need radiation or chemotherapy?

It is not uncommon, unfortunately, for dogs to get multiple MCTs, either simultaneously or sequentially. A wise approach is to regard them initially as separate events, unless there is strong evidence that they are related, such as an affected regional lymph node. A usual course of action is to treat each new MCT the same way, i.e., with surgery that includes wide margins and one plane of tissue excision, and then submit the tumor for grading. Chemotherapy is indicated if there is evidence of the spread of the disease, if the grading confirms high risk, and if appropriate margins could not be achieved during excision. Whatever the reason, opting for chemotherapy or radiation for our canine friends is never an easy decision, as we will discuss in more depth later.

In Bob's case, luck was on his side: he is still alive and doing well, more than two years after his surgery. Mrs. White made a decision to end all medical treatment for her dog after the excision (removal by cutting off) of the mast cell tumor, even though full wide margins could not be achieved. After the excision, the tumor was sent to the laboratory for histologic examination, and was graded 2 on a scale of 4, which meant the tumor would potentially, but not necessarily, spread. If it did spread, Bob's owner knew it would likely be difficult to deal with later on. Even so, Mrs. White took her chances, and so far her choice to decline chemotherapy or leg amputation for her Basset Hound has turned out to be a wise one.

Shystress, also afflicted with a tumor, turned out to be a most unusual case. A shy rescue dog that looked very much like a Husky, two-year-old Shystress was definitely not a high-risk dog for mast cell tumors. This dog was brought in to our clinic because of her sudden lack of energy, and an egg-sized mass in her ventral (lower) neck that seemed to have sprouted overnight. The large mass was firm on palpation, and definitely not painful to the dog. Its location indicated that it might be an inflamed lymph node. Subsequently, we performed an aspirate, which was inconclusive: the cells present revealed very little, other than a high degree of inflammation. The formulated treatment plan for Shystress included general anesthesia to allow us to incise the skin and expose the lump, then either excision or at least a biopsy to determine the behavior of the lump. When we exposed the lump, our findings were grim: judging by the color and structure of the mass, it was definitely not a lymph node. But that was not all: most alarming was the fact that this lump had grown to completely surround the right jugular vein.

Was the lump benign or malignant? At this point, did it matter much? Of course it did. As discussed earlier, we had two clear directions to investigate: if the lump were an aggressive mast cell tumor, portions of the jugular vein would need to be resected (cut); and if the lump were benign, there would be no need to start messing with this major blood vessel draining blood from the head. What was our best option with Shystress? We needed to take a full bore biopsy to reveal more about the lump before executing swift and excessive scalpel moves.

The biopsy results came as a total shock to all of us. Against all odds, the lump in Shystress's neck turned out to be a grade 3 (out of 4) mast cell tumor. Aggressive surgery would be required, involving the removal of at least five centimeters of Shystress's right jugular vein, effectively shutting down her blood drainage from this vein.

To her owners' relief, Shystress recovered uneventfully from this soft tissue surgery, which included a week of post-surgical drainage from the large neck incision. However, the difficult part of the treatment plan was about to begin. Would Shystress's owners, like Bob's, elect to end all treatment with surgical removal of the tumor? Or would they be more aggressive and opt for chemotherapy, since this tumor was engulfing a major blood vessel?

In the end, Shystress's owners opted for a mild form of chemotherapy that did not make Shystress sick at all, and did not involve extensive medical visits that would be stressful for Shystress. During most of her six months of chemo, Shystress did very well. Before she received her last treatment, however, Shystress's health started to deteriorate, so we began a medical investigation to find out why. Fearing a fatal spread of her previous mast cell tumor, her owners were much relieved to discover the simple reason behind her sudden health decline. Shystress, originally a rescue dog, had learned to look after herself well; and during her hunting escapades, she had indulged in too many of her favorite delicacies: mice! Apparently, Shystress hunted the little creatures down so swiftly that she sometimes swallowed them whole, without bothering to kill them first. As a result, Shystress was infected with roundworms and tapeworms. A highly effective deworming medicine, given in a single dose, soon put Shystress back on the road to recovery. Against all odds, her mast cell tumor problem never recurred.

Sadly, Shystress's luck did eventually run out. The Husky cross was just six years old when she was found dead, hunted down by a marauding cougar in the area.

Just as for humans, early detection of malignancies (cancerous tumors) increases the chances of survival for dogs, in many cases with fewer aggressive medical and surgical interventions. As illustrated through the examples of Bob the Basset Hound and Shystress the Husky mix, all lumps and bumps that appear suddenly and grow quickly, no matter what the age or breed of the dog, should be closely monitored to decrease morbidity (disease) rates. Checking for suspicious lumps can easily be made part of a dog's play activities or grooming sessions, both ideal opportunities for stroking the animal's body thoroughly and noting anything unusual. In fact, if this is done routinely with the dog from puppyhood, there will be full acceptance – and, for most dogs, delight at the extra attention.

As a dog lover, you can…

- Be aware that, with age, your dog may develop harmless lumps and bumps, which should be monitored for any changes.

- Ensure early detection of potentially harmful lumps and bumps by making it a habit to stroke your dog all over during either play or grooming.

- Pay attention to any lumps or bumps on your dog that appear suddenly and grow quickly.

CHAPTER 20

Dumb and Furious: the rage of rabies

My seventeen-week-old puppy just came home with a skunk tail in his mouth, and boy, does he ever smell! What can I bathe him in to remove the skunk smell?

This type of question is often asked by dog owners whose dogs have strayed too close to annoyed skunks. When a skunk is harassed and on the defensive, the animal's instinctive reaction is to project a foul-smelling liquid from two glands adjacent to the anus. This liquid spray is profoundly offensive, and eliminating it is always a priority for the owner, however difficult a task it might be.

In the case of Harley the husky-cross puppy, however, something immediately struck me as worrisome. The real concern here was not about the dog getting sprayed by a skunk and smelling terrible: it was about the possibility that the feisty pup may have killed a skunk.

"Did Harley kill the skunk, Mrs. Marley?" I asked the pup's owner, who was still covering her nose to mask the awful odor, "Or did he find it dead somewhere?"

"I don't really know," she admitted, "It might have been dead already, but I'm not sure…"

"Do you know if Harley ate any of the skunk?" I asked.

"He might have, I guess," she said, frowning with uncertainty, "But I couldn't say for sure. I just know that he carried the tail home as a trophy!"

The bigger issue here was that rabies could be transmitted by skunks, which led to my next question. "Is Harley vaccinated against rabies?"

"No," Mrs. Marley replied, looking worried now, "Not yet."

I cringed inwardly at her response – she really did have something worth worrying about here.

The routine protocol for rabies vaccination is that puppies are not vaccinated for the deadly virus until they are twelve weeks of age in the USA, or sixteen weeks of age in Canada, and they do not receive a booster until a year later. If the vaccine is given prior to twelve weeks of age, it is unlikely to be efficacious, due to the presence of maternal antibodies still circulating in the puppy's body – assuming the dam was properly vaccinated. These antibodies from the dam can interfere with the uptake of the vaccine. At twelve weeks of age and beyond, however, this problem no longer exists.

Even if Harley did not kill the skunk, the question remained: could he contract rabies simply by chewing on a rabies-infected skunk tail? In reality, this was not likely, as the rabies virus is labile (very fragile) and does not survive long outside the body of a live mammal; however, it was possible.

"So what should be done in this case?" Mrs. Marley inquired.

My answer, unfortunately, was not overly encouraging. There is very little wiggle room for creative solutions in cases of suspected rabies. All protocols regarding this zoonotic disease (i.e., a disease that can be transmitted from animals to people, such as salmonella or anthrax) are put into place by government-run regulating bodies.

"Is the dead skunk's brain available for testing?" I asked Mrs. Marley, "That would certainly make things easier."

"I did look for the dead skunk," Mrs. Marley told me, "But I couldn't find it… not even by smell!"

Without the option of testing the wild animal's brain, I explained to her, we didn't have much choice. In this situation, Harley had to be considered exposed to rabies. Based on that, the protocol required that we quarantine Harley at home for ten days. During that period of time, Mrs. Marley would need to contact us immediately if Harley showed any signs of change in either behavior or health. Also during that ten-day period, the puppy should not go for walks, on leash or otherwise; should not run loose; and should be restricted to backyard exercise only. Contact with children would have to be vetoed, since too many dog bites occur with young children. In addition, Harley should not go into boarding kennels, should not go on vacation, and should not have contact with other people. All of this was put into writing for Mrs. Marley, and we emphasized to her that this had become a public health issue, for which treatment protocols are rigidly dictated by health authorities and must be taken seriously. Every couple of days, a member of our veterinary team would be in contact with Mrs. Marley to see how Harley was doing, and to encourage her in her efforts.

If Harley were to develop signs of rabies, what would Mrs. Marley observe? Clinical signs of rabies present themselves in either "dumb" or "furious" forms, both of which cause abnormal behavior. Shortly before dying of the affliction, animals with furious rabies appear mad, i.e., frothing at the mouth and lunging and biting at anything that gets in their way, whether moving or stationary. The frothing at the mouth is caused by paralysis of the larynx, which prevents the animal from swallowing its own saliva. In the dumb form of rabies, paralysis of the lower jaw and drooping of the head may be the first signs of a rabies infection. The paralysis quickly spreads to the rest of the body, and death follows soon after due to paralysis of the intercostal muscles, which are responsible for respiration.

Rabies has been known and feared for more than 4000 years. Highly infectious and contagious, this disease of the nervous system was very prevalent in the nineteenth century, and only began to be controlled when Louis Pasteur developed a vaccine against it at the end of that century. This lethal virus currently exists in almost all parts of the world, and is responsible for an estimated 55,000 human deaths a year, mostly in Asia and Africa. According to Darwin's well-known theory of evolution, only the fittest survive. This does not necessarily mean the strongest, but it does mean that the most well adapted organisms will survive.

If an award could be given to the living organism that best exemplifies Darwin's theory, the rabies virus would most definitely be nominated. Not only can it infect any vertebrate animals (i.e., those with spinal columns), but it can do so in the most pernicious and judicious way. If a being is not vaccinated against rabies, and gets exposed to it, death by suffocation is almost guaranteed as a result of this viral infection.

If we assume, then, that Harley did indeed kill a rabid skunk, let's find out what would happen to the rabies virus and to Harley.

Since the virus is concentrated mostly in the saliva and central nervous tissue of a rabid skunk, it would have to make contact with Harley's tissues through a break in the skin, or through the moist tissues of the mouth, nose, and even eyes, before it could penetrate the pup's body. That would most certainly have happened if Harley and the rabid skunk had tangled in a biting, snarling bloody match that mangled bodies and tore flesh as they tried to kill each other.

After it managed to invade the canine body, the virus would start its slow migration to Harley's brain. Its first stop? The local muscle cells adjacent to the bitten area, where it would get its bearings for a couple of days before penetrating local nerves. Once settled into the nerve tissue and en route to its final destination, the brain – a journey that could take anywhere from twenty days to a year – the virus would remain totally hidden from the body's immune system.

Once in the brain, the trouble would really begin: the rabies virus would at that point become transmissible, and clinical signs of the disease would become evident. Initially, a change of personality would occur, turning a friendly dog like Harley into one that was shy and withdrawn; and the larynx would go into spasms, causing a change in the voice. Over the next couple of days, "mad dog" syndrome would manifest, with the rabid animal showing no fear at all and possibly hallucinating. This stage would be followed by paralysis: with the larynx in effect "frozen", we would observe excessive drooling or "foaming at the mouth". The muscles controlling respiration would eventually shut down, and at that point Harley would suffocate and die.

The intriguing part of the evolution of the rabies virus is that it remains sheltered from the immune system while hiding in the nervous system. The only opportunity for the virus to be attacked by the host's immune system is immediately after the bite, before it enters the local nerve cells, or at the end of the disease process, when it leaves the brain to be secreted in saliva or other body fluids. Unfortunately, the time spent outside nerve cell tissue is very brief, hardly long enough for the rabid animal's immune system to mount a proper attack against the virus. Therein lies the great difficulty in controlling a rabies infection after a bite has occurred.

The good news in this case was that Harley never developed rabies, but the spirited fellow nearly went crazy with all his unleashed energy over the ten days. However, the pup's "possible but not certain" encounter with the disease certainly exemplifies how marvellously well adapted the rabies virus is to our world. Having survived several millennia, the rabies virus can easily infect a broad spectrum of hosts and, within each host, is able to go into hiding in the nervous system so rapidly that the affected host's immune system is rarely ever able to mount a vicious and successful cellular attack against the invader. For this reason alone, the rabies virus is guaranteed ongoing success at survival and transmission, unless vaccination is implemented on a planetary level. If you are a movie lover, you may recall that this infinitesimally small virus played the leading role in the movie *Cujo*, based on the novel written by Stephen King and featuring rabies as one of the most feared infections of all times.

To complete the picture of rabies infection, let's take a closer look at the following common scenario. Mr. Autobody Worker takes his two fearless Jack Russells, Diesel and Bolt, to the dog park. Diesel, who is the stockier of the two and has an inbred tendency to leap at people's faces with great persistence, is doing his very best to annoy a leashed, medium-sized healthy-looking mutt. Eventually, when the mutt's patience wears thin, the frustrated dog turns on Diesel and starts biting him. Mr. Autobody Worker, horrified, runs to Diesel's rescue, grabbing the mutt by the neck. Not a wise move. The mutt, as expected, promptly whirls around and bites Mr. Autobody Worker on his wrist, puncturing the skin.

· If we skip the ensuing verbal exchange (by this point very loud, not at all courteous, and largely unprintable) between the two dog owners, and go straight to the relevant facts, this is what we discover: the mutt was not vaccinated for rabies, but Diesel was; and Mr. Autobody Worker was not vaccinated for either tetanus or rabies (as is often the case with people in the general population). Both Diesel and Mr. Autobody Worker have bleeding wounds from the mutt's bites.

If we concentrate our thinking efforts only on potential viral infections, we know that we need to first of all deal with Mr. Autobody Worker, who requires a tetanus injection. Dogs are not susceptible to tetanus (or they are naturally resistant to it), so this is not an issue for Diesel. The mutt most likely bit Diesel because of his annoyance, not because he was rabid. However, no one can prove this for sure, so safety measures must be undertaken, especially since the incident involved a person who was also bitten by an unvaccinated dog.

The steps to be taken after a human is exposed to an animal bite depend on a number of factors. If the animal in question is dead – which is obviously not the case with this mutt – then its brain can be "harvested" and tested for rabies after decapitation. There are no reliable tests for rabies on a living animal. Since we know, however, that death follows quickly after the rabies virus has penetrated the brain and becomes contagious in the saliva, a living animal that has bitten someone should be confined for ten days. An animal infected with the rabies virus will most certainly exhibit clinical signs of rabies and die within that period of time. During the ten-day isolation period, administration of a rabies vaccine to the animal is not recommended, to avoid any possible confusion between signs of rabies and signs of vaccine reaction, such as lethargy.

People are often confused about the quarantine period and about the decapitation of an animal to check for rabies infection. To clear up any ambiguity, let's take a second look at the two different scenarios presented above. In the first case, if Harley was bitten by wildlife, Harley would be the bitten one. If the brain of the skunk – the biting animal – had been recovered, it would have been tested for rabies, and Harley would not have been required to suffer through quarantine for ten days. His quarantine time was based on the uncertainty of rabies infection; we were waiting to see if he would in fact come down with rabies after being bitten.

In the case of the mutt, there was a ten-day quarantine to see if the mutt, as the biting animal, was contagious with rabies in his salivary glands at the time of the bite. Another option would have been to euthanize the mutt, decapitate him and send his brain for analysis. Clearly, this was not warranted, as our index of suspicion for rabies was very low. If Diesel had not been already vaccinated for rabies, he – as the bitten one – would have had to endure a ten-day quarantine period as well.

The noteworthy points highlighted in this chapter are twofold: firstly, that the rabies virus has thrived for several millennia in human populations, yet is preventable with the use of an effective vaccine; and secondly, that the rabies virus is commonly and easily transmitted to mammals – including humans, our canine companions, and farm livestock – by backyard wildlife such as raccoons, bats, foxes, and coyotes, so these animals are best kept wild and away from human settlements.

Despite initial suspicions of infection, Harley the puppy, Diesel the Jack Russell, and the nameless mutt all turned out to be rabies free. Other dogs, sadly, are not so lucky. Every companion animal that ventures outside – and even those who do not – should be vaccinated for rabies; this simple measure could save a dog's life.

A final note: laws regarding biting animals and their rabies vaccinations are highly regional, so it is best to check with your local animal regulation department and health regional board for specific procedures to follow in the event of an animal bite.

As a dog lover, you can…

- Make sure your dog is vaccinated against rabies.

- Prevent any contact between your dog and wildlife that could potentially be carrying rabies.

- Do your part to keep wildlife wild and away from human-populated areas.

CHAPTER 21

The Fly is Deaf: therapies proven and unproven

The only thing I remember about my inorganic chemistry classes at McGill University has nothing at all to do with chemistry: it is an anecdote about how a person of science can err in reaching conclusions. This memorable anecdote, about a fly that becomes deaf, is a useful reference as we wend our way through the vast field of medical research.

The story takes place in a medieval laboratory, where a conscientious scientist is bent over his work table, completely focused on the experiment he is conducting. Carefully, he sets a fly on the wood block before him and, with tweezers, removes one pair of the fly's wings. Then he sits back and directs the tiny insect: "Fly, fly!" And the fly flies. Meticulously, the scientist dips his feather quill into the ink bottle and scripts: "Upon removal of one pair of wings, the fly can fly." He then removes another pair of wings, instructs the fly to fly again, and notes a similar result on his parchment paper: the fly can fly. Finally, the scientist removes the third and last pair of wings from the fly, and instructs the tiny creature to fly. But the fly does not fly. The scientist reaches for his ink bottle and writes: "When the fly has no wings left, it becomes deaf."

The following discussion of modalities of treatment delves into those that may be helpful; those that, while perhaps not helpful, are likely harmless; and others that are downright dangerous to health, and worthless in terms of preserving life. This is a straightforward task, so let's get started.

We begin with a phone conversation I had with a client. "Mr. Baker, I understand you are getting frustrated with Rollo's interdigital cysts," I said, "They are a difficult condition to treat, and we have tried to keep these cysts under control with some antibiotics, which have certainly helped. But the cysts tend to recur when Rollo is off antibiotics. It would help, however, if you kept Rollo out of the water while these cysts are trying to heal."

Interdigital cysts are cysts that grow between a dog's toes, front or back, and are common in Labrador Retrievers such as Rollo, a four-year-old chocolate Lab. The etiology (cause) of interdigital cysts is not fully clarified, but we do know they can originate with hormonal dysfunction (e.g., hypothyroidism), allergies, conformation problems, infestation by ectoparasites (parasites on the outside of the body, such as mites), or the presence of penetrating foreign bodies, such as plant spicules. For any clinician, interdigital cysts are a frustrating medical problem, as they tend to recur. They may also cause physical pain to the animal, which leads to distress and frustration for the owner.

All of these factors had been addressed with Mr. Baker when Rollo was first diagnosed with this ailment. Even though he had been forewarned about the unpredictable prognosis of this condition, he was understandably frustrated, and in search of answers.

"Maybe I should seek help for Rollo through alternative medicine," he persisted, "Can you please refer me to a specialist in alternative medicine?"

"With pleasure," I responded, with nary a hint of sarcasm, "Shall I refer you to a specialist in integrative medicine, complementary medicine, TCVM (Traditional Chinese Veterinary Medicine), holistic medicine, naturopathy, pure homeopathy or allopathy homeopathy, VOM (Veterinary Osteopathy Manipulation) or homotoxicology?

Or would you prefer to see an herbalist, acupuncturist, osteopath, chiropractor, mystic healer, or shaman?"

For a moment, the only response from Rollo's dumbfounded owner was silence. "I don't know the answer to that," he finally admitted, clearly taken aback.

Here is where a discussion of "alternative medicine" and "conventional medicine" is perhaps warranted. Conventional or western medicine is generally based on scientific evidence, which involves sound clinical trials and methodology. A clear clinical benefit can be demonstrated and defined. Alternative medicine is often based on anecdotal evidence, and is therefore more unpredictable in its application and outcomes. Herbal products are produced and distributed under different rules than drugs, so the strength, purity and dose of an herb cannot be precisely gauged. Owners may also think that a product labeled an "herb" is harmless and soothing.

So Mr. Baker did some research on his own and, after discussion with a friend who was a human naturopath, he decided that the best treatment for Rollo was the use of bloodroot. Bloodroot (Sanguinaria canadensis) is an herb, one of the ingredients in the most popular escharotic (caustic, burning) salves available today. Bloodroot causes surface necrosis (tissue death), and special precautions should be taken with dogs to prevent licking of the salve, as it may be caustic internally. In fact, Vaseline is often applied at the edge of a medicated lesion to prevent the burning effect of bloodroot on adjacent tissues. Once a lesion has been burnt by bloodroot, the large open sore that results might take several weeks to heal.

Let's divert briefly for a small parenthesis here: perception is reality. If bloodroot were named vincristine or cyclophosphamide, and recommended by an oncologist (a medical specialist who deals with malignant tumors) as part of a chemotherapy protocol, many pet owners would decline its use, based on its extreme toxicity. If, however, the herb is recommended by a herbalist as part of a holistic treatment program, it becomes more readily accepted by pet owners, who assume that it is harmless and soothing.

In reality, would any oncologist recommend the use of bloodroot to treat skin tumors? Most likely not – and for good reason. Often, the strength, purity and dose of the product cannot be precisely gauged – never mind the absence of well-designed, randomized, double-blind clinical trials attesting to the efficacy of the product for different types of skin tumors. Use of such an unproven·product would leave any well-insured oncologist wide open to malpractice lawsuits.

If bloodroot is to be effective at burning a skin tumor, the tumor must first of all be very small and superficial, since an open skin defect will most certainly result from its application. Furthermore, bloodroot has thus far failed to demonstrate any intrinsic anti-tumor activity, or any preventive benefit when it comes to metastasis (spread of tumor cells).

A scalpel blade in the hands of an experienced surgeon, on the other hand, provides the possibility of excising a skin tumor completely, even when the tumor is large and deep, often without leaving a significant open gaping wound. In cases where excision is not warranted, cryotherapy (therapeutic use of cold) can be effective, but again the skin tumor must be relatively small – as required in cases of treatment with a bloodroot salve. The problem with the last two treatment modalities – cryotherapy and bloodroot – is that tumor margins cannot be evaluated for complete removal, nor can histopathology (microscopic study of diseased tissue) be conducted to learn about the behavior of the tumor, past, present, and future. As you can see, there are obvious pros and cons to every treatment modality. That one is labelled "alternative" and the other "conventional" should not dictate whether or not a particular treatment is worth using. End of parenthesis.

How did Rollo fare with his bloodroot treatment? Very well, according to his owner! The Lab's treatment consisted of daily applications of the black salve, which apparently burnt the cysts and the surrounding tissues quite effectively over a period of a few weeks; then another few months were needed for second-intention healing of the gaping holes left between the toes. All in all, Rollo's treatment process took five months of salve application, cleaning, and bandaging, and ended in February. By then, the Lab's toes were almost normal looking.

However, the question remains: did bloodroot really fix the problem? Or did time do its magic, as it does in many cases of interdigital cysts that spontaneously resolve on their own, especially when kept dry – as in the fall and winter seasons in northern climates when dogs stop going swimming? Was bloodroot actually the cure here? What actually did the trick remains an enigma, but I suspect Mr. Baker was not really convinced of the benefits of bloodroot. When Rollo developed more cysts the following summer, Mr. Baker requested a course of antibiotics to address the problem.

Every time we encounter an illness, three outcomes are possible: a cure, palliation, or suppression. A cure is self-explanatory: when a remedy or a drug is given to a sick animal, the animal improves completely without recurrence of the symptoms. In the example of a dog with a bite wound on the leg, the wound is cleansed and the dog is prescribed a course of antibiotics. Ten days later, the bite wound is completely and uneventfully healed; the dog is thus cured of this acute wound. In another example, a dog hit by a car develops a pneumothorax (presence of air in the chest surrounding the lungs, which impairs normal breathing) from the trauma. After chest drains are inserted for a couple of days to remove the excess air from the chest, and the leak in the lungs seals itself, the dog is cured.

In palliation, the remedy (or drug) works and the symptoms go away, but when the action of the remedy wears off, or the drug is stopped, the symptoms return. A classic example of this is ear problems in Retrievers, which are often prevalent in the summertime when the dogs go swimming and get their ears full of water. These otitises (ear infections) usually respond very well to antibiotics and anti-inflammatory medication, but typically return as soon as the medication is stopped. There is obviously an underlying problem that has not been addressed; in Retrievers, that underlying issue is often atopy (an allergic reaction with a hereditary predisposition, which causes reaction to specific allergens, often inhalants such as pollen). Until the allergies are resolved, the medications only provide palliation of the clinical signs of the external otitis.

Suppression, in the example of otitis, is a result of the clinical signs (redness, swelling, and oozing inside the ear) disappearing even though the animal is not healed. This is illustrated in the case of a dog that becomes very lame: when the owner gives the animal OTC (Over The Counter) anti-inflammatories, the lameness seems to go away. However, this is only suppression, since the dog is overweight and suffers from hip dysplasia. Every time the dog is dosed with OTC anti-inflammatories, he feels better and moves more freely, but this illusion of improvement is deceiving. In truth, the dog's joint cartilage is becoming even more ulcerated, leading to more lameness as the dog ages or exercises.

Any time a clinician needs to establish a treatment protocol, the first aim should be of course to achieve a cure. With that aim in mind, we look to an integrative approach that is least harmful to the dog and will yield the greatest benefits. Turning back to our example of the lame dog with hip dysplasia, administering anti-inflammatories alone would be pure madness and dreadfully short sighted. The dog would certainly feel better, but the gain would be short term because the dog is morbidly obese and his joints have already undergone degenerative changes.

A more appropriate integrative approach would combine a sensible weight loss program, to reduce strain on the dog's joints from extra weight; a supplement such as glucosamine that is FDA, NASC, or GMP approved, to help rebuild his damaged cartilage; a proper exercise program, to rebuild his atrophied muscles; some massage therapy or physiotherapy, to increase the range of motion of its stiff joints; and finally, an anti-inflammatory that is either chondroprotective (chondro refers to cartilage) or at least chondroneutral, so that all of the above treatment modalities could be executed without pain or discomfort to the dog. In such a case, cure is not likely since the joints have already begun their degenerative process, but a decent quality of life is probable with some weight loss and a GMP, FDA or NASC (regulating bodies) approved joint supplement, and only the occasional use of an anti-inflammatory.

This chapter could easily become a book if we were to cover all aspects of proven and unproven medicine, and their judicious use. But since we cannot, the main points to remember are the following: first, know *what* you are treating, regardless of the modality of treatment. This translates into the three basic rules of all medicine – diagnose, diagnose, and diagnose. If a dog has a primary lung tumor and is coughing blood-tinged phlegm, an erroneous diagnosis of pneumonia would create much needless pain and a shortened lifespan for the suffering dog. Too many cases with dismal outcomes were either not diagnosed at all, or misdiagnosed. The choice of treatment should always be based on an accurate diagnosis, and from there an understanding of disease pathology will direct the choice of treatments.

Second, once a diagnosis is reached, we should explore modalities of treatment not on the basis of glowing anecdotes or single-case studies, but rather on the basis of established evidence. Both types of medicine – proven and unproven – would be better off for discarding useless interventions and treatments that fail to yield consistent and effective results.

Third, practitioners of both fields of medicine need to remain open-minded and respectful, and learn to play nice with one another to improve treatment outcomes. Unproven medicine has a long way to go before gaining widespread acceptance, unfortunately, given current perceptions of scientific implausibility due to the paucity of valid clinical evidence to support its claims. As already required of proven medicine, all unproven remedies and treatment interventions should be submitted to randomized, controlled clinical trials, to ensure their reliable efficacy and allow for comparison.

Practitioners of both fields of medicine know all too well that many diseases, simply left alone, will heal over time without medical intervention. Given this reality, credit should be awarded where it is due: to the body, which possesses an amazing and inherent ability to heal, if given a chance.

In closing, I share with you the words spoken by a fellow emergency veterinarian as he headed out the door at midnight after his last shift: "And remember, animals will heal *despite* what you do to them!"

My colleague's wise words echo those of Voltaire: "The art of medicine consists of amusing the patient while nature cures the disease."

And finally, we must not forget the wisdom of Pien Ch'iao (fl. B.C. 255), who wrote: "Men worry over the great number of diseases, while doctors worry over the scarcity of effective remedies."

As a dog lover, you can…

- Ensure that an accurate diagnosis is in place before exploring treatment options for your dog.

- Approach all treatment options with a critical but open mind.

- Avoid the temptation to choose treatments based solely on glowing anecdotal claims or opinions; demand scientific evidence from reliable sources.

- Be wary of treatments that merely mask symptoms rather than addressing their underlying cause.

- Work with your health professionals in developing an integrative treatment plan specific to your pet's needs.

- Be aware that, in some cases, new medications may not have beneficial outcomes, even when administered by an experienced veterinarian, and may lead to deleterious side effects. Ask questions.

CHAPTER 22

Lost But Not Forgotten: when dogs go missing

The day it happened was an easy one to remember: it was Halloween and the trees were brilliant with fall colors when Jake and Arluk, two Husky Malamute crossbred dogs, went missing from their small town in the Canadian Rockies. The dogs had been out with their owner on a short hike close to town, loping happily along beside him over trails thick with fallen leaves, when they spotted a deer in the distance. Yipping with excitement, they bolted after the animal.

When they did not return immediately, their owner, Dean, began calling for them. No response. Wasting no time, Dean dutifully followed all of the proper steps (described below) to find them. He knew they usually came back when they had tired of the chase, and he was hopeful they would this time.

By then, darkness was approaching, and with all the little ghosts and goblins out trick or treating that evening, there was a lot of activity and confusion on the streets. Neither dog was found that night, nor in the days following. Even so, their owner persevered with posting ads and asking the two local veterinary clinics and local pound to be on the lookout. Dean never gave up looking for his beloved dogs: he hiked far and wide searching for Jake and Arluk in the mountains, camping solo for several nights in different mountain valleys, always calling and whistling for them.

When winter set in, he intensified his search, fearing the dogs would die of cold exposure. Deep down, he knew they were still out there, somewhere, but he found no signs of them, ever. Dean talked about his missing dogs constantly, at the coffee shop, at the gas station, and at the grocery store. All the locals knew Jake and Arluk, and Dean was determined to keep them present in everyone's mind. Even tourists passing by heard about the missing dogs, although they were not certain whether Jake and Arluk were part of the local lore, real missing dogs, or elusive ghosts in the valley.

And then, one sunny morning early in the spring, to the bewilderment of all the local townsfolk, Jake and Arluk plodded into town, right down the centre of main street, ignoring vehicular traffic. They were heading home. Their gait was slow, almost painful to watch. Both dogs were incredibly emaciated, with scars on their faces, and they looked beyond tired. Jake was limping badly on his right hind leg. It was a surreal scene: two weary mountain warriors making a humble return.

Though we will never know what happened to Jake and Arluk through those frigid winter months, we can speculate that they likely survived in the mountains by preying on small animals; we know this because they were passing worms in their excrement. Judging by their scars, they probably got into a few fights with the area wolves too. If only they could talk – what stories would they tell? And why did it take so long for them to find their way home?

In the end, what matters is that Jake and Arluk were finally reunited with their overjoyed owner, who raced madly down the street to greet them. Those who witnessed Dean's tears of joy and the ecstatic yipping of his dogs that day could not help but share in their joy, and the emotional reunion quickly became the talk of the coffee shop, the gas station, and the grocery store. It had been five long months since Jake and Arluk's disappearance, but the bond between the three of them had never weakened. It took just over two months back at home for both dogs to rid themselves of their gut parasites and fur mites and regain their normal body weight. Jake had injured the cranial cruciate ligament in his right knee, so was by then fit enough to undergo surgery for repair. The dogs' adventure soon became little more than a distant memory for everyone concerned – although their relieved owner now keeps a much closer eye on them whenever they are out hiking together.

Lola's story begins very differently. She was certainly no deer-chaser, nor would it ever occur to her to stray from her owner's side. In fact, Lola's life had been unfolding uneventfully until she met two Good Samaritans who – as it turned out – nearly got her killed. If you were to meet Lola, a Rough Collie, you could not help but notice that she looked just like the canine movie star Lassie, with the same endearing eyes. Unlike Lassie, however, Lola was not out to save the world, only herself. You see, Lola was a shy girl, and did not seek human companionship from anyone except her single owner and his friends.

One September morning, though, Lola's world went topsy-turvy. That day, Mr. Hastie, her owner, left her sitting in the passenger seat of his Acura in downtown Calgary, as he usually did when he attended short meetings in the area. The windows were rolled down an inch to make sure she would not get over-heated in the shade-covered parkade. Even though it was not her favorite place to be, Lola sat there obediently, waiting for him, knowing that the trade-off for her patience would be a walk in the park later. Then came the unexpected: although Lola could not see a storm brewing, she could hear the rumbling of distant thunder. She had never panicked during thunderstorms, but for some reason Lola was feeling uneasy about this particular one. As the rumbling drew closer, she started to drool and pant, and compulsively hopped between the front seat and the back. She was becoming more and more frantic as the storm approached, and simply trying to displace nervous energy with activity.

Good Samaritan #1, heading for his car in the parkade, noticed the commotion in the Acura. Concerned, he tried to unlock the door to let Lola out, thinking she was getting too hot (which was not the case). Unable to fit his hand in through the window crack, Samaritan #1 managed to break the passenger window and open the car door. But it was no friendly Lassie that leapt out: Samaritan #1 did not even get a grateful lick or a thankful paw shake out of Lola. All he got was a fleeting view of Lola's furry rump as she took off, panicked, into the early morning Calgary traffic. And that was the image that remained imprinted in the confused brain of Mr. Hastie as he approached his vehicle.

By then, Samaritan #1 was feeling bad. *Very* bad. Mr. Hastie, an Englishman and a gentleman, was feeling worse: he knew Lola was definitely not traffic-wise, as she had lived on an acreage just outside the city limits for her entire life. Worried, Mr. Hastie set out to drive around the neighborhood, hoping to find Lola.

After eight days of fruitless searching for Lola, Mr. Hastie found himself giving way to despair. He had contacted the local shelters daily, but there had been no reports of Lola's rescue or any sightings of her. On the ninth day, however, he did get a call from one of the shelters: a female Rough Collie had just been brought in, very matted and thin, but she did not seem to answer to the name Lola when called. Although Lola had been wearing a collar with ID tags at the moment of her escape, no accessories were reported on this stray Collie at the shelter. Even so, Mr. Hastie was convinced that it had to be Lola. From what he'd been told, Good Samaritan #2 had found what he assumed to be a stray dog trotting slowly, tongue hanging sideways, in the ditch paralleling Highway 22, a mere four kilometers from Mr. Hastie's house. Mr. Hastie immediately got into his car and headed off to see for himself. As he anxiously drove to the shelter, he kept glancing at his passenger seat, praying desperately that Lola would be sitting there beside him on his way back from the shelter.

"Lola, my girl!" exclaimed Mr. Hastie when he saw the bedraggled dog. Hearing his voice, Lola began frantic 360s in the small kennel where the shelter attendant had placed her. The little dog was beside herself, dancing in circles, lifting her paws one after another upon seeing her owner. As her kennel door was opened, Mr. Hastie crouched down on his knees to greet his precious Lola, who wriggled in panting ecstasy when she reached the safety of his arms. Being shy and a bit wary, Lola had not responded to her name when called by a stranger in a strange environment. As for her tags and collar, they had indeed disappeared – as is often the case with stray dogs. Samaritan #2 obviously thought he was doing a good deed by picking Lola up and delivering her safely to the local shelter; but in this case, Lola left on her own would likely have reached her home within an hour.

Poor Lola! After eight days of travelling over thirty kilometers from the downtown parkade where she had escaped in a panic from Mr. Hastie's car following her release by Good Samaritan #1, Lola had almost managed to find her way home when, barely four kilometers from her house, she was scooped up by Good Samaritan #2, who assumed that this dog wandering along in the ditch was lost. Thankfully, Mr. Hastie had made himself and Lola known to the local shelters, which in the end made for an efficient "lost and found" scenario.

What should you do when you realize your dog is lost? Below is a timeline of recommended actions to take once you realize your canine friend is unexpectedly at large. Keep this emergency guide on hand in case your pet goes missing; it certainly helped Lola get home safely.

Day One: Do not waste time! Work in an organized way, simultaneously with a couple of other people if possible. Within the first three hours, ask family and friends to search around the immediate area, up to a three-kilometer radius from where your dog was last seen. While you are out searching, have someone else make phone calls to your local humane society, animal shelters, veterinary clinics, and fire departments, and provide a detailed description of your dog. Contact your neighbors, and ask them to be on the lookout.

In the evening, once it becomes too dark to search any more, create a "Missing Dog" ad that includes a recent picture of your dog. If you don't have a photo of your pet, find a picture in a book or on the Internet and modify it to look like your dog. Describe your dog in such a way that an average person would recognize him if s/he saw him. Include identifying details, such as collar and dog tags, but keep in mind that retrieved dogs are often found without those items, as in the cases of Lola, Jake and Arluk, so do not rely solely on them. Tattoos and identifying features, such as unusual colorations, scars, or a missing toe, are very helpful. Refrain from including your dog's microchip ID number, however, as this may help a thief who decides to claim the dog as his own once in possession of such knowledge. Think about it: if you were the animal's bona fide owner, why would you walk into a veterinary clinic and ask to have the dog's microchip ID number read? (A special hand-held microchip reader is used to scan the chip.) You would obviously have access to that information elsewhere. Such an action should arouse a high level of suspicion.

When creating your ad, be very specific, as in this example: "LOST: a black dog with white face and front paws; SPAYED female; 25 Kgs. Got away from (location where lost) at (date and time of day). Wearing a blue collar with license tag. She is on heart medication. Family pet. REWARD. Call (your phone number)." If the dog is a purebred and female, it is useful to indicate that she is spayed, so that she will not be stolen for her breeding potential. Please consider *not* divulging the amount of the reward in the ad: only the person who has found your dog should ultimately have that knowledge. If the reward is too high, some finders may wonder about the value of your dog and decide to keep him.

Day Two: Intensify the search. Make at least fifty photocopies of your ad. Post your ads on bulletin boards in high-visibility areas such as gas stations, postal depots and grocery stores in your area. Start spreading the word to your local mail carriers, joggers, bikers and anyone else you see walking around the search area. Arluk and Jake were fortunate that their owner, Dean, excelled at this task.

Call your area shelters again, and give them a detailed description of your pet. Better yet, start making shelter visits every other day, especially if your dog is not a purebred. Mr. Hastie, Lola's owner, excelled at this task. At the shelter, ask to be shown to the restricted area where injured dogs or other problem dogs are held, just in case the shelter has not identified your dog. Do not expect overworked volunteers to distinguish one black dog from another. If a rescued dog has become dirty and matted, or lost weight, it may be difficult for strangers to identify your pet. If you have not found your dog within a couple of days, expand the radius of your search area by several kilometers. Call shelters even beyond the area you think your dog might have wandered.

Life saving tips for your dog's safe return

1. Plan ahead in case your dog becomes lost. Prepare a file that includes a picture of your dog, a record of his ID tag, tattoo and license numbers, and/or microchip ID information.

2. Strongly consider a tattoo for your pet, or a microchip that can be detected with a scanner at veterinary clinics and local animal shelters. If your pet is held at an animal shelter, its survival time will increase with the presence of either identifying method.

3. Have on hand the phone numbers for local veterinary clinics, the animal rescue league, the humane society, and animal shelters in your area, and possibly in neighbouring districts as well.

4. If your dog has a medical problem or genetic defect, say so clearly in the ad. This will be helpful for two reasons. First, unscrupulous people will be less likely to consider breeding a dog that has a known medical problem. Second, stating this gives urgency to your ad, and elicits compassionate efforts which may otherwise be absent.

5. Leave at least one important detail out of the description. The sad reality is that desperate dog owners can be taken advantage of in such circumstances, especially when a reward is mentioned. For instance, if someone calls to say s/he has your dog, ask if there is a small white marking under the right armpit (axilla). If s/he says yes, and your dog does not have such a marking, hang up. However, if the person says no and you feel a sense of honesty on their part, simply say you made a mistake and ask the person to look for the correct marking that has not been revealed in the ad. You can then share with the rescuer the name of your dog so s/he can see if the found

dog will react. Keep in mind, however, that shy dogs like Lola do not necessarily respond when called by a stranger.

Remember, it is not uncommon for dogs to remain missing for over a week, and then return home totally on their own. Do not despair, and do not give up. Keep going back to the shelters, always armed with pictures of your dog.

Finally, search regularly for your dog on the several "Lost Pets" websites, and check with rescue organizations for your specific breed if you own a purebred. Many rescuers will travel a great distance to help their favorite breed in need.

Ultimately, a practical search plan, when coupled with assistance from neighborhood resources and a measure of good luck, can lead to a happy reunion between a lost dog and his owner – as was the case for two adventurous deer-chasing Husky Malamutes, one shy Rough Collie, and a pair of very relieved and grateful owners.

As a dog lover, you can...

- Ensure that your dog is properly identified with either a tattoo or microchip.

- Keep a file of basic information about your dog to assist in finding him if he gets lost.

- Organize a search without delay if your dog goes missing; enlist help from neighbors and friends to expand the search.

- Post "Missing Dog" ads around your neighborhood to alert people to keep an eye out for your dog.

- Contact nearby animal shelters and veterinary hospitals in case your lost dog is taken there; leave your contact info so you can be reached, and be sure to check back regularly.

CHAPTER 23

Poetry in Motion or Death in the Fast Lane: greyhound racing

My father, now deceased, was well aware of my ambition to work with animals, even when I was a teenager. And he would take every opportunity to trip me up, especially on animal welfare issues. As far as he was concerned, it was all part of my education.

"How about going to the dog races?" he suggested one day.

"Sure, when do we go?" I responded. The idea seemed exciting to me: seeing the fastest dogs on the planet – Greyhounds – running hard and doing their very best. But that illusion didn't last long.

"Never!" my father answered, and then went on to address some of the welfare issues around farming out racing dogs. Back then, I certainly did not understand the full extent of dog racing as a commercial and gambling activity. Today, as a veterinarian, I do, and I find it ugly. Every time I have seen a Greyhound in my practice, it has been a rescue dog from the track. The reason is simple: the racetrack produces an enormous number of surplus Greyhounds, and if not adopted, these surplus animals end up dead.

The vast majority of Greyhounds in the USA are registered with the National Greyhound Association (NGA), and are bred for the sole purpose of racing. These dogs by far outnumber American Kennel Club registered dogs (i.e., the non-racing Greyhounds).

The best racing dogs will be retired as breeding stock, while the "rejects" from the racetrack – the ones that are injured, too old, or too slow – will be adopted if luck is in their favor. The rest get disposed of – often in questionable ways that we may not wish to hear about; such closely-guarded "industry secrets" are not meant for the public. Indeed, the Alabama Greyhound massacre in 2002 brought to light a horrific truth: that racing Greyhounds are nothing more than racing machines, to be executed when no longer useful. An *Associated Press* article of May 22, 2002, "Ex-Pensacola Security Guard Admits Killing Greyhounds," reported that the remains of approximately 3000 Greyhounds from Florida were discovered on the Alabama property of a former racetrack security guard. He was routinely killing unwanted Greyhounds with a .22 rifle, a job he had been doing for four decades.

The harsh glare of publicity on the Alabama Greyhound massacre made it difficult for the Greyhound racing industry to justify such killing sprees in the name of gambling events that exist solely for the entertainment of spectators. Given the nature of dog track racing, this profit-driven industry has an abysmal record when it comes to keeping animal welfare issues at bay and maintaining a clean image.

In the same year as the Alabama Greyhound massacre, a January 1st *Associated Press* release, "Two Charged in Deaths of Former Race Dogs," reported that a former Greyhound kennel owner and his assistant faced felony charges for selling more than 1000 Greyhounds for medical experiments. Unbelievably, the two claimed to be running an adoption agency for Greyhounds!

The year 2002 was definitely an "annus horribilus" for the Greyhound racing industry's public relations. That year, they made the news with cruelty to animals due to inadequate transportation conditions for racing dogs, as reported in the *Miami Herald* article, "Inquiry Launched in Death of Dogs - Greyhounds Likely Died From Heat," on August 13, 2002. Several Greyhounds died on a transport truck during a forty-five kilometer trip between Naples and Miami;

ventilation and temperature control were deemed inadequate for the crated dogs. Indeed, common practice in the industry is to carry up to sixty Greyhounds in one truck, with two or three dogs per crate, and to line the truck floor with ice rather than providing proper air conditioning. The back of these trucks can apparently reach temperatures in excess of 38°C (100°F) on a hot summer day. Needless to say, overcrowding and excessive heat are deadly conditions for animals who cannot sweat in order to cool themselves.

If you are born a Greyhound, the one key to survival is to be speedy. But even speed has its pitfalls. During a three-year span, almost 500 Greyhounds were injured while racing on Massachusetts tracks, as reported in the *Boston Herald* article, "A Most Dangerous Game: Report Cites Racing Dog Deaths," on July 20, 2005. The good news was the public's resounding reaction: enough human hearts were touched by the Greyhounds' plight that in November of 2008, Massachusetts held a vote to ban Greyhound racing, which passed by a margin of 56 percent to 44 percent. Racing in that state ceased in 2010. Since Greyhound racing is governed by state law in the USA, regulations range from total prohibition in some states to no specific regulations in other states, which blindly rely on the industry's self regulation.

Greyhound kennels consist of indoor crates stacked on two levels, with female dogs usually kept on the upper level and males on the lower level. While the space allocated to each dog varies by location, typical crate size is one meter wide by one and quarter meters deep by one meter high. While living at the racetrack, the dogs will spend most of their time in these kennels. When out of their kennels, Greyhounds are customarily muzzled at all times.

The United States is not the only country permitting dog racing that is governed solely by the industry's self regulation; like-minded countries include Great Britain, Ireland, Australia, and New Zealand. As awareness of the plight of Greyhounds has grown, rescue groups have been established all over the USA in an attempt to place unwanted Greyhounds into loving homes. But there is much more work to be done. In the United Kingdom, according to the BBC's *Inside Out* on

February 24, 2003, only one in four retired Greyhounds finds a home as a family pet.

Reputable adoption groups, despite their limited funding, save as many retired Greyhounds as they can. In many cases, however, this can be a tall order. Racing Greyhounds often have little in the way of socialization before they are offered for adoption, and they can have trouble adjusting to life as companion animals. These dogs have spent almost their entire lives in crates, or on the track, so understandably they are not used to the intricacies of modern living, with its odd noises, smells, and new experiences. For example, some Greyhounds may become quite distressed at climbing stairs for the first few times. Trained as "sight" hounds, these dogs are conditioned to chase a lure; these characteristics, unfortunately, commit them to life on a leash when taken outdoors for walks. Adopted Greyhounds can spot moving targets, such as squirrels, from a great distance. If allowed, they will engage in a deadly chase of the target, which can end up badly either for the target or for the Greyhound that is oblivious to vehicular traffic.

Interestingly, a common problem of rescue Greyhounds is tail injury. Because the animals are not aware of their personal space in a house, their tails can whack every coffee table in sight. Not only do they leave behind broken articles strewn on the table, they often emerge from their clumsy navigation with injuries to their tails. Further injuries result when their tails get in the way of closing doors, or flop under moving rocking chairs. To make matters worse, a tail injury usually heals poorly due to the tail's poor skin elasticity and diminished blood flow to its extremity, often requiring a partial amputation.

In my medical interactions with these rescue Greyhounds, I have invariably been touched by their gentle and trusting nature. Although adoption helps, the only way to ultimately stop Greyhound abuse is to put an end to track racing. In light of our countless opportunities for gambling in the twenty-first century – especially via the Internet and ever more numerous casinos – we might wonder why people still have the urge to spend their time placing wagers on dogs at a racetrack.

Dog lovers everywhere, I appeal to you to call a halt to any support of Greyhound racing, by refusing to patronize or bet on dog races. Only through concerted efforts by those of us who care about the welfare of racing dogs will we finally put an end to this cruel and barbaric industry.

Greyhounds deserve so much more than a life in crates or on the track, racing for their lives everyday – and suffering hasty "disposal" when they can no longer turn a profit for the business. These beautiful animals are truly poetry in motion, and they belong in loving homes with people who will protect them.

As a dog lover, you can…

- Become informed about the true scope of Greyhound abuse in the dog racing industry.

- Join the effort to end Greyhound abuse by withdrawing all support for dog racing and related betting events.

- If contemplating adoption of a retired Greyhound, first consider the animal's history, and be willing to devote the necessary time and patience while the dog adjusts to a new and unfamiliar environment.

CHAPTER 24

Look Who's Coming for Dinner: rat poisoning in dogs

Wesley leapt about in excitement when he heard the word "farm." To the spirited West Highland Terrier (Westie), this meant a visit to his owner's parents' sheep farm in the foothills of the Rockies. Can you imagine being a white Terrier and having access to all that dirt to dig up, with gophers galore all around, tempting and teasing you? This was so much better than spending time at the doggy daycare where everything was way too civilized. The farm visit was to be only an evening affair but, if the gopher hunting was good, that would be plenty of time for Wesley to get down and dirty and satisfy his Terrier instincts by chasing the pesky rodents. And the little dog did just that. Judging by how dirty and tired the Westie was on the way home later that evening, Mr. and Mrs. Bogner were confident that Wesley had had a grand time at the farm while they were dining with Mrs. Bogner's parents.

It was not until nearly two weeks after the farm visit that something seemed to be amiss with the little West Highland Terrier. The Bogners noticed that Wesley seemed totally out of breath and unusually tired: he even declined the chance to go for his usual late afternoon walk. Their worry level crept up a notch when Wesley refused to get up for his dinner. Unbelievably, he was not even tempted by table scraps. Something was definitely *off*. By the time Wesley sneezed up some blood, Mr. Bogner was already pulling the car out of the garage. Mrs. Bogner lifted Wesley into her arms and hurried after him. There was no question of what to do next – all three headed off to the emergency veterinary hospital.

Wesley was a wreck on arrival: he was unable to stand on his own, and blood was dripping out of both nostrils. Would it be any better if blood had been dripping from only one nostril? Possibly, yes. In a dog as young as three-year-old Wesley, unilateral (one-sided) nasal bleeding would point to the likelihood of a foreign body lodged in the nasal cavity. A tumor in the bleeding nostril was another possibility, but Wesley was unusually young for a cancer diagnosis.

What could cause bilateral (two-sided) bleeding, as in Wesley's case? This often indicates a more systemic (whole body) condition. Or, if it were cancer or other forms of rhinitis (inflammation of the upper nasal passages), bilateral bleeding would mean it was relatively severe. After a quick look in Wesley's mouth, we could already formulate a broad diagnosis based on the pallor of his mucous membranes and the presence of several petechial (red, spotty) hemorrhages. These hemorrhages, which resemble red pinpoints, indicated a coagulation problem – a sign that we should keep looking for more evidence. Sure enough, upon inspection of Wesley's inguinal (groin) area, we discovered more pinpoint hemorrhages. What about his labored breathing? On chest auscultation, we heard gurgling sounds on both sides of his thorax: this alone was a bad prognostic indicator, as it meant Wesley was likely suffering from a general bleed-out. No time to waste! We needed to do some whole body radiographs, pronto.

But first we needed to take a small blood sample for laboratory analysis. Did Wesley have an adequate platelet count? How anemic was he, from losing blood internally? If this were a general bleed-out, not due to platelet dysfunction, Wesley would have a decreased red blood cell count (anemia) along with a decrease in total proteins. In taking the blood sample, we saw immediately that Wesley's blood definitely could not coagulate: the site of venipuncture (where the vein was punctured to obtain a blood sample) was becoming very bruised from blood leaking into the subcutaneous (under the skin) tissues.

From here on, we treated Wesley like an expensive piece of porcelain, with extreme care and wrapped in towels to avoid any banging that might induce or aggravate his bleeding propensity. On radiographic images, we could see that his small chest was filled with fluid. Time for a quick chest tap: a small amount of lidocaine (a local anesthetic solution to induce tissue freezing to numb pain) was injected behind the seventh rib, where a shaved clean area had been prepared and a needle inserted. Through aspiration, we drew three milliliters of whole blood into the syringe. This confirmed that Wesley was bleeding out.

The two most likely causes of the bleed-out were a hemolytic crisis, in which Wesley's body would basically be destroying his red blood cells for unknown reasons; or exposure to rat poison. Drugs to address both problems were being calculated and drawn up as we questioned Mr. and Mrs. Bogner about the Westie's lifestyle.

"Has Wesley been exposed to rat poison lately?" I asked his concerned owners.

"No," they both answered, with simultaneous head shakes. "We live in the city, so vermin is not a problem," Mrs. Bogner explained, "And Wesley hasn't been anywhere in the last week or so, except for his regular visits to doggy daycare."

Where there is any room for doubt, we as clinicians need to ask more specific questions to solicit any forgotten details. So I tried again: "Has Wesley been anywhere in the last two weeks where gopher, rat or mouse poison could have been used – either outdoors or in an attic or basement?"

The look of bewildered shock on both Mr. and Mrs. Bogner's faces told me they'd just remembered an important detail. Fumbling through her purse, Mrs. Bogner pulled out her cell phone and rapidly began dialing her parents' phone number. Indeed, rat poison was used at the farm to control vermin. And Wesley had been out feverishly hunting that evening, while the Bogners were having dinner. They were certain of that because he had returned to the house covered in dirt.

Certainly Mrs. Bogner's parents were not the first, or only, people to use gopher poison liberally on their property. Mankind and vermin, such as mice and rats, have been at odds since the dawn of time. Vermin spread disease, nest in our food storage areas, damage our crops, infest our homes, and leave unwanted excrement as their calling card. We may be able to send men to the moon, but permanent pest control seems to elude us, even in the twenty-first century. To complicate matters, the average citizen in North America can take rodent control and extermination into his own hands with just a trip to the local hardware or grocery store to buy rat poison, also known as rodenticide. And this is precisely what Mrs. Bogner's father had done. Extermination of vermin might be the desired outcome, but collateral casualties are not so desirable. Who are these collateral casualties? Mostly, our canine companions – like Wesley!

Rodenticides come in three different categories. The one that concerns us most is the traditional anticoagulant rat poison, which is the most common cause of rodenticide toxicity in veterinary patients. Thankfully, there is an antidote, so death by rat poison ingestion can be avoided if detected early enough.

But let's start at the beginning, and find out what actually happens in rat poisoning cases. Typically, a dog will find pieces of food that might look like crumbles of granola bar, often tinted with a distinctive green dye. Dogs – not exactly whiz kids at discerning colors – are attracted by the smell and the palatability of these products. Once ingested by the animal, the anticoagulants, such as warfarin, begin to act internally, with no visible external effects for at least a couple of days. Then a slight jostle, push, or shove turns the internal trickle into catastrophic bleeding.

Whether or not we enjoy learning about complex metabolic functions, we must at least marvel at how efficient the mammalian body is at hemostasis (the stopping of blood flow). This intricate process involves the activation of cellular systems of coagulation proteins/factors, multiple enzymes and an end product called fibrin, which binds platelets together for the permanent healing of a blood vessel tear. Once an injury occurs, a coagulation cascade follows, and the twelve coagulation factors (I to XII) trigger one another to fulfill their special roles in stopping the bleeding. Clotting factors II, VII, IX, and X are called K dependent factors, for reasons that are about to become obvious. These clotting factors are produced by the liver and activated when a blood vessel tears and a clot must be formed to seal it. The activation process requires the presence of Vitamin K, and as long as there is plenty of Vitamin K available, clotting will occur normally. Whenever anticoagulant rodenticides are used, their mechanism of action is to abolish Vitamin K recycling. Basically, this means that as soon as the active Vitamin K reserves in the body are depleted, there can be no more significant blood clotting – which translates into a life-threatening situation for the afflicted being. Depletion of Vitamin K typically takes a couple of days after rodenticide ingestion; at that point, dangerous, uncontrollable bleeds or hemorrhages start to occur.

When this process happens within a canine body, external bleeding is not usually obvious. We would notice only that the dog seemed weak and/or cold. If we looked at the gums, however, they would appear pale, possibly with little red spots as a result of superficial bleeding. Sometimes bloody urine or stools are evident, or the dog will have sudden nosebleeds (epistaxis). If the dog vomits, any presence of blood in the vomit should be cause for alarm. Signs of bleeding in more than one body location are a strong indicator of a blood coagulation problem, especially if we part the dog's hair to look more closely at the skin and notice red patches or bruises on different areas of the body. At this point, appropriate testing is urgent and treatment should be started. If, however, the dog has suffered from severe bleeding and its red blood cell count is significantly low, a blood transfusion may be required to stabilize the patient. Even though the antidote is given simultaneously, it may not be physiologically active for another six to twelve hours, hence the need to stabilize the patient with additional blood.

In cases where the patient has just recently ingested the poison, blood clotting will not be a problem yet. But if we are aware of the dog's dietary indiscretion, inducing vomiting is a good way to rid the animal's body of the poison. However, using the antidote is generally prudent whether or not vomiting has been induced, simply as an added safeguard. Without question, if there is evidence the dog is bleeding, the antidote is certainly required.

What exactly is the antidote for rat poisoning? Simply Vitamin K! The antidote dosing process is usually started with an injection. When the dog is stable, or does not tolerate the injections anymore, tablets (wherever available) can be prescribed. Another noteworthy caution: since there are several classes of anticoagulant rodenticides, users are urged to keep the wrapping material or box label of the rat poison used, to identify the active ingredients involved. This information is crucial, as the length of therapy will depend on it.

Typically, Vitamin K therapy will continue for at least a couple of weeks. When therapy is discontinued, a coagulation test is performed forty-eight hours later to confirm whether or not there are still active rodenticide effects in the patient's body. If the test is positive, a couple more weeks of antidote therapy may be indicated. At this stage, the pet owner must be very diligent about returning on schedule for the recheck coagulation test. Failure to do so, even by a day or so, could allow catastrophic bleeding to start all over again.

What about a dog that actually eats a poisoned rodent? What course of action should we take? This becomes something of a dilemma, as it depends on how much anticoagulant rodenticide the rodent actually absorbed, for how long, and which generation of rodenticide was used. The newer generation products, such as diphacinone, would boost the risk significantly. The best preventive strategy for this common cause of poisoning in our companion dogs is an obvious one: be very cautious about using rodenticides in your own home. Dogs, with their powerful sense of smell, will often seek out and find the rat poison. When visiting someone else's house, be sure to inquire about the use of such products. If you have any doubts at all, leave your doggy friend at home or keep him on a tight leash!

What had actually happened to Wesley that caused his rat

poisoning? Had he eaten the gopher poison directly that evening? Or had he eaten gophers that had ingested the poison? Since no one was present to witness the event – and Wesley's not talking – we will never know for sure. But considering how very sick Wesley became, he had likely ingested a large dose of poison directly. In the end, the resilient little Westie survived his ordeal, recovered well, and carried on his joyful dog's life as though nothing had ever been wrong with him.

As a dog lover, you can…

- Be ultra-cautious about using rodenticides in your home if you have resident dogs.

- If you must use rodenticides, store them securely where curious dogs do not have access.

- When visiting other homes, ask whether the homeowners use rodenticides anywhere on the property; if so, keep your dog securely leashed and supervised, or leave him at home.

- Become familiar with the symptoms of rat poisoning in dogs.

CHAPTER 25

The Irresistible Puppy: what to avoid when adopting

Mrs. Morton had a heart of gold. At seventy-seven years of age, she was still living on her eighty acres of farmland, caring for six older horses that were spending their twilight years gracefully and purposefully, mowing down all the grass year after year. Mrs. Morton managed to get around the horse paddocks amazingly well, considering she'd had two hip implants within the past five years. Although Mrs. Morton had lived alone for some years, she never complained of loneliness. But she must have felt the sting of her solitary life, since she walked into our veterinary hospital one day cradling a black Cocker Spaniel puppy in her arms.

"His name is Thunder," she announced with pride, cuddling him to her chest. "I just purchased him from the pet store. The clerk said he was lonely because his brother had been sold yesterday."

What was wrong with this picture? "Everything!" I wanted to shout. But I bit my tongue and restrained myself.

The little Cocker Spaniel was adorable, no doubt about that. Nestled comfortably in Mrs. Morton's arms, Thunder watched his new world unfolding before his eyes, clearly enjoying his regal position. Almost immediately, my eyes zeroed in on something odd: what was that red lump in the corner of his right eye? It was glaringly obvious even from six meters away. On closer inspection, the red lump revealed itself to be an eye condition called "cherry eye," or in more professional terms, "a prolapsed nictitating membrane." The condition, either intermittent or permanent, manifests as prolapse and exposure of the third eyelid gland, which is responsible for tear production. A little surgery would be required to tack that rogue gland back within the eye socket where it belongs, in order to avoid future chronic inflammation.

"Mrs. Morton, what about Thunder's eye?" I inquired.

"Oh, I am aware of it," she answered cheerfully, "The clerk said it is normal for the breed!"

"The clerk is right indeed," I said, "But is there any provision in your sales contract regarding the surgical cost to repair this condition, if need be?"

"I'm not sure," Mrs. Morton admitted, "But I was also told that Thunder is cryptorchid. What exactly does that mean?"

"Well, it might sound like some kind of flower from Hawaii, but it's not, unfortunately," I told her, "Cryptorchid is a condition in which only one testicle has descended in the scrotum – the other one is still hiding in the abdomen or the inguinal canal. This condition is genetically inherited, and the retained testicle is thirteen times more at risk of cancer than if it were present in the scrotum."

Mrs. Morton's excited demeanor was fast dissolving. She looked worried.

"Apparently Hitler was cryptorchid," I added, to diffuse her growing aggravation. Thunder's new owner was slowly coming to realize that her puppy might have been an unwise choice.

"Mrs. Morton," I went on, "If that testicle is still not descended by the time Thunder is six months of age, we can neuter him then and retrieve the missing testicle."

I sensed Mrs. Morton's next question by the uncertain look on her face.

"Yes, unfortunately there is an additional expense if we search for the 'missing in action' testicle," I said gently, "Because it involves a separate incision." My heart went out to her – it was clear that Mrs. Morton was starting to lose confidence in what had initially been such a rewarding shopping experience at the pet store.

How could we not be sympathetic? Mrs. Morton had been taken advantage of at the pet store – it was that simple. Living on her own, with limited pension revenues, Mrs. Morton was by no means well off financially – and adopting Thunder had suddenly forced unexpected medical care expenses on her. If cryptorchidism and cherry eye were the only two medical problems that Thunder would face in his lifespan, Mrs. Morton would be indeed be fortunate. The odds were against it though.

By now, you may be wondering, "What can possibly go wrong with a Cocker Spaniel?" Here is a list of genetic diseases reported in Cocker Spaniels:

- Patent ductus arteriosus
- Pulmonic stenosis
- Endocardiosis***
- Atopy***
- Primary seborrhea
- Food hypersensitivity***
- Hypothyroidism***
- Cranial cruciate ligament rupture
- Patellar luxation***
- Chronic hepatitis
- Immune mediated hemolytic anemia***
- Hemophilia B
- Factor X deficiency
- Immune-mediated thrombocytopenia***
- Sebaceous gland tumours
- Perianal (hepatoid) gland adenomas
- Acquired vestibular disease secondary to otitis interna***
- Intervertebral disc disease***
- True epilepsy***
- Idiopathic facial paralysis
- Entropion***

- Ectropion***
- Distichiasis***
- Lacrimal punctual aplasia***
- Keratoconjunctivitis sicca***
- Primary glaucoma***
- Cataract***
- Generalized progressive retinal atrophy
- Central progressive retinal atrophy
- Struvite bladder stones
- XX sex reversal
- Spontaneous thymic hemorrhage

Dear reader, you guessed it: when three stars are present, the condition is relatively common to the breed! Thunder would be enormously lucky to avoid any allergy problems, to either food or the environment, which could lead to chronic ear infections (otitis externa and interna). And these problems could be seriously compounded if Thunder were to become hypothyroid (a condition in which the thyroid gland underperforms and slows down the entire body metabolism).

Within three days of having her Cocker Spaniel puppy at home, Mrs. Morton called to say that Thunder had had relentless watery diarrhea ever since he came home with her. When she brought him in again, a stool sample revealed that Thunder was infected with parasites – specifically, a protozoan called Giardia, the well-known cause of Beaver fever. He presumably contracted the disease through contact with other puppies at the pet store. A Giardia infection can be controlled with the use of a proper anti-protozoal drug, administered for a few days. But in Thunder's case, there was another risk. Because Giardia is considered a zoonotic disease (transmissible to humans), we had to inform Mrs. Morton that she needed to take certain precautions to avoid becoming infected herself.

"Mrs. Morton, did the pet store tell you where Thunder came from?" I asked, "Does he have any registration papers?"

"Oh, yes," Mrs. Morton responded, "I have some papers for him. He was registered with the Continental Kennel Club, and he came from a private breeder."

I cringed inwardly. As sweet as she was, Mrs. Morton had done no research on the breed of dog she had just purchased. This looked very much like a case of impulse puppy buying. "Private breeder" is a correct term, as there are no public breeders. But puppy mills and backyard breeders also fit the definition of a private breeder, which can be broadly defined as either a person or corporation that breeds dogs.

As for the Continental Kennel Club registry, dear reader and erudite dog lover, let us pause together here and step into the world of cyberspace to search "Continental Kennel Club" which should not be confused with the more regulated CKC, ie "Canadian Kennel Club". Go ahead – I will be waiting for you on the site. Are you there yet? Great, now drink down the rest of your coffee (or wine), as I do not wish to be responsible for the inevitable spurt up your sinuses in mid-gulp when you see the information on this registry. Let's look first at the "canine registration application," which can be completed online – you simply have to fill in the blanks.

While you read, I will point out to you the most shocking parts, with my comments tagged on – so if you still have that coffee mug in hand, be forewarned!

- Bloodline: *optional* (No pedigree required – obviously lineage is deemed superfluous.)
- Tattoo #: *optional* and microchip #: *optional* (No need to identify said dog as said dog; feel free to misrepresent your dog, as it will never be proven.)
- DNA certification #: *optional* (ditto the above)
- Breeder: *optional* (No one cares whether the dog came from a certified breeder or a puppy mill breeder – apparently this is better left unknown for legal reasons.)

When so much information is deemed "optional," how could we possibly view this club as professional? Any dog, of any type, from anywhere would evidently qualify for registration.

Let's look further: The parent section of the form requires both the sire's and dam's names, and their respective CKC (Continental Kennel Club) numbers. If they do not have member numbers, no problem! All you need are two witnesses to attest to the names of the dam and sire. Yes, mind-boggling as it seems, you have read this information correctly: the witnesses need to vouch for the *names* of the dam and sire, not their *breed!*

I am not sure whether Mrs. Morton was impressed that Thunder came with a registration number from the CKC, but I most certainly was not. Disheartening as it was, my information-seeking Internet session did prompt me to create a list of warning signs, to guide people like Mrs. Morton in becoming more consumer-savvy when considering a puppy purchase. The following is my list of cautions.

You should think twice about getting a puppy if:

- You have not seen the puppy's dam, its littermates and the environment into which the puppy was born.
- The breeder meets you at the end of his driveway with a puppy in hand, ready to sell it to you at half price.
- The breeder insists on meeting you at a rest area on the side of the highway.
- The breeder insists that an obvious defect, visible from six meters away (e.g., cherry eye) or so audible that you need earplugs (e.g., a Pug puppy's loud breathing, due to stenotic nares, or too-small nostrils), is normal for the breed.
- The breeder has no sales contract, and does not volunteer a phone number for future contacts.
- The breeder tells you specifically what food to feed your puppy, and when to get – or not get – vaccines for the pup, and reminds you that if you do anything differently, even on the advice of your veterinarian, your sales contract will be immediately nullified.
- The breeder tells you that there is no need to get the puppy vet checked, since most vets are incompetent and all are in cahoots with big drug companies.
- You are told that the puppy is OFA (Orthopedic Foundation of America) certified. The OFA certifies dogs for hip and elbow dysplasia, which can cause crippling disease even in young dogs. In order to be certified, the dog must be two years of age, so typically when you buy a puppy, the animal's parents

will have the certification, *not* the puppy. (Note: A preliminary evaluation can be submitted for a dog at four months of age, but a definite rating will not occur until two years of age.)

Let us divert briefly from the list for a quick anecdote. During a research trip to a local pet store some time ago, I noticed a ten-week-old Golden Retriever for sale. The advertisement stated that the puppy was OFA certified.

Intrigued, I asked one of the pet store clerks to clarify the ad. "Do you mean her parents had their hips certified?" I asked.

The sales associate rolled his eyes three times and let out a very vocal sigh before he told me, very slowly and loudly "No, *her* hips were!" as he pointed to the ad.

"How strange," I said, "I was taught that a dog had to be two years of age for OFA certification."

"Where did you hear *that?*" he asked, rolling his eyes once more.

When I told him I had learned that in veterinary school, the sales clerk didn't back down one bit. He insisted – with more rolling of his eyes – that I had it all wrong.

What was most depressing about the incident was my certainty that Mrs. Morton had gotten her information from just such a person as this. Whether the guy was badly misinformed or just flat-out deceptive, the repercussions for a puppy adopter would be much the same – dismal.

Let's continue now with the cautionary list. **You should think twice about getting a puppy if:**

- You are told that a puppy is CERF (Canine Eye Registration Foundation) certified. CERF is dedicated to the elimination of heritable eye disease in purebred dogs, through examination, registration and research. Both OFA and CERF have a policy that dogs must be permanently identifiable with a tattoo, a DNA profile or a microchip. Many puppies, especially "designer" puppies, are sold without any permanent identification.
- The seller tells you that OFA and CERF certifications are over-rated, unreliable or totally unnecessary.

- The seller apparently practices veterinary medicine without a license, since he provides you with a list of all the "treatments" he has already dispensed to the puppy.
- The seller does not have a health certificate for the puppy. Remember, a health certificate is not the same as a sales contract; it guarantees nothing, but it shows at least some concern for the well-being of the puppy.
- The puppy does not have all its baby teeth, is younger than eight weeks, or is not yet weaned.
- The breeder tells you that the puppy's registration papers are in the mail, or they are from an association that neither you nor your veterinarian has ever heard of.
- The breeder cannot knowledgeably explain to you both the problems and the assets of the breed, and no pedigree papers are on the table.
- The breeder is unsure about who the father of the puppy might be.
- The breeder is not familiar with the breed standards, or is unable to articulate how well the puppy's parents conform to those standards.
- The breeder is not able to explain the pedigrees of the puppy's parents, or the attributes and talents of this particular breed of dog – aside from adding money to his kids' college funds.
- Either of the puppy's parents has an unpredictable or unsound temperament.
- The breeder owns both parents, yet cannot intelligently explain why these two happened to be the perfect match for his breeding goals.
- The seller cannot tell you why you should *not* consider this puppy, based on your needs (e.g., he cannot anticipate behavioral catastrophes that could arise from having a Great Pyrenees dog living in a tiny condo).
- The seller has puppies of various breeds for sale at the same time.
- The breeder does not have either a spay or neuter agreement for the puppy, or suggests that the puppy could be bred at the first sign of heat.

- The seller is unfamiliar with medical terminology such as cataracts, hip dysplasia, and luxating patellas.
- The seller tells you the puppy will make a great "lifestyle accessory"!

Did Mrs. Morton have any recourse as far as compensation for Thunder's anticipated medical expenses? The answer to that depends on what was stipulated in her sales contract. The parasite issue was well defined as the owner's responsibility, whereas the cherry eye condition, clearly a pre-existing condition, was not acknowledged. A quick phone call to the pet store confirmed the store's policy, too often applied in these cases: Mrs. Morton could return Thunder and choose another puppy. By now, of course, Mrs. Morton did not want to lose her Thunder, especially since there was a discernible implication that Thunder would likely be put down if returned. So from that point on, it was all up to Thunder, Mrs. Morton and me – we would have to make it work!

If Mrs. Morton lived in Florida, she would have had much greater legal recourse under the state's Puppy Lemon Law. Florida has one of the best pet buyer protection laws in North America. The law, thankfully, applies to both dogs and cats, and requires animal vaccinations and examinations prior to sale. The law contends that a pet dealer may not knowingly misrepresent the breed, sex, or the health of dogs and cats offered for sale within the state of Florida.

The definition of "pet dealer" is explicitly written to include active hobby breeders, since it comprises anyone who sells in excess of two litters or twenty dogs per year, whichever number is greater. Consumers have fourteen days to document infectious diseases (such as Giardia, in the case of Thunder), and a full year to document congenital or hereditary defects (such as Thunder's cherry eye). The lemon law provides for replacement (through either refund or an alternate animal), plus reimbursement of veterinary expenditures related to certifying illnesses, up to the price of the dog.

If Mrs. Morton had purchased Thunder in Florida, she would have been protected by its lemon law, but unfortunately no such law exists in Canada, and not every state in the USA has one. Although there may be shortcomings with the lemon laws, they do place the responsibility of bad breeding and bad husbandry squarely in the laps of pet dealers. If lemon laws are far-reaching enough and enforced properly, we should see fewer dogs with crippling genetic diseases, such as hip dysplasia, enter the breeding pool; pet dealers would be wary of incurring too many expenses associated with the sale of affected dogs.

In Thunder's case, Mrs. Morton resigned herself to the added financial burden, since she could not imagine parting with her Cocker Spaniel puppy. For other puppy adopters, however, the outcome of a bad decision can be decidedly worse – as it was for one kind-hearted banker and his two puppy adoptees.

Mr. Corbett purchased Stocks and Bonds, two chocolate Labrador Retrievers, at a large pet store. The pups were almost four months old when Mr. Corbett first saw them, and their cage was so small that the two little brothers could not lift their heads above shoulder level without hitting the cage ceiling. Although Mr. Corbett was looking for only one puppy, he could not bear the thought of having to choose which one to leave behind. So, as you might have guessed by now, he left the store with two new puppies.

Within a day of acquiring Stocks and Bonds, Mr. Corbett brought them both in for new puppy checkups. Both dogs were in very good physical condition, and as playful as all Labrador puppies should be BUT they tumbled and stumbled together. Then they tumbled and stumbled some more – so much so that I finally raised my concern with Mr. Corbett.

"Have you ever seen the puppies *not* tumbling and stumbling?" I asked him, as we watched the playful twosome frolic about the room.

"Well, I've noticed that both puppies have kind of an odd gait," he said after a momentary pause, "But I assumed it was from being so cramped in the small cage at the pet store."

"Perhaps," I conceded, "But if that's the case, Stocks and Bonds should get progressively better over the next few weeks, as they get a chance to exercise normally in open spaces."

The next time Mr. Corbett called, ten days after adopting Stocks and Bonds, the news was not good: there had been no improvement at all – in fact, quite the opposite. Both puppies were becoming more and more lame, almost dragging their hind ends, sometimes practically running on their knees when bolting around the house. They walked with their rear ends weaving as though they were drunk, sideswiping one another and causing an occasional yelp.

Although the pups were too young for a proper radiographic evaluation of hips, knees and elbows, we scheduled a preliminary one to figure out the cause of their painful and irregular gait. Amazingly, both Stocks and Bonds cooperated fully during their X-rays, dispensing face licks to anyone that got too close to their faces. They lay still when asked to, and voluntarily took a spread-eagled position on the X-ray table for full radiographic views. As soon as they were let down off the X-ray table, they resumed playing in the exam room, despite their crippled gait.

I gasped when I read the radiographs: both puppies had identical problems, with almost equal severity. At their tender age, Stocks and Bonds were already affected with severely dysplastic hips, which did not bode well for them in the long run. As they reached maturity – and a weight of over thirty-two kilograms – there was a good chance that one or both hips in each dog would luxate (i.e., pop out of its joint).

Needless to say, Mr. Corbett was devastated. What were the treatment options for his Lab puppies? Before investigating any further, some research was in order. First of all, Mr. Corbett needed to review his sales contract with the pet store, to find out whether the pet store was willing to shoulder some of the costs of the looming financial storm. Mr. Corbett had paid nearly $2000 for the pair of puppies: did they have a registered pedigree? Who was the breeder? Certainly s/he should be informed of the serious hereditary condition discovered in this line of puppies – assuming, of course, that the breeder cared to know. Were the sire and dam of these puppies OFA certified?

On the orthopedic side, a consult with a specialist in orthopedic surgery would need to be included in our review of possible options for managing pain and ensuring long-term quality of life for Stocks and Bonds. In the meantime, we sent the pups home on anti-inflammatories and medication to help rebuild their joint cartilage, which seemed to be eroding fast. Soon after, Mr. Corbett confirmed that the puppies were about 50 percent improved within three days of starting the medication. His research had revealed that the puppies apparently came from a "private breeder" who often supplied puppies to the pet store. Furthermore, Stocks and Bonds had no pedigrees, and their parents had never been OFA certified. The pet store offered to reimburse Mr. Corbett for the two puppies, if he wanted to surrender them. He, like Mrs. Morton, was put in the no-win situation of either surrendering them to a certain death, or keeping them and assuming a large debt load in return for their affection and many face licks.

Unfortunately, the news from the orthopedic surgeon was less than encouraging: his best recommendation was immediate euthanasia for both puppies. Stocks and Bonds were too young to have new hips surgically implanted, as their bones would continue to grow for another four months or so. Because they were puppies and very active, there was a good chance that at least one hip would luxate. If that occurred, a femoral head resection would be required immediately. Basically, the head of the femur (thighbone) would be surgically removed and a fibrous pseudo-joint would form to replace the hip. This procedure is considered a salvage procedure and would involve a two-month recovery time with limited exercise. During that time, there was a strong possibility that the other hip, forced to bear all the weight, would end up luxating too; this would necessitate another femoral head resection. All this to tide the puppies over until they were old enough to get new hips implanted. And the cost of such surgeries? The orthopedic surgeon quoted upwards of $15,000 per puppy, barring any complications. As a banker, Mr. Corbett understood the financial implications all too well. Even so, he needed time to absorb all the information and formulate a plan.

Mr. Corbett made contact with us a week later and presented the following assessment: he had made a mistake purchasing Stocks and Bonds from the pet store without doing any research. It was most unlike him: he had acted out of compassion, but without logic. This, he realized, was going to cost him dearly, both financially and on a personal level; he would deal with the pet store for being irresponsible at a later date. As for medical care for Stocks and Bonds, he planned to continue to medicate them, as their quality of life had improved with medication thus far. If one of the puppies ended up with a luxated hip before it reached the required age for hip implant surgery, he would regretfully have the puppy euthanized, considering the grave prognosis offered by the orthopedic surgeon.

In the end, Mr. Corbett lost both of his puppies before they reached one year of age. Within a month of each another, both Lab pups luxated a hip. The double loss was heart-wrenching for all involved, especially the puppies' grieving owner, who had done his best given the grim circumstances. Mr. Corbett had evaluated the situation well: it was not about money, but about future quality of life. Even so, it was a painful lesson for him, one he wished he had not had to learn. He had done far more research before buying a new vehicle that would last him only three years before he resold it, yet he had acquired two companions that were supposed to be at his side for up to fifteen years, and had never gone beyond the emotional "cute puppy" stage with his research.

To redeem himself in the long run, Mr. Corbett adopted a five-year-old mutt from an animal rescue group after he lost his Labrador Retriever puppies. Yen, a Shar-Pei Labrador cross, was with Mr. Corbett for three years before the banker was transferred to another country, and the twosome left to enjoy life elsewhere.

Impulse buying may lead to buyer's remorse, but in the case of puppies, it can lead to much more: potential health or behavioral catastrophes that are often beyond either the emotional or financial capacity of a new owner. To his credit, Mr. Corbett took full responsibility for his puppies, but some people, unfortunately, simply abandon their "faulty" dog or surrender the animal to a shelter. Some problems, whether behavioral or physical, might be detected by shelter personnel, but sometimes they are not. When they are not, the adopted puppy is often returned to the shelter within a few weeks.

By the time a puppy has been deemed unsuitable by two or three adoptive families, the little fellow is usually an emotional wreck, confused by multiple relocations and the various commands and demands of different homes. If a compassionate, patient, and understanding owner does not show up in time, the near-adult puppy, having outgrown his "cute and cuddly" stage, will likely find himself on the receiving end of a lethal injection, or in a gas chamber.

As a dog lover, you can…

- Avoid impulse buying in your search for a suitable companion dog.

- Research a dog's background thoroughly before considering adoption; find out as much as you can about the breed and its potential problems, both physical and behavioral.

- Review the "cautions" list in this chapter.

CHAPTER 26

Why Plan for a Doggy C-Section?
breeding and bulldogs

Emma was one of my favorite dogs. She belonged to a wealthy family, and shared the love and affection of her owners with Damian, a seventy-three kilogram Bull Mastiff. Damian had been through his own share of medical trials and tribulations, most notably a lip tuck done at eighteen months of age when his owner realized how much drool could leak from his mouth, especially when he shook his head. She had initially tried to deal with the problem by painting the walls of her house a pearl grey color that would camouflage the slobbery drool. As she soon discovered, however, the camouflaged drool had a distinct and rather unpleasant odor – and there were probably liters of drool on those walls.

From then on, everywhere she went, she carried a tea towel draped over her arm, much as a butler would when serving dinner, to wipe any drool that escaped Damian's lips, especially after a drink of water. But she soon tired of the constant jowl wiping and tea towel washing. Putting Damian outside for most of the day was not really an option, except in the summertime. Mastiffs are not equipped to live outside, as they have a thin hair coat much like that of Dalmatians and Boxers. Unlike breeds such as Labrador

Retrievers, Mastiffs never seem to grow an undercoat and therefore cannot spend much time in sub-zero temperatures. As a last resort, the Mastiff's frustrated owners turned to surgery: in order for Damian to become a socially acceptable pet, his exceptionally droopy lips would have to be tucked so the excessive drooling would stop. Fortunately, the lip tuck did the trick, and all lived happily ever after. Oh, if only that were true… but in this case it was not.

Once Damian's problem was resolved, Emma became the family's new problem. Because she was so cute and adorable, her owners had decided to have her bred so they could have more little Emmas running around. Nobody in Emma's family knew anything about the troubles and woes of her particular breed when it came to breeding problems. You see, Emma was an English Bulldog, and by most estimates 95 percent of English Bulldogs are born by Caesarean section. Before we continue with the saga of Emma's pregnancy, let's backtrack and investigate her breed a little further.

Typically, the English Bulldog of today is kind and gentle, nothing like the original breed that started in England, most likely as a descendant of the Mastiffs that were introduced by Roman conquerors. (As a point of interest, some historians disagree, insisting that the Bulldog is in fact an *ancestor* of the Mastiff.) From what we know, our own ancestors were a blood-lusty bunch, and the Bulldogs became a favorite outlet for their aggression and cruelty. In the 1600s and 1700s, Bulldogs were commonly used for bull baiting (as well as bear baiting when bears were available), a popular gambling sport of the day. A bull was lashed to a post, and bets were placed on trained Bulldogs that would leap at the hapless animal, latch onto its snout and attempt to suffocate it. Needless to say, many Bulldogs were maimed in the process, swung into the air by crazed bulls and flung over the frenzied crowds. Goring wounds and broken backs were not uncommon injuries for these fighting dogs. Courage and ferocity were essential temperament traits bred into the Bulldogs to sustain them through a bullfight. Physically, Bulldogs had distinctive traits that allowed them to remain low to the ground away from the bull's horns, and strong, agile bodies for leaping and hanging on to bull snouts. The Bulldog's lower jaw jutted out further than the maxilla (upper jaw), creating a distinctive underbite that also worked in its favor, allowing the dog to grip onto the snout of the bull and still breathe through its recessed nose.

In 1802, a bill to abolish bull baiting was issued in the British House of Commons, but it was not until 1835 that an Act of Parliament finally made the sport illegal. From then on, the number of purebred Bulldogs began to decrease rapidly.

English Bulldogs have evolved significantly since their fighting days. The breed is now a medium-sized dog with narrow hips and a large skull, approximately equal in circumference to the height of the dog at the shoulders. The Bulldog face, as measured from the front of the cheekbones to the end of the nose, should be as short as possible. You can see where we are going with this: narrow hips and a big flat head require that large newborn-puppy faces move through a birth canal that sits within a narrow pelvis. In addition, the muzzle – typically very short – has a lower jaw that protrudes well beyond the upper jaw and angles upward at the front, with many deep facial folds or wrinkles that can easily trap moisture.

Based on this description, even someone with very little imagination can figure out a few drawbacks of the Bulldog physique. These dogs cannot swim very well, due to their compact shape and small rear end. They cannot go for long walks on hot summer days, as they will hyperventilate quickly due to chronic airway obstruction. They cannot join you while you build a snowman in the winter, as their coat is too thin and they would likely freeze. And more importantly, their arrival into this world more often than not requires surgery on their mother.

An English Bulldog bitch will have difficulty whelping on her own for two main reasons: first, the birth canal is often too small for the large heads of the puppies; and second, the heavy breathing which accompanies labor contractions can prove very difficult for the bitch, considering the abnormal anatomy of her face. As she struggles to breathe, her throat can swell up, leading to hypoxia (lack of oxygen). Ensuing complications include cyanosis (turning blue), collapse (fainting), and death.

Emma's family was familiar with none of this breed information when they had her bred. But once the deed was done, our only choice was to start monitoring her pregnancy by doing reproductive hormonal profiles in anticipation of a C-section before her due date, which was approximately sixty-three days after breeding. As is commonly done in dog breeding, however, Emma was bred three times at forty-eight hour intervals to ensure pregnancy. So her due date potentially spanned a full week, which complicated our planning somewhat – but better too soon than too late. We settled on a due date sixty-one days after her first breeding date, and decided that if the last breeding had been the successful one, she could be cut open on day fifty-seven and the puppies would still be viable. As it turned out, the C-section was uneventful, but only one puppy was present for delivery. The expense of the stud fee, the hormonal profiles, and the C-section was decidedly high for just one puppy, and this explains why English Bulldogs are relatively expensive dogs to purchase.

Unfortunately for Emma and Damian, their loving family eventually split up: the mother and children moved to the coast with Emma, while poor Damian – unwanted by his family – was adopted by a compassionate family friend. During the inevitable upheaval of the divorce and the move, no one noticed that Emma had gone into heat again – except a neighbor's dog, who could not believe his good luck! However handsome Emma's new boyfriend was, he was no purebred. The amorous fellow was black and he was big, weighing in at twenty-seven kilograms.

By the time someone finally figured out what had happened to Emma, she was well on her way to becoming a mother once more. She was soon back at the animal clinic for her hormonal profiles and a scheduled C-section. These puppies were going to be *big*.

In due course, Emma gave birth to seven puppies with a wide range of color markings and body shapes. They were actually so ugly they were cute! To prevent any more wayward trysts, Emma was spayed during her C-section, but she was still able to nurse her puppies until they reached four weeks of age. All of the puppies eventually found homes, as people were very sympathetic to the plight of the family. As you have probably realized by now, breeding English Bulldogs is not for the faint of heart or those with thin wallets!

All breeds of dogs have health conditions common to their particular breed, and the English Bulldog is no different. Many conditions, in fact, are the direct result of characteristics considered desirable in the breed. At the moment, English Bulldog breeder clubs are in turmoil over that very issue. The British Bulldog Breed Council was threatening legal action against the country's Kennel Club over a January 2009 announcement made in *The Times* and reported by Valerie Elliott: "Healthier new bulldog will lose its Churchillian jowl – Kennel Club standards will improve welfare." With this overhaul of breeding standards, the classic British Bulldog is destined to give way to a healthier dog with a leaner body and longer legs, and less of a sunken nose in a shrunken face – despite the storm of protests unleashed against the change.

The Kennel Club, committed to animal welfare issues, stated: "The breed standards have been revised so they will not include anything that could in any way be interpreted as encouraging features that might prevent a dog breathing, walking, and seeing freely." Seems reasonable, don't you think?

As a dog lover, you can...

- Familiarize yourself with the physical problems common to the English Bulldog before you consider adopting a dog of this breed.

- Carefully consider the complications of pregnancy for a female Bulldog, if you are planning to adopt or breed one, and be prepared for the expense of a C-section.

- Support only breed standards that are favorable to the animal's health and do not contribute in any way to physical problems.

CHAPTER 27

Pet Food Recall:
will it happen again?

In 2007, over 150 million dogs and cats were living as companion animals in the USA during which time every pet owner had significant cause for worry. Reportedly, thousands of pets were dying of kidney disease, related to the ingestion of commercial canned pet food. The major concern was the mystery behind the tragic deaths: no one knew which ingredient was killing these pets, and which foods were safe to feed. Pet owners began to lose faith in commercial pet food, and rightly so. Ongoing investigations revealed that pet food manufacturers themselves did not know exactly what was in their pet food. Iams, owned by Proctor and Gamble, was the first commercial pet food manufacturer to sound the alarm and move full throttle on the problem. This action forced Menu Foods, the leading North American manufacturer of private-label wet pet food products, to announce one of the largest consumer product recalls in North American history, with over 60 million containers of food ultimately recalled.

As later discovered, the concomitant presence of melamine (a plastic precursor) and cyanuric acid (a chemical used to stabilize chlorine in swimming pools) in the canned food was the cause of kidney failure in pets. These two chemicals, when combined together, formed insoluble crystals that obstructed kidneys, leading to painful renal (kidney) failure. Menu Foods had not only let down seventeen large retailers, including Walmart, Petsmart, Loblaws, and Safeway, but also fifty-three producers of dog food and forty-two producers of cat food, whose brands Menu Foods had been contracted to produce. More importantly, Menu Foods had let down thousands of pets that suffered an untimely and painful death, and shaken the public's confidence not only in the safety of pet food, but in the safety and security of the entire food chain.

In the following question-and-answer series, we will address some of the most common questions and clear up some of the mysteries around the pet food recall.

Was the contamination limited only to pet food? No.

Had the contaminated pet food entered the human food chain? Yes. Prior to the food recall announcement, excess or salvaged pet food was routinely fed to domestic animals, such as pigs, which were a source of food for humans.

Which food sources contained melamine? Wheat gluten and rice protein from China.

Why was melamine added to the gluten? Profit was the primary motivator. Melamine was deliberately added to inflate the perceived amount of protein (tested as nitrogen) present in the food, and therefore fetch a better price.

Why was the melamine not detected? Because it was fraudulently used, this chemical was intended to "fly under the radar." Melamine was inserted into the concentrate for one reason only: to deceive the buyer corporations into believing that they were being supplied with a high-quality protein concentrate. Melamine is a nitrogen-rich product that measures like protein in standard testing. Pet food labels read "crude protein" content because it is just that, an estimate based on the nitrogen content. As a nitrogen-rich compound, melamine can falsely elevate crude protein measurements.

Why was wheat gluten imported from China rather than being produced in North America? Here again, the motive was profit. Believe it or not, the USA has become a net importer of food; North America is obviously running out of protein, and cheaper prices command higher market shares. Cheap wheat gluten and rice protein products were purchased because they were less costly.

Was the wheat gluten and rice protein concentrate imported by Menu Foods from China considered pet food quality? No, actually the contaminated product was labelled for human use. Enough said.

Should people avoid purchasing food that contains wheat gluten or rice protein? Not if buyers are concerned about melamine contamination, since a screening process is now in place for exactly that reason.

Are other products used in pet food still coming from China or Asia? Yes, taurine (an essential amino acid for cats) and premix (vitamins and minerals added to pet food) are imported.

Why are we still importing products from China or Asia? Again, profit is the impetus. China can produce goods more cheaply than we can, and North Americans love a bargain!

How can we find out if a particular company uses ingredients from China? Call the company's 1-800 information number and ask.

Could a similar food recall occur again in the future, or has the lesson been learned? Without improved regulations, we could certainly face another tragedy of this sort, and not just with pet food.

Is there any possibility of a mandatory pet food recall if another harmful contaminant is found in the future? No. Neither the FDA in the USA nor the CFIA (Canadian Food Inspection Agency) in Canada has any authority to order a mandatory recall of pet food.

Understandably, the pet food recall created confusion and doubts among pet owners, and many – like Mrs. Brown, owner of a female Dalmation – came to us with their questions, seeking clarification on food safety for their dogs.

"What's the best pet food for a dog like Millie?" Mrs. Brown asked, when she brought her Dalmation into the clinic.

"First of all, what are your criteria for 'best' pet food?" I asked in return, "Is your decision based on price, or is it based on the quality of ingredients, or the variety of them? How important are the availability and the safety of the food? How about convenience – is that a factor for you?"

At that point, Mrs. Brown sensibly interrupted my barrage of questions, and answered in the best possible way, "I would like a food that will ensure optimum health and longevity for Millie." Well said!

Millie belongs to a breed that is plagued by several diseases. Dalmatians have the highest incidence of deafness – either unilateral (affecting one ear) or bilateral (affecting both ears) – of all breeds. Dalmatians are also susceptible to a very peculiar bladder stone, formed by the deposition of uric acid crystals, that can give the hair coat a "bronzed" appearance, and allergies that can be either environmental or food-related. A copper storage disease, although not exclusive to this breed, is a fairly common cause of liver disease in Dalmatians. Luckily, Millie did not suffer from any of these problems at the moment, but if she were to develop any of these ailments other than deafness, a food evaluation for specific health needs would be in order.

Dietary recommendations for Millie should be based on her nutrient needs, the ability of certain diets to provide proper nutrition, and Mrs. Brown's expectations. In other words, Mrs. Brown needed to find a nutritionally complete food that conformed to her desired levels of convenience and price, and was in accordance with her personal values. There were plenty of options that could achieve her objectives, including commercial pet food, home-cooked food, and raw food. Mrs. Brown, for personal convenience, preferred to use commercial pet food. This is worth repeating: commercial pet food was chosen *for Mrs. Brown's convenience,* not for Millie's.

Could Mrs. Brown expect Millie to live a long healthy life on commercial pet food? Yes, if we rely on the past to provide answers for the future. Large-breed dogs, with a few exceptions, are now expected to live twelve to fifteen years; over two decades ago, having a large-breed dog live a day beyond twelve years was only wishful thinking. Adequate nutrition, even if we do not concede its contribution to longer life expectancy, is likely not a hindrance to longer life.

So why are some dog owners reluctant to feed commercial dog food? Understandably, the massive food recall of spring 2007 came as a major wake-up call for all pet owners and pet food manufacturers, and raised numerous questions. What are the ingredients in dog food? And where do those ingredients come from? If large manufacturers were unable to answer those questions in 2007, how are consumers supposed to feel informed, or safe, about their pet food choices today?

In fact, some tools are available to pet owners to verify that their choices are wise ones. We need only look to the rash of food recalls in the human food industry to realize that these tools are not foolproof, but they certainly contribute to making an informed decision. But let's start at the beginning. Earlier in this chapter, the words "nutrients" and "ingredients" came up; understanding the difference in meaning between these words is an important start. Basically, a nutrient is a substance that provides nourishment, whereas an ingredient is simply an element of a mixture or food. In the world of nutrition, we can accurately say that animals require certain nutrients, which are found in different ingredients. For example, chicken meat is an ingredient that contains the nutrient, protein, just as rice is an ingredient that contains the nutrient, carbohydrate.

Therefore, when we read a food label and note the list of ingredients, we need always to ask, "Do these ingredients provide the nutrients that my dog requires?" One very contentious issue with commercial pet food is the presence of grain in the list of ingredients. If dogs are facultative carnivores – as opposed to cats, which are obligate carnivores, and humans and bears, which are omnivores – then why are they fed grains such as corn, wheat, or soy?

If we use the "the wolves in the wild" argument to say that the dog's ancestors did not forage for grains, we must also acknowledge two credible points that refute that argument. First, the domesticated dog has evolved alongside communities of humans for over 10,000 years, during which time we would be hard pressed to find societies that did not grow some kind of grain as a basic ingredient in the human diet (excluding Arctic communities of course). Since domesticated dogs had to scrounge at the fringe of human societies, they probably evolved with some grain as part of their diet too. Second, when wolves hunt down their prey, the choicest place to start their meal is usually the gut pile (entrails), followed by muscles, bones and fur. What is found in the gut pile of herbivores, which are the primary prey of carnivores? The digestive tract is usually filled with partially digested carbohydrates, such as grasses and grains. What nutrition do grains provide? They provide a little of everything: protein, carbohydrate, and fat, provided they have been processed enough to allow adequate digestibility. If they have not been properly processed, these three nutrients will be unavailable to your companion carnivore.

Mrs. Brown, generally a busy woman and already well informed, was not keen on attending a seminar on animal nutrition, but she did want some quick guidelines on how to choose a pet food. Mrs. Brown had agreed that the food should be nutritionally complete, safe for Millie, and convenient and affordable for her. She had also decided that commercial pet food was her best choice, but which one? And how would she choose from more than 1000 commercially available brands? Mrs. Brown had many questions that needed answers before she could make up her mind. Below is a sampling of her questions.

Mrs. Brown: "Is it true that the ingredients are listed in order of weight on the package?"

Me: "Yes, that's true. Generally, the first five ingredients make up the majority of the product. The difficulty in assessing the first few ingredients is that not all companies compare their ingredients on a 'dry matter' basis. So chicken may show up as the first ingredient because it was weighed as is, with all the moisture still in it (i.e., not on a dry matter basis), whereas the second ingredient, such as corn, may have been weighed after all the moisture was extruded (on a dry matter basis), making it appear as a smaller proportion of the diet than it really is. Furthermore, certain manufacturers will use several types of carbohydrates, such as brown rice, white rice, and oatmeal, to lead the consumer to believe that animal protein – chicken, for example – is the main ingredient, when in fact the various grains comprise the main source of energy in the diet."

Mrs. Brown: "In a single pet food, how many sources of ingredients are there?"

Me: "Generally over ten sources. Multiple sources are required to provide all the necessary proteins and amino acids, carbohydrates, fat, vitamins and minerals, flavors, antioxidants, binders and preservatives. The more numerous the sources, however, the more difficult it becomes to regulate the safety and conformity and reliability of the ingredients, and the more complex the supply chain becomes. Therefore, a longer list of ingredients does not automatically equate with a better diet."

Mrs. Brown: "Some pet owners advocate buying food only from the Big Four – why is that?"

Me: "The Big Four (Iams, Hill's, Purina, Royal Canin) are major pet food manufacturers that have detailed quality control programs and extensive research programs that are unaffordable to smaller pet food companies. The Big Four certainly have better control of their products, as demonstrated by the effective removal of their products from the market in 2007."

Mrs. Brown: "Some pet owners suggest buying only from small, local pet food companies instead of the big multinationals – is there any advantage to that?"

Me: "That depends on how you measure advantage. The service may be more personal, but small companies that do not sell beyond state lines require only a business license to operate, and are not held accountable to meet certain standards that larger, more far-ranging companies have to comply with. There is a greater chance for small 'niche' food companies to escape scrutiny unless there is a consumer complaint. And it goes without saying that small operators find it more difficult to maintain the high quality control measures put in place by the Big Four. Smaller local pet food manufacturers often produce diets that do not meet AAFCO requirements, or have not been submitted for evaluation by AAFCO."

Mrs. Brown: "What does AAFCO have to do with pet food?"

Me: "Everything. AAFCO stands for Association of American Feed Control Officials – this is a voluntary organization that strives to regulate the quality and safety of animal foods in the USA. Unlike the FDA, AAFCO has no regulatory authority, hence its inability to enforce mandatory food recalls. AAFCO offers the best safety measure we currently have, so companies are wise to use it, despite shortcomings such as limited testing on food trials."

Mrs. Brown: "Is it true that 'holistic' or 'natural' pet food is likely not what it claims to be?"

Me: "In terms of pet food, there are currently no legal definitions or enforcement for the terms 'holistic' and 'natural', so these terms can be very misleading when applied to pet food packaging. Since most premixes, or ingredients that make up premixes, and amino acids such as taurine come from Asia or China, where the sourcing of ingredients is uncertain and poorly regulated, 'holistic' and 'natural' pet food manufacturers have to avoid such ingredients and still provide balanced diets, which becomes a tricky task to accomplish."

Mrs. Brown: "What should I look for on the label of a pet food?"

Me: "An entire book could be written to answer that question. As a shortcut answer, I'd suggest calling the manufacturer's 1-800 number for answers to all your questions about the food. Here are a few questions to start with. Where do the ingredients come from? If not AAFCO approved, how do I know the diet is balanced? Who formulated the diet – a certified nutritionist? Do you manufacture the diet yourself, or do you contract a co-manufacturer, such as Menu Foods, to produce the food? If there is no complete guaranteed analysis of ingredients on the bag, why should I purchase the food?"

Mrs. Brown: "Is it not simpler just to look at the list of ingredients, and if they look adequate, then go ahead and buy?"

Me: "No. If the diet was not submitted to AAFCO for feeding trials, then we don't know anything about the digestibility of the ingredients. Just because whole chicken is listed does not mean that tendons, ligaments, beaks, and feet are nutritious. If grains are listed, were they processed properly to ensure digestibility? How were the carrots, peas, blueberries, and cranberries transformed to ensure that their entire nutritional content was not destroyed in the heating process to form kibble?"

Mrs. Brown: "If Millie likes the food, that says something, right? Is that not good enough?"

Me: "Children love soda pop, chocolate bars, and potato chips. But does that mean those foods are good for them? The same reasoning applies to animals."

Mrs. Brown: "What about the presence of byproducts? Are they harmful?"

Me: "No, many people eat byproducts such as chicken livers (pate, foie gras) and beef kidneys (steak and kidney pies in the UK). AAFCO has defined meat byproducts as the non-rendered, clean parts, other than meat, derived from slaughtered mammals. Meat byproducts include, but are not limited to, lungs, spleen, kidneys, livers, blood, bone, partially defatted low-temperature fatty tissue, and stomachs and intestines freed of their contents. They do not contain hair, horns, teeth, and hooves. They are suitable for use in animal food.

Some small 'boutique' pet food manufacturers claim their food does not contain byproducts, yet have included organs such as livers and hearts in their food, simply because they are unaware of the legal definition.

In the past, there was some concern that low-grade ingredients, such as feathers and beaks, were used in pet food, but any food manufacturers that meet AAFCO guidelines will exclude these items from their food products."

Mrs. Brown: "Why are byproducts put into the pet food in the first place?"

Me: "For economic reasons, mainly. There are billions of domesticated chickens, pigs, and cattle slaughtered every year in North America to feed the human population. Most people prefer to eat muscle meat, which creates a huge byproduct surplus. This surplus is effectively used in pet food. If not, we would have insurmountable heaps of rotting organs in depotoirs across the continent. We must also remember that byproducts can be an excellent source of nutrients. For example, the heart muscle contains the precious amino acid, taurine, which is essential to the well-being of cats."

Much like you, dear reader, Mrs. Brown is a dog lover who wants to feed her companion animal what is best for her. But narrowing down the choices of food was no easy task, and she found the complexity of pet nutrition enormously overwhelming. She is not alone in her predicament. To complicate matters further, the field of nutrition is hardly static. No indeed, this is a very dynamic field, in which new paradigms are discovered, new truths are unveiled through research, and knowledge constantly evolves. At this point, we still do not have a clear and comprehensive understanding of complete nutrition as it relates to pet health. What we do have is a basic understanding of minimal nutrient requirements for growing pets, and from there we merely build on the assumptions that we believe to be accurate. As pet owners, health professionals, and pet food manufacturers, we all have much left to learn. And the 2007 pet food recall taught us *not* to take food safety for granted.

In the meantime, we have to settle for what an adequate diet might be, and what Mrs. Brown should look for in a pet food as she strives to maintain and nurture Millie's heath. An ideal pet food diet is one that contains the necessary nutrients (versus ingredients), in the right proportions, and in a digestible form so that each nutrient is fully available to the dog. Obviously, the diet has to be palatable (pleasant tasting), so the dog is willing to eat enough to maintain its body condition. In short, the diet must be physically available to the end user, and affordable for the owner. Due to the increased complexity of our food chain and quality control regulations (or lack of), every dog owner needs to do some detective work to ferret out the best pet food to optimize their dog's health and longevity.

Do I feed commercial pet food to my dogs? Yes.

As a dog lover, you can…

- Do thorough research so you can take an active role in selecting the best pet food for your dog's specific needs.

- Get into the habit of checking pet food labels for ingredients and nutrient analyses.

- Look for a contact number on the food bag and call to inquire about the formulation of the diet, ie., origin of ingredients, preservation methods, AAFCO testing…

- Stay abreast of current information and new research findings in the field of pet nutrition, so that you are equipped to make wise choices.

CHAPTER 28

Spay Now or Pay Later: the risks of not spaying

O n February 12, 2008, the City Council of Los Angeles gave final approval to a new law requiring that all dogs and cats in the city be spayed or neutered after the age of four months, with some specific exemptions allowed. The ordinance was signed by the mayor on February 26, 2008, making Los Angeles the national leader in this serious effort to humanely decrease the number of pets abandoned and euthanized each year. With the new law, LA was taking direct action to reduce the number of animals killed in city shelters every month, thereby freeing valuable resources. Violations were subject to three levels of fine, starting at $100 to urge compliance, and resulting in a misdemeanour after the third violation.

A brief interjection here, to set the record straight for those of you who – like many of my clients – find your tongues stumbling over the correct terminology. For the record, females are spayed, not spaded (no shovels involved in the procedure). And males are neutered, not tutored (they're already smart enough).

What were the drawbacks to the spay/neuter law in Los Angeles? As far as social repercussions, it created one very unhappy group of people, namely dog and cat breeders. The advent of this law created a serious challenge for breeders wishing to keep a wide selection of their dogs or cats unaltered. In financial terms, the breeding business would likely see more exposure of its practices, possibly driving it out of the black market. On the medical side, however, the reaction was generally welcoming: the majority of practitioners in the veterinary community agreed that spaying or neutering a dog has more positive health effects than negative ones.

Before we go any further, a review of canine estrous cycles is in order. Female dogs come into heat every six to eight months or so, starting in their first year of life. A bloody vaginal discharge, lasting approximately a week, heralds the onset of estrous, or heat, and is followed by one to two weeks of canine harassment: local male dogs will literally scale six-foot fences and chew through drywall to reach a bitch in heat once her vaginal bleeding has ended. The good news? Spaying your dog will make this nightmare go away. In Los Angeles, spaying is not only a good idea – it is now the law.

In North America, the procedure generally involves removal of the uterus, which has two horns, and both ovaries. This is major surgery, and easier to perform in young dogs than in older dogs. The popular adage in veterinary medicine, "spay now or pay later!" certainly holds true. Since an older dog is bigger in size than it was at five or six months of age, surgery requires a bigger incision through the abdomen to reach the reproductive organ. According to veterinary estimates, up to 75 percent of adult dogs are overweight to some extent, which can further complicate the procedure. The need for surgical exploration through a few inches of abdominal fat to reach and manipulate ovaries the size of almonds increases overall surgical time, which in turn increases the cost of the operation. The good humor and patience of a surgeon also decrease markedly when gloved fingers get greasy and slippery from manipulating excessive adipose (fatty) tissue! As the reproductive organ matures, blood vessels supplying it become more significant and require additional ligations (knots) to prevent hemorrhages. This also increases surgical time and boosts risk to the patient.

The following two cases illustrate exactly how the decision *not* to spay early can lead to serious health issues for female dogs. Lacy, an eight-year-old Yorkshire Terrier, visited our veterinary hospital for a wellness exam, including a closer look at a small lump near a mammary gland. Lacy was originally supposed to be bred, but her pronounced underbite (a dental malocclusion in which the lower jaw is longer than the upper jaw) prevented her from successfully competing in the show ring. Her owner kept her despite this genetic flaw, but as a consequence never bred her. Moreover, Lacy had become her owner's daughter's favorite pet.

Clinically, Lacy perfectly fit the profile for developing mammary cancer, the canine version of breast cancer. A female dog spayed before her first heat will have a near-zero chance of developing mammary cancer. After the first heat, however, the rate of incidence climbs to 7 percent, and after the fourth heat the risk is nearly 25 percent (one in four!). This high incidence does not seem to change further with increased number of heats after the fourth one. As you can easily see here, an early spay done by six months of age would completely prevent a debilitating and potentially fatal form of cancer.

Was it too late for Lacy to be spayed, once her mammary tumor had been surgically removed and she was well past her fourth heat? No, in fact spaying is important even in female dogs that already have mammary tumors. This is because many mammary tumors appear to be stimulated by estrogens, so removal of the ovaries, the source of estrogens, will help slow down tumor spread. As it turned out, Lacy was fortunate: her pathology report came back indicating a mammary adenoma, instead of the more malignant adenocarcinoma. A mammary adenoma is a relatively benign tumor with little chance of metastasis (spreading). However, her owner would need to remain diligent, as more mammary tumors could appear in the future, and those might not be benign. Classically, mammary tumors follow the 50:50 rule, ie about half of the dogs presented to veterinarians with mammary masses have benign lumps, and half have malignant disease. Appropriate surgical removal of the malignant masses will prove to be curative in half of the dogs with malignant disease. As for Lacy, early diagnosis and surgical removal were the keys to her prolonged survival, as well as being spayed, even though it was later in life.

Unlike Lacy, Alley had been bred several times before her medical crisis arose. Alley, a Golden Retriever, was a drop-dead gorgeous blond. Barely past middle age at six years of age, she had a tail that never stopped wagging, even at the vet's office. So far she had had three litters of puppies, but raising the last litter had been unusually hard on her: she had developed mastitis (breast inflammation) and lost two puppies as a result. When Alley came in, she was barely able to stand on her own in the exam room, and her tail was hanging limp and motionless. She was febrile (feverish), had been drinking excessively over the last twenty-four hours, and her abdomen seemed slightly enlarged. She had vomited bile twice that morning.

"Has Alley been in heat in the last six weeks or so?" I inquired. Unfortunately, the answer to that was yes. From what we could see, Alley had likely developed a life-threatening condition called pyometra (pus accumulation in the uterus). This was quickly confirmed through a blood sample that indicated a high white blood cell count and a radiographic study revealing a very large fluid-filled uterus.

No time to waste: we promptly set Alley up with IV fluids, antibiotics, and a surgery monitor hooked up to monitor blood pressure and oxygen saturation levels, then wheeled her into surgery to have her pus-filled uterus removed before she collapsed completely and died. This was a very delicate surgery, so we needed to take every precaution while lifting the uterus, filled with approximately one liter of pus. If the uterine wall weakened and tore during removal, the abdomen would become contaminated with pus. This would drastically decrease her chances of survival after surgery. Luckily, Alley's uterus, although pus-filled, was not extended to the point of rupture. The uterus and accompanying ovaries were ligated and removed uneventfully from the Retriever's abdomen. After receiving large doses of painkillers, Alley was able to go home that night; she was staggering as though she'd drunk a few too many martinis, but health-wise she was perfectly stable.

Even though pyometra is common in unspayed females, most

dog owners are not familiar with the condition. The treatment, which almost invariably is surgical removal of the pus-filled uterus as demonstrated by Alley's case, is expensive. Without treatment, the chances of the animal dying are extremely high. Spaying prevents this very debilitating and potentially fatal condition.

By now we know that pyometra is an infection of the uterus that generally occurs with older female dogs in middle age, following a heat cycle. The hormone progesterone, which primes the uterus for potential pregnancy, serves its function by causing proliferation of the blood-filled lining of the uterus. In pyometra cases, we assume that, during a heat cycle, bacteria in the vagina ascend to the uterus and cause infection. The affected uterus then swells dramatically, filling with pus, bacteria, dying tissue, and toxins. Any owner of an aging bitch can easily lose track of her heat cycles, as they often become irregular. There is no end to cycling in female dogs that compares to menopause in women.

Although Lacy the Yorkie and Alley the Golden Retriever did survive their health crises, both were exposed to considerable risk and endured needless suffering that could have been prevented through early spaying. On the other paw, there is emerging evidence about the health consequences of spaying dogs very early in life and it behooves you as a responsible owner to become very familiar with the implications of this.

As a dog lover, you can…

- Spay your female dog before her first heat to avoid potential health complications and additional expenses later.

- Become familiar with the serious medical conditions that can befall an unspayed female dog.

- Consult with your veterinary practitioner if you have any questions about spaying or not spaying.

CHAPTER 29

Obesity: 5/5 is a bad score

What would you suspect is the common thread in the following three dog cases?

Cujo, a nine-year-old white Miniature Poodle, was brought in to see us for a moist cough, which was especially severe at night. Cujo also had difficulty moving around; running to the door was no longer part of the little dog's daily activities. In short, Cujo suffered from "exercise intolerance."

Hypotenuse, a large mixed-breed female dog owned by a math teacher, came in with a history of drinking water and urinating excessively. Her appetite had increased considerably over the prior few weeks, to the point of persistent "counter surfing", – an activity that involved standing on her hind legs with front paws on the kitchen counter, and "hoovering" any food within her reach. She had never indulged in such behavior in the past.

Windsock, a stocky yellow Lab belonging to an airline pilot, was much too young to give up retrieving sticks, her longtime favorite pastime. But lately her habit had taken a downturn: she would start to play with her normal enthusiasm, leaping and bounding to catch the flying sticks thrown by her owner. But after the fourth or fifth toss, she would flag, looking quizzically at her owner as if to say, why must this game go on? At that point, she just wanted to lie down and rest her aching body. But Windsock was only eight years old – much too young to act so old.

By now, astute reader and dog lover, you have likely guessed what was wrong with each of these dogs. Cujo suffered from heart disease. Hypotenuse would be diagnosed with diabetes mellitus as soon as a urine sample was taken (to check for sugar in the urine). And young Windsock was sore because she suffered from elbow dysplasia, a condition common to large-breed dogs that can eventually lead to elbow joint degeneration, otherwise known as arthritis.

But have you guessed the common thread in these cases? All three dogs were grossly overweight, in excess of 20 percent of their ideal weight. For example, Windsock the yellow Lab weighed in at thirty-eight kilograms. Based on the amount of fat covering her rib cage and sternum, we would estimate her ideal body weight at around twenty-seven to twenty-nine kilograms. Windsock was literally covered in a layer of fat: even persistent searching fingers using deep pressure could not feel the bony ridges of her rib cage. In fact, Windsock had a body condition score of five out of five!

On this scale, the higher the number, the more fat the dog has – so 5/5 was nothing to crow about. It was more like the booby prize. The ideal body condition score is 3/5, which indicates a slim and fit physique with a desirable silhouette. But lower scores can be worrisome too: a score of 1/5, for instance, indicates a dog that is grossly underweight. All three dogs described above suffered from conditions that were either predisposed by obesity or aggravated by obesity.

In medical terms, obesity is defined as a pathological condition of excessive energy storage in the form of adipose tissue in the body. Most definitions go on to state that this excess results in adverse effects on health and longevity both in dogs and in humans. Although obesity is recognized as the most common nutritional problem in dogs and cats, most owners do not seem to perceive or acknowledge this condition in their companion animals. This was especially well illustrated through a body condition score (BCS) study, in which dog owners and dog experts were asked to evaluate a BCS in 201 dogs. The results were very revealing indeed. The experts considered 79 percent of the dogs to be above ideal body weight, while only 28 percent of the owners estimated their dogs to have a BCS above ideal body weight. Worse yet, this misinterpretation by owners occurred even though they had access to an illustrated BCS chart. The implication here? Most pet owners do not recognize their overweight dogs as overweight without professional guidance. Is this denial, or loss of the concept of normalcy? While we cannot say for sure whether willful blindness is ever a factor, we do know that the dog owners in this particular study could not plead ignorance, since a BCS chart was provided.

Since the adverse effects of obesity on the health of companion dogs are easily quantified, there is no good reason why pets should be allowed to become overweight in the first place. Think about it: why should companion animals have to run any risk at all? While owners might face a host of social, psychological, and physiological obstacles to maintaining their own ideal body weight, all should find it relatively easy to prevent their pets from becoming overweight. And while treating is always more difficult than preventing, reducing a dog's weight once the animal becomes obese is still possible.

How does obesity happen? The answer is simple: dogs, just like humans, become overweight when their energy intake exceeds their energy expenditure (i.e., there is a "positive" energy balance). The excess energy is stored primarily as triglycerides in adipose tissue, where one kilogram of fat produces 7700 kcal (kilocalories) of energy. Weight loss is achieved by putting the overweight dog into a negative energy balance, where the energy expenditure is greater than the energy intake. This goal can be achieved by increasing exercise, decreasing caloric intake, or both.

Increasing a pet's energy expenditure or exercise level generally requires a firm commitment on the part of the owner, and may not always be possible given individual circumstances (e.g., the dog in question is a Dashchund, and reluctant to go for walks or climb stairs). For that reason, most animal weight loss programs center on dietary intervention. The key to restricting energy intake is to have a notion of the animal's current energy intake, and reduce it just enough to maintain normal physiological functions but not the deposition of fatty tissue. In practical terms, this involves evaluating every piece of food that enters the mouth of the overweight dog, whether given by the owner, the friendly neighbor the dog visits every day, the adoring grandfather staying for a visit, or any of the children in the household. And what about the uneaten cat food left in a bowl on the floor, instead of at a height the dog cannot reach? Leftovers from other household pets can also fatten an already pudgy dog.

While owners can easily calculate and measure the appropriate reduction in caloric intake, implementing a restrictive diet is often more difficult, since feeding is often perceived as the primary bonding activity between pets and their owners. A common recommendation by clinicians is that all treats stay, but they must be cut in half in the first two weeks of the weight loss program, and again cut in half during the following two weeks. Treats are useful for their bonding effect, not as a source of nutrition or energy, the latter being the job of meals.

To be fair, we must ask the question: are all overweight pets chubby simply because of too much food/energy intake? The answer is obviously no. Hormonal imbalances can trigger a deposition or abnormal distribution of adipose tissue. Hypothyroidism, a condition in which the thyroid gland is impaired, will cause clinical signs that are both gradual and subtle in onset, with lethargy (fatigue) and obesity being the common symptoms. Cushing's disease, also known as hyperadrenocorticism, affects the adrenal glands; the afflicted dog will appear very pot-bellied and be constantly ravenous for any food type. In hormonal cases, obviously, these conditions need to be treated medically to resolve the obesity problem.

Would Cujo's heart disease be easier to manage if the dog were not so overweight? Of course: if Cujo did not have to carry around an extra one an a half kilograms on a small body of seven kilograms, he would be exerting his heart much less, and the oxygen requirement for all of his muscles, including the heart muscle, would be much decreased. Until Cujo loses some weight, he will find any movement exhausting, and require large amounts of medication to prevent his lungs from filling with fluids as a result of his failing heart. Undeniably, his long-term quality of life is affected by his being 20 percent overweight. So is his longevity.

Hypotenuse's diabetes was likely a consequence of her lifelong obesity. Although in people, the link between obesity and non-insulin-dependent diabetes is well know, such is not the case for dogs. In medical circles, abnormal insulin secretion has been well established as a potential consequence of obesity in dogs, but the exact mechanism by which this occurs still needs to be clarified.

Of the three, Windsock was the lucky one. Her lack of stamina and the mild lameness in her right front leg were clinical signs that resolved over time. An appropriate diet with significant caloric restriction enabled her to consistently lose 1 percent (and no more) of her body weight every week for a period of just over three months. Her owner was astonished by how much better the slimmed-down Windsock was feeling. Unfortunately, Windsock's arthritic joints were irremediably damaged, but the removal of her backpack of nine kilograms of fat certainly lessened the continual wear and tear on her joints. Her dependence on anti-inflammatory drugs has also decreased since she became leaner. Financially, this is very good news for her owner, as the cost of treating an arthritic, large-breed dog can easily run over $100 per month.

Even in Windsock's case, however, some uncertainties remain. It is difficult to say, for example, whether her arthritis resulted in reduced activity, which then led to obesity, or whether the obesity was a causative factor in the development of the joint disease. Windsock's genes, her diet, and environmental factors have all interacted to create her phenotype, or what she has become physically – whether this is destined to be good health or ill health, a long life span or a short one.

The important point for every dog lover to remember is this: who we become physically as humans, or what our animal companions become physically as dogs, is largely dependent on three factors, only one of which we can control to any extent in terms of its impact. The three factors are genetics, environment, and nutrition. Once we are conceived, our genetic code is already set, and – barring possible damage through certain insults (e.g., radiation exposure or excessive sunlight exposure) – remains relatively fixed. Once we have been born into this world, not much can be done to improve our genetics; that hand has been dealt.

The second factor is the environment, which can be difficult to .control or change. Windsock lives where she lives due to the preferences and obligations of her owner. Whether the climate is humid, the smog is abundant, or there are too many stairs to climb, Windsock's surroundings are what they are.

The third factor, nutrition, is the one factor we can manipulate – oftentimes with tremendous impact. What we feed our dogs and the quantity we feed them are variables fully within our control, unlike genetics and the environment. The onus then is on us to control the dietary intake of our companion animals to prevent body condition scores beyond 3/5. The most compelling research on the topic of obesity in recent years was conducted by Purina, one of the Big Four pet food producers. Purina's study examined and followed the lives of forty-eight yellow Labradors until the death of the last one at the age of fifteen years. The research study concluded, with a high degree of certitude, that lean-fed dogs lived, on average, about two years longer, and experienced the onset of arthritis about two years later. These are significant findings for dogs that typically live twelve to fifteen years and thrive on being super active.

In a world where two-thirds of our human population goes to bed hungry every night, the knowledge that over half of our canine population in North America is obese, or becoming obese, is increasingly difficult to reconcile. Only two segments of society benefit from this affliction in our companion animals: the pet food industry, and the veterinarians who treat the many obesity-related problems. Sadly, I am part of this latter group and have seen far too many hefty dogs. In my practice, each pet visit at our veterinary hospital starts with a weigh-in and an assignation of a BCS. If the animal's BCS score is not an ideal 3/5, a nutrition and pet lifestyle discussion becomes part of a comprehensive consultation.

As evidenced in the cases of Cujo the Poodle, Hypotenuse the mutt, and Windsock the Lab, extra body weight can lead to health problems, impede physical activity and diminish enjoyment of life for our cherished companions. A weight loss program can often turn the tide, as it did for Windsock, but for some dogs the damage caused by obesity may be irreversible. Our only wish for our animal companion patients and their owners is "stressless wellness and a normal waist line for all!"

As a dog lover, you can…

- Become aware of the health consequences of obesity in dogs, as well as strategies to prevent the accumulation of extra weight.
- Maintain a healthy weight in your dog through proper nutrition and exercise.
- Resist over-feeding treats, even when your pet begs for more.

CHAPTER 30

Wanted and Outlawed: vicious dogs

Not long ago, a young associate veterinary clinician presented me with the following problem and a possible solution. She had just seen Mrs. Williams, who brought in her Buddy (a neutered black-and-tan Rottweiler cross) for a physical exam and to have a rapidly growing lump on his nose checked. Buddy had always been the sweetest dog imaginable – until you did anything related to a physical exam. Buddy seemed to sense when the actual physical exam was about to start, and his face would abruptly transform: one moment he was a friendly, face-licking sweetheart, and the next moment he was a jaw-snapping, in-your-face snarling demon. Needless to say, this display of ferocity could be mighty intimidating, especially since this big boy weighed in at a muscular thirty-three kilograms.

Thankfully, Mrs. Williams was always very understanding: she knew that Buddy was not easy to work with. On this day, he would need a sedative injection before we could proceed with any physical manipulation. Based on this and other incidents of working with aggressive dogs that can wear anyone's patience thin, our associate veterinary clinician proposed that we profile notoriously vicious dogs. If implemented, the policy would work like this: whenever an appointment was scheduled, the receptionist would inquire about the breed of the dog coming in to see us. If the dog happened to be on our "profile list," the next question would be whether a muzzle would be required. If the answer was yes, then we were not open for business as far as this dog was concerned. And if the dog owner became upset about the policy, we could safely assume the dog was probably an aggressive one, so nothing would be lost. *Voilà* – our new "aggressive dog" policy! At least that was the idea.

The new policy proposal made some sense to me, as I had just dealt with a similar case myself two days prior. Mr. Gibson was a client with several Maremmas (large, white livestock guard dogs originating from Italy) charged with looking after his farm animals, namely alpacas, sheep and poultry. Maremmas are beautiful dogs to work with, and very popular on the eastern slopes of the Rocky Mountains where cougars, bears and coyotes are major predators of farm animals. Ideally, a farmer would own at least two of the dogs for this type of work. One dog would do its rounds by day, while the other one rested; at night, the dogs would reverse their roles, making sure all shifts and all livestock were covered. I knew that Mr. Gibson bred Maremmas and had several of these dogs on his ranch, so his recent request came as no surprise.

"Could you please look after Kitty's medical problem?" Mr. Gibson had asked.

"Of course, no problem," I responded. How could I decline? My experience thus far with Mr. Gibson's dogs had been nothing but positive and favorable, and I naturally assumed that Kitty was another one of his self-assured and pleasant Maremmas. Often in the veterinary world, ignorance is bliss: I was completely unaware that Mr. Gibson was not only a farmer; he also owned a steel and iron shop on the east side of a nearby town, in the rougher part of town. As I found out later, he liked to boast that not one break-in had occurred at the shop since Kitty was brought in seven years earlier. Even his employees feared Kitty, so the dog was chained up during the day and released at dusk to patrol freely around the shop. Truth be told, Mr. Gibson himself did not feel confident in his own ability to handle Kitty, so the dog handling duty fell to Bert, the janitor. Bert and Kitty had a superb working relationship: whatever Kitty desired and wanted, Bert would always agree. "No need for confrontation" was Bert's motto. Bert was the only one that fed Kitty, which gave him a slight advantage over everyone else. If Kitty started to growl or misbehave, Bert simply gave her some food treats to appease her, a strategy that – unbeknownst to him – served to further reinforce her aggressive behavior. Remember, all this was background information gathered during – not before – Kitty's appointment!

On the scheduled morning, Kitty was duly delivered for a 9:30 appointment to check a pus-filled and blood-oozing mass on her abdomen. At 9:25, the receptionist called my attention to a most interesting sight outdoors: a tall man, approximately 1.9 meters and weighing less than eighty kilograms, was running or, more precisely, *flying* over the ground behind a leashed, fifty-nine kilogram Rottweiler that was trotting from tree to tree, sniffing and peeing at will. The Rottweiler was Kitty! This was a bad omen – a very bad one indeed. During my twenty years of practice, only three dogs had managed to pierce my skin and flesh, and two of them had been Rottweilers (Rotties) weighing over fifty-nine kilograms. Although the breed had not been banned from our veterinary hospital, I certainly had an acute familiarity with the pain that a jaw-locking breed such as the Rottweiler can inflict. So as I watched the scene unfold outside the clinic window, my extra-cautious instincts automatically kicked in. It was obvious to all of us watching that Bert had no control over Kitty. Wherever she wanted to go, featherweight Bert followed with a steady spiel of acquiescing puppy talk: "Good girl, Kitty... slow down, Kitty... come on now, Kitty...."

As it turned out, Kitty had a mass about three inches in diameter located in her distal mammary gland (the one closest to her groin). Proper medical protocol would have dictated, at the very least, a fine needle aspiration or a biopsy to see whether the mass was benign or malignant, comprehensive blood work in preparation for surgery, then removal of the oozing, smelly mass and a spay at the same time to prevent more potential mammary gland tumors from developing. In addition, chest radiographs were needed, to check for evidence of metastasis from a possible mammary gland cancer. However, Kitty was no Golden Retriever: she had no intention of dispensing face licks, her tail was not wagging, and any eye contact with her, however fleeting, instantly elicited overt aggression with ferocious, lip-curling growls.

Kitty's moment at the veterinary hospital was restricted to that day only, according to Mr. Gibson's instructions. So be it: Kitty would be sedated, blood drawn and analyzed immediately, and chest X-rays done while she was sedated. Then, if all went well, we would proceed with a complete lumpectomy (lump removal) and spay. "If all went well" referred to one primary aim: that Kitty could receive an intra-muscular injection of a sedative without drawing any human blood. The only way this could possibly occur was if Bert put a muzzle on Kitty. To my amazement, Bert did it! He actually sweet-talked Kitty into accepting a muzzle. Since luck was on our side, I promptly requested that Bert put a second muzzle on her for additional safety. With two muzzles as a barrier between Kitty's teeth and nearby vulnerable skin, we proceeded full steam ahead with all intended medical and surgical interventions. That evening, Kitty was released to go home to rest, with Bert nearby to watch over her.

The histopathology report, released three days later, confirmed that the mass had been a malignant adenocarcinoma tumor, and verified for us that the surgical removal of the mass, coupled with spaying, had indeed been the right course of treatment. In ideal circumstances, removal of the affected mammary gland plus the adjacent one may have been a safer bet to prevent possible spread of the cancerous tumor – but frankly, circumstances were anything but ideal in this headstrong Rottweiler's case.

As it turned out, Kitty recovered uneventfully from her multiple interventions in a single swoop; the cancer had been removed, and she returned to her guard dog duty. Five years later, when she became too crippled with arthritis to continue her nightly patrols of the shop, Kitty was euthanized. In the end, she had lived a good long life, and served her purpose well.

Dealing with a large and aggressive dog like Kitty is exhausting, both physically and mentally. The clinician's duty in such a case is to make sure that the dog is properly chemically immobilized to cause no physical harm to any living, breathing being within reach, while at the same time ensuring that the animal is not receiving a fatal overdose of sedating chemicals. Several veterinary hospitals and clinicians have completely banned known aggressive dogs from their practice for obvious safety reasons. Whether fair to the dog or not, the single-minded aim of such a drastic move is to protect veterinary staff and other animals under their care. In fact, the practice of banning certain breeds of dogs – not only from some public places but from entire cities – has gained considerable ground worldwide, becoming entrenched in the bylaws of several municipalities while drawing major controversy in others.

Is this banning of entire breeds a sensible idea? In our search for answers, we need to first of all investigate what has happened to one of the most maligned dog breeds of modern times, a breed of dogs that has been subjected to genocide in one of Canada's most avant-garde cities, and cruelly pitted against each other in dog-fighting bouts that led to the twenty-three-month jail sentence for a multimillionaire football star. Yes, I am referring here to the ill-reputed Pit Bull, the city of Toronto, and the convicted football star Michael Vick.

But wait a minute, I said "Pit Bull." What exactly is a Pit Bull? And since the Pit Bull is not an AKC recognized dog breed, what am I talking about? This is precisely the problem with breed-specific laws, or BSLs. In simple terms, a BSL – or anything related to breed-specific regulation or prosecution – is based on a specific breed and not a specific dog. For example, in Miami-Dade County, Florida, the law forbids owning or keeping Pit Bulls, American Staffordshire Terriers, Staffordshire Bull Terriers, or any other dogs that substantially conform to any of these breeds' characteristics. In Miami-Dade County, therefore, any dog that *looks* like a Pit Bull, such as a Boxer cross (that shares no recent genetic ancestry with Pit Bulls), is also targeted, not just aggressive Pit Bulls. The main problem with the law directed at Pit Bulls is that it presents formidable legal hurdles, since

Pit Bulls are not a specific breed. Rather, the label refers to a generic kind of dog with powerful jaws and a strong front end. The American Staffordshire Terrier, recognized by the AKC, fits this profile. Now for an interesting dilemma: if we cross an American Pit Bull with a Boxer, do we have a Pit Bull type of dog that will be banned, or a mutt that escapes the Pit Bull regulations? Furthermore, do we have accurate DNA testing for American Pit Bulls or Staffies (American Staffordshire Terriers)? No, we do not.

Let's amuse ourselves for a moment with a real-life anecdote before we get too serious on this topic. Some time ago, Mrs. Mosteller, wearing a fur coat and travelling by Mercedes with a chauffeur, made a grand entrance into our veterinary hospital, practically exploding with joy as she introduced her new puppy. At her side was her twelve-year-old daughter, Page, who was equally excited over Mimosa, the new puppy.

"Mimosa came from a reputable breeder in Texas, and cost nearly $2000," Mrs. Mosteller proudly informed us, "She is breeding quality." Her royal cuteness, Mimosa, eight weeks old, looked suspiciously like a Pit Bull to all of us. As the exam progressed, I questioned Mrs. Mosteller about Mimosa, and it soon became obvious my questions were starting to irritate her.

"Mrs. Mosteller, Mimosa really looks like a Pit Bull," I persisted, "Are you sure this is the breed of dog you wanted?"

Annoyed, Mrs. Mosteller finally decided to set me straight. "I have papers to certify that Mimosa is a registered purebred Staffordshire Bull Terrier," she insisted.

"Oh, dear Lord," I blurted in spite of myself, "Staffordshire Bull Terrier is just another name for Pit Bull!"

Mrs. Mosteller gaped in shock as her hand flew to her mouth. The poor woman looked like a deer caught in the headlights. Turning finally to her daughter, she stammered: "We bought a *Pit Bull?*"

The confusion is indeed understandable: there are too many breed names, and too many breeds look alike. Let's have some fun now as we peruse together the website page titled "Find the Pit Bull" (www.pitbullsontheweb.com/petbull/findpit.html), which presents photographs of twenty-five different purebred dogs, of which only one is an American Pit Bull. Go ahead, take a minute and find the site. The exercise is well worth it.

So how many pictures did you look at before you found the Pit Bull? As dog lovers, we must promise one another not to reveal our score, unless it is a perfect one. Embarrassingly enough, not one of my colleagues got a perfect score, and they would be appropriately labelled as "dog experts." This comparison of several breeds of dogs emphasizes a very salient point: when a dog attack occurs, people without pertinent knowledge of other aggressive dog breeds may falsely identify the offender as a Pit Bull. By examining the website pictures, we can better understand just how closely aggressive and menacing breeds resemble one another. We can also see a number of external physical traits that should forewarn a person that dogs of certain breeds have been bred to kill. By perusing these pictures, can we reliably decide how many breeds – if any – should be targeted by breed-specific laws (BSLs)?

As a matter of sad interest, look carefully at the dog belonging to the Presa Canarios breed. This is the breed of dog that killed a San Francisco woman named Diane Whipple in 2002. That fatal dog bite incident sparked great controversy over keeping such large and menacing dogs in apartments. This breed, along with the Dogo Argentino, is often cited as the most dangerous and vicious dog breed in the world. Some people use the following analogy to argue their point: if we are not allowed to keep large animals such as sheep and goats within city boundaries, then would it not be reasonable to have regulations against keeping such large dogs in small urban settings? What do you think?

On the other paw, the most horrifying example of lack of breed predictability especially where size is concerned is the October 9th, 2000 death of a six-week old baby which was killed by her family's Pomeranian dog as reported by the Los Angeles Times. The average weight of a Pomeranian is less than two kilograms and Pomeranians are not generally thought of as a dangerous breed although they have been bred historically as watchdogs. While the baby's uncle left the infant on the bed with the dog while preparing her bottle, he found upon his return the Pomeranian mauling the baby who died shortly afterwards.

Ownership of a so-called "Pit Pull" creates four potential complications: finding a city to live in that does not have a Pit Bull BSL, renting a house, getting home insurance, and travelling on a commercial airline with your black-listed dog. If you own a Pit Pull, you would be well advised not to think about moving to Toronto, or for that matter, the entire province of Ontario, Canada. On October 24, 2008, the Ontario Court of Appeal re-affirmed a law banning Pit Bull type dogs in the entire province. Under this ban, owning, breeding, transferring, abandoning or importing Pit Bulls is illegal in Ontario. Ouch! That law definitely has a bite to it.

Renters will attest to the difficulty of finding a house in which the landlord will accept dogs, especially if they are large dogs. If you simultaneously own a Pit Bull and are seeking shelter, keep in mind that these two are almost 100 percent mutually exclusive, unless you are prepared to purchase a house of your own – outside the province of Ontario, that is.

If you have somehow found a home for yourself and your companion Pit Bull, have you checked into home insurance yet? The insurance industry has a tendency to clamp down on some dog owners, and Pit Bull and Rottweiler owners may well find themselves in the target category, depending on their city of residence. Insurance companies frequently employ two favored strategies: one is to simply refuse to sell any policies to owners of certain breeds, and the other is to create a coverage policy that excludes dog bites and other dog-inflicted injuries. Is a policy such as this worth the calculated risk to a Pit Pull owner?

By now, you and your Pit Bull are likely growing restless in your new home and may wish to visit relatives in San Diego. Let's suppose that we are back in September of 2002, one month after American Airlines banned Pit Bulls from their flights. What are the chances that you and your restless canine will be flying anywhere? Perhaps loading your dog and your luggage into your pickup would be a better bet.

More to the point, why would American Airlines establish such a ban, profiling only one type of dog? Mostly because AA had a very bad experience the month prior, when a Pit Bull in the cargo hold escaped from its cage, deep in the belly of an airplane heading to New York from San Diego. Apparently the Pit Bull expended a good deal of energy during its ensuing rampage, gnawing at electrical cables the size of garden hoses, chewing through the bulkhead, and damaging a cargo hold door. The Boeing 757 ended up being out of service for nine days to repair the many canine-inflicted injuries. Although there was no mention of the cost associated with the incident, the Pit Bull owner reportedly did not to have to cover that bill. In an interesting side note, however, the incident was reported on BBC's *World News* in the following manner: "As well as destroying cabling, the masticating Mastiff gnawed a hole in a bulkhead and damaged the cargo hold door in the incident last month." What just caught your eye, astute reader and dog lover? Even though the original news article and AA both referred to a Pit Bull as the culprit behind the aircraft damage, the BBC later referred to a "Mastiff." So which was it? We, of course, would recommend a visit to the "Find the Pit Bull" site on the Internet to clarify this matter. And again, we promise, the score can be kept a secret. Another little note for your reflection before we move on: if the dog responsible for the grounding of a Boeing 757 had been a Golden Retriever, would AA have dared to put a ban on that breed?

Before leaving the entire Pit Bull BSL saga, let's pause for a moment to take note of a rather interesting position by the co-founding president of PETA (People for the Ethical Treatment of Animals), Ingrid Newkirk: that Pit Bulls and their close breed relatives *should* be banned. Apparently the consensus is that Pit Bulls can be used as deadly weapons. In People v. Nealis (1991, 232 Cal. App. 3d Supp. 1), a dog had been commanded to attack, so the court held that the animal was a deadly weapon. Similarly, in People v. Henderson (1999 Daily Journal D.A.R. 11862), a case of Pit Bulls used to threaten police, the court held that the dogs were deadly weapons – not necessarily because of their breed, but because the defendant was using them as such.

The danger associated with this breed is well established. Pit Bulls, along with Rottweilers, apparently accounted for over half of all reported canine-inflicted deaths in the two decades ending in 1998. Since Pit Bulls were created for blood sports, with the specific purpose of violence, they are often treated cruelly to make them as vicious as possible, and routinely abandoned or executed if they do not exhibit the desired vicious behaviors. They are also kept as protection by many drug dealers, and as such they are chained, starved, beaten, and trained to attack people and other animals.

This horrific abuse, and its associated tragedy, prompted PETA rep Ingrid Newkirk to take a stand in favor of banning all Pit Bull breeding. In her view, Pit Pulls are probably the most abused dogs on the planet, and people who truly care about dogs would not likely be affected by a ban on Pit Bull breeding. The fact that many animal shelters in Canada and the USA have a low-kill policy is hardly a secret. But listen closely: if you say low-kill fast enough it sounds very much like no-kill, and perhaps this is no accident. Among shelter workers, it is also no secret that Pit Bulls entering their facility will likely end up on death row, not adoption row. Understandably, then, the position taken by many is that if we are to stop killing Pit Bulls, we must stop breeding new ones.

Now that you have a clearer understanding of some of the pitfalls of banning Pit Bulls, dear reader, let's move on to the broader topic of dog bites and breed bans in general. First of all, let's review some solid dog bite statistics. A survey by the national Center for Disease Control and Prevention in Atlanta (CDC) confirmed that dogs bite nearly 2 percent of the US population – more than 4.7 million people – annually.[1] This represents almost 800,000 bites per year, with one out of every six rated serious enough to warrant medical attention. Apparently more than 50 percent of dog bite incidents happen to children.

---

[1]Sacks, J. J., Kresnow, M., & Houston, B. (1996). Dog bites: how big a problem? *Injury Prevention, 2,* 52–54

Hard as it might be to believe, dog bites are the second most frequent cause of visits to emergency rooms.[2] Every year, nearly 3000 letter carriers are reportedly bitten by dogs (US Postal Service), for an overall general statistic that an American has a one-in-fifty chance each year of being bitten by a dog (CDC).

Surely, among all these numbers, there must be room for some healthy skepticism. If an average American has one chance in fifty of getting bitten, then what is the risk to people working with dogs, from groomers to animal shelter workers and veterinary staff? The HSUS (Humane Society of the United States) seems to be in accordance with the CDC, as it also states that there are over 4.5 million dog bites each year in the USA.

The question is: how much can we rely on this number? Not a great deal, unfortunately, since 4.5 million is considered merely an estimate of the number of dog bites. There is no central reporting agency for dog bites; they are reported on a voluntary basis, or when significant bodily harm has occurred. Therefore, specific details of offending breeds, sex and age of dogs, circumstances around the biting incident, and other information are not computed. One important statistic, however, stands out amid this imperfect data recording system: of the millions of dog bites, less than thirty are fatal each year. Though extremely small, this number is tragic nonetheless, especially as young children are often over-represented in the fatality group. Less than thirty dog bite fatalities make up an incidence of less than thirty divided by 4.5 million (0.0007 percent). We should be extremely cautious in using this number to make sweeping legislative or regulatory demands. Compared to annual fatalities for vehicular accidents and gun-related activities, for instance, 0.0007 percent is a minuscule number to warrant such a flurry of legal interventions.

---

[2]Weiss, H. B., Friedman, D. I., & Coben, J. H. (1998). Incidence of dog bite injuries treated in emergency departments. *Journal of the American Medical Association (JAMA)*, 279, 53

A paper published in 2000 in *JAVMA*[3] lists the top ten dog breeds involved in fatal human attacks in the USA over a twenty-year period ending in 1998. In descending order of importance, they are: Pit Bull types, Rottweilers, German Shepherds, Husky types, crossbreeds, Malamutes, Dobermans, Chow Chows, Great Danes, and finally, the quintessential life-saving St. Bernards.

In examining the list, we can understand why some breeds are included. Although we can estimate a dog's temperament by looking at its breed characteristics, breed alone cannot be considered the major contributing factor of temperament. Typically, a Retriever retrieves, a Pointer points, and a Setter sets. We can also say that a hound sniffs and howls, and a guard dog guards, but these last two do not retrieve, point, or set very well. While it may be difficult to argue against some genetic component to temperament, many more environmental factors need to be considered as equally important, such as the dog's socialization and training. The available data on dog bites is just too vague to support launching legal action against certain breeds. Not only are we lacking accurate numbers and specific details of dog bites in North America, we are also lacking one other important number: the total number of dogs belonging to an "offending" breed in the general canine population.

If you are just entering the second half century of your life, you probably never heard of Pit Bull attacks when you were a child. Back then, however, German Shepherds, Boxers, and Dobermans would likely have scared you, since they were the breeds of dogs making headlines for dog bites. The point is this: since dog breeds change and evolve over time, targeting a specific breed would likely only shorten the time span in which the breed could thrive. A more effective and often-suggested approach would be to target chronically irresponsible

---

[3]Sacks, J. J., Sinclair L., Gilchrist, J., Golab, G. C., & Lockwood, R. (2000). Breeds of dogs involved in fatal human attacks in the United States between 1979 and 1998. *Journal of the American Veterinary Medical Association (JAVMA)*, 217, 836–840

dog owners and people with questionable intentions that persist in turning harmless breeds into aggressive killers. Restrictions placed on specific breeds fail to address the larger problems of canine abuse and aggression training.

So how do we deal with dogs that bite? First, we as a society must be reminded that, even though dogs have evolved within human communities for thousands of years, dogs of all breeds have the potential to bite. If, as a society, we want to play it safe, only stuffed dogs should be allowed into our neighborhoods. Beyond that, we must also remind ourselves that biting is a natural activity for dogs. Given that reality, all dog owners should be fully responsible for the actions of their dogs, including taking the necessary steps to socialize and train their dogs to become good canine citizens and not bite fellow citizens – whether animal or human. The overriding difficulty with that expectation is that most legislation deals with dog bites *after* the fact: if a dog is menacing but has not yet bitten, often nothing can be done legally until a bite wound has occurred and is reported.

Remember the policy on aggressive dogs proposed by our young associate veterinarian? In short, she had suggested profiling vicious dogs and refusing veterinary services to dogs of profiled breeds. Would you acquiesce to such proposal? Perhaps a more reasonable option, in light of the information presented in this chapter, would be to continue with our dog-specific profiles and not breed-specific profiles. At our hospital, all dogs in need of medical attention are given a chance, no matter how aggressive they are. The only applicable rule is that, if a dog shows overt aggression toward people or other animals, it must be muzzled while in their presence. If a dog like Kitty requires a muzzle, the owner or guardian of the dog should be able to apply a muzzle. If the owner feels threatened while attempting to apply a muzzle, or fears injury from a dog bite, then the veterinary team reserves the right to not attend to the needs of such a menacing dog, for obvious safety and liability issues.

On an interesting tangential note, an informal survey among peers revealed that veterinary professionals share a common fear of being bitten by four consistent breeds of dogs above all others: Chow Chows, Cocker Spaniels, American Eskimos, and Shar-Peis!

In over twenty years of practice, I have never once had a Pit Bull, or any related breed, inflict harm on my staff or me. When it comes to most other dog breeds, managing behavior is much like a poker game: the ones to watch closely are the ones that don't give away their intentions. Within the context of a veterinary hospital, Rottweilers are relatively easy to deal with: they are poor poker players. If they have aggression on their mind, they do not hide their feelings – a growl and a bite will come fast, fair and square, no surprises, cards on the table! Dashchunds and Cocker Spaniels, on the other hand, are clever poker players; they can be a threat because they are so cute that it's hard to imagine they could possibly have aggression on their mind. They certainly can be fierce when they choose to be, but are manageable due to their small size. German Shepherds are the *uber* poker players, giving the illusion that all is well until cornered to have their teeth looked at; then these major sweethearts transform in a flash, leaving teeth marks on human flesh. Retrievers are among the worst poker players: an involuntary wag of the tail always gives away a good hand. Jack Russells are not far behind: at the sight of a good poker hand, they joyfully leap into the air a dozen times at least.

If I was pressed to breed profile, the winning poker player would definitely be the cool, calm and composed Border Collie: this high IQ dog would have all the cards memorized and the odds calculated in its brain. Irish Setters, though, should never be allowed to sit at a poker table: they cannot stay still long enough to play a full hand, and they would distract everyone. As for Akitas, they would no doubt end up the lone poker players at the table, after intimidating and scaring off all other players, either with their fearsome looks or nasty bites.

In closing this chapter, I leave you with a worthy caution from an insightful but anonymous source: "When dogs are outlawed, only outlaws will have dogs." A slippery slope indeed.

As a dog lover, you can…

- Remember that biting comes naturally to dogs, and that none carry a foolproof guarantee of safety when it comes to dog bites.

- Train your dog to be a sociable animal that can be around people or other animals without biting them.

- Take full responsibility for the actions of your dog, especially when he misbehaves, frightens someone, or bites.

- Take all necessary safety precautions with your dog, including fitting him with a muzzle for any situation that requires it.

CHAPTER 31

Death on Wheels:
car rides gone wrong

My journey had been a long one with many detours along the way, but finally, with nine and a half years of university and three degrees to my name, I had arrived at my moment of truth. On my first night shift at a large emergency veterinary hospital, I was on my own directing a medical team. Our aim was to save animal lives, alleviate suffering, and remain compassionate as we did so. Marshall was our first case through the door that night. When I saw this badly injured Golden Retriever, the enormous weight of my responsibility came crashing down on me as fast as the wheel of the running Jeep that had ripped into Marshall's body. My mind was awhirl with questions: what if I was over-educated and under-skilled? Did I have what it would take to save this dog? All the knowledge we accumulate is worthless if we cannot put it into practice for the betterment of others.

Three, two, one, and action! We were looking at significant damage here: torn flesh, a torso covered in blood, a right front humerus fractured with bone piercing through the skin, shallow breathing, heart arrhythmia, anisocoria (one pupil larger than the other, likely indicating head trauma), and a low body temperature that was dropping fast. As if time were suspended, the medical team started moving like a well-oiled machine, working in perfect unison: inserting an IV line, stopping external hemorrhages, providing thermoregulation, initiating pain management, medically managing VPCs (Ventricular Premature Complexes, common heart arrhythmias in trauma cases, easily diagnosed with an EKG), and sending a blood sample to the lab to assess internal damages. Then Marshall was on the X-ray table: was there a hemothorax (blood in the chest cavity)? Were the spleen, the liver and the bladder intact? How bad was the right humerus compound fracture, with the front leg facing backward and pieces of bones protruding from the flesh?

Only after all this work was done, roughly fourteen minutes later, was I able to speak to the Retriever's owner.

"How did Marshall get under the wheel of a moving vehicle?" I asked her.

"He was riding in the Jeep with me," his owner explained, near tears, "And he tried to jump out while it was moving!"

I nodded; this was hardly a first. Marshall had done exactly what so many other dogs that come in during emergency shifts do: when riding in the back of an open truck, they jump out while the vehicle is still in motion. But Marshall's case was worse than most.

"It's an open canopy Jeep," Marshall's owner continued shakily, "But I thought if I secured a tie from Marshall's collar to the safety bar, that would prevent him from falling out the back."

She was right on that count. Marshall never touched the ground, because the tie was short enough to prevent that – but the tie was too long to keep him fully secured in the Jeep. So when he jumped out, the tie kept him stuck under the back wheel as the owner frantically stomped on the brakes to bring the vehicle to a stop from a running speed of over ninety-six kilometers per hour. Frankly, I was surprised that Marshall had not been either strangulated or killed from a broken neck.

Fortunately, our patient was a resilient dog. After merely a week of hospitalization, Marshall had recovered completely from his vehicular accident and was released from our care. The young

Golden Retriever did what his breed does best: wagged his tail and hopped about in excitement when his owner came to pick him up. Marshall did not even seem to notice that his front leg had been amputated at the shoulder: he jumped onto the back seat of his owner's vehicle without hesitation. Life on three legs was just fine for Marshall!

Vehicular trauma in dogs usually happens in one of four ways, and all relate to dogs being improperly secured. Firstly, Marshall would never have lost a limb if the tie had been short enough to prevent his four legs from reaching over the side of the vehicle. Using such a short tie, however, means that every time the owner wants to hook or unhook the dog, he has to jump onto the truck bed to secure or release the dog. Many people do not want the bother of doing this, so they use a longer tie that can be affixed from the side of the flat bed.

Secondly, unsecured dogs riding in the back of open pickup trucks run the risk of hurting themselves as they impact the ground once they decide to jump off – or fall off after losing their balance. If the vehicle is moving fast enough, fractures of limbs and pelvis are often the painful result of their joy ride.

Radar, a Portuguese Water Dog cross, exemplifies the third way vehicular trauma can occur in dogs. The day of his accident, Radar was in the back of the car, becoming increasingly anxious. His owner had just taken him to his favorite park to meet his canine friends. Now, on the way home, he could not settle: he was panting excessively and pacing on the back seat. His owner thought that perhaps he needed to have a bowel movement, as he had had very loose stools during his walk earlier. So she pulled off the highway onto the shoulder lane and opened her car door. She went to grab Radar by the collar to put a leash on him, but never had the chance to do so: Radar bolted out and was immediately struck by an oncoming car. He was literally dead in the fast lane. The owner, in shock after witnessing her dog die so brutally in front of her, phoned our veterinary hospital for help: a staff member drove to the site of the accident and picked up Radar's body from the shoulder lane where he had been flung by the impact of the vehicle. His rear end was smeared with diarrhea, which likely explained why he needed out of the car fast. The driver that struck Radar never stopped.

The fourth and final way that a dog can be injured or killed as a result of vehicular transport is the obvious one: by not being secured with a seat belt, thereby becoming a projectile. This was what happened to Monty, a loyal Border Collie that travelled everywhere with his owner, Rick. Monty was equally happy whether working cattle on Rick's ranch or taking a break to ride in the truck en route to the feed store. On their many journeys together, the Collie always sat on the front passenger seat, where Rick could extend a hand and pat him on the head.

One frosty November morning, Monty accompanied Rick in the truck for the last time ever. That day Rick hit some black ice, swerved, and ended up hitting a tree in the ditch. His car was an older model and did not have air bags. Rick ended up with a mild concussion and recovered uneventfully. But his dog was not so lucky. Monty's body was thrown against the dashboard resulting in severe chest trauma. Monty never recovered: within minutes of the impact he was drowning in his own blood, and he passed away on the passenger seat where he had fallen after his collision with the dash. Rick, wanting to keep his cherished dog close by, buried him on his cattle ranch. But there would be no more shared journeys for these two.

Over the years, I have treated numerous dogs for injuries due to vehicular transport. Some I have helped to heal, others I have helped to die, always with great sadness. Some of them were thrown like projectiles through windshields. Others suffered spinal fractures after hitting the vehicle's ceiling and falling unevenly against the side of a car seat or dashboard as the vehicle rolled off the road. Others simply jumped out of car windows that had been rolled down for fresh air.

Although naysayers would point to the shortcomings of safeguards such as seatbelts for dogs, very short ties to secure the animals in the back of pickup trucks, and well-fastened crates in the rear of vehicles, these devices can truly be life saving for many canines. Had such a device been used in Marshall's case, the happy-go-lucky Retriever would not have lost a leg. And Radar and Monty, both well-loved dogs, would likely still be alive today.

One final note, be aware that driving with your dog unrestrained on the front seat or on your lap may lead to a ticket for the unsafe operation of a motor vehicle.

As a dog lover, you can…

- Secure your dog well whenever he rides in the open back of a pickup truck.

- Never allow your dog to exit a vehicle near traffic areas without proper restraints.

- Transport your dog by vehicle only inside a secured crate or with a proper seatbelt.

CHAPTER 32

Watch that Mouth: dental disease

W hat would you say is the most common disease in dogs and cats? No, it is not heart disease. Nor is it liver disease, or kidney disease. The *most* common canine and feline ailment is dental, or periodontal, disease. If left untreated, dental disease will affect at least one of these three organs – the heart, the liver and the kidney – to some extent.

Given that I emphasize dental care for all my patients, I was somewhat surprised to see Pudgy coming back for a dental cleaning already. After all, Pudgy was only six years old, and his teeth had been cleaned just a year ago. But where there is concern, due attention must be given. So after an examination of Pudgy's mouth due to a recurring foul odor, we went full steam ahead with another ultrasonic teeth cleaning. This time I suspected we would need to do an extraction as well, since Pudgy's upper premolar was loose, causing the dog to pull away when pressure was applied to that tooth.

Over 85 percent of dogs and cats over four years of age have some form of periodontal disease. The disease starts with the formation of plaque, which is composed of saliva, bacteria, and food particles. Plaque will deposit within two days of having a professional teeth cleaning done if no other forms of oral hygiene are applied. And if plaque is not promptly removed with proper mouth hygiene, it will mineralize and become hard calculus, or tartar.

As I reminded Mr. Tatomir, this was especially important in Pudgy's case, given his history thus far. And "forgetting" was hardly an excuse.

"Next time you go camping with Pudgy," I admonished him, "And you somehow forget your own toothbrush and Pudgy's, you should head to the nearest civilized retail outlet to get yourself some new toothbrushes, especially if you intend to camp out for more than two days."

Mr. Tatomir nodded sheepishly. "But what if it's only for an overnight stay?" he asked.

"If it's just overnight, then you can relax and kick back," I told him, "At worst, there might be some halitosis – bad breath – to keep the bears away, but there won't be any permanent deposition of plaque or gum damage."

Wasn't Pudgy a little young to be having his second ultrasonic teeth cleaning? If he were a large-breed dog with a well-aligned mouth, my response would be yes. But Pudgy was a Pug, and like all Pugs he adored people and loved nothing more than to lick their faces. However, his halitosis made everyone back away from his generous face slurping. The problem with Pudgy the Pug's mouth, as for most dogs belonging to brachycephalic breeds (i.e., dogs with pushed-in faces, such as Boston Terriers, Pekingeses, and Bulldogs), was that his teeth were very crowded and did not line up properly. Dogs of this type commonly have teeth that are stacked sideways, making it easy for food particles to hide in many pockets, and accelerating the process of plaque and calculus deposition.

The other problem with Pugs, and for that matter all dogs of brachycephalic breeds, is that they are not exactly a joy to put under anesthesia, which is of course a necessary prelude to performing thorough mouth cleanings and teeth extractions. Intubation (the process of putting a tube down past the larynx into the trachea, to allow passage of gas and oxygen to the anesthetized patient) is the tricky part in dogs like Pudgy, since his breed often presents with an elongated soft palate that makes intubation difficult.

If Pudgy were allowed to get excited about this process, he could start to pant heavily and inflame his larynx, which would then become edematous (swollen with fluid), preventing a healthy flow of air. This could quickly lead to a state of asphyxiation and possible death. So to avoid such a catastrophe, we put together an anesthetic protocol for Pudgy that was tailored for brachycephalic dogs. Once under the influence of an anesthetic gas called Isoflurane, Pudgy was physiologically stable: his mean arterial blood pressure as well as his systolic and diastolic pressures were all within normal ranges, and his oxygen saturation level was well above 95 – a happy place to start. Because Pudgy was a small dog with very short hair, he would gradually lose body heat over the next hour while under anesthesia. In order to prevent hypothermia (low body temperature), we surrounded Pudgy's body with two heating blankets and measured his rectal body temperature every ten to fifteen minutes, to ensure that it remained around 37–39°C.

Pudgy's dental exam revealed stage two periodontal disease. The plaque had irritated the gums and allowed bacteria to survive below the inflamed gums, where they were hard at work degrading the tooth support structure, but fortunately the loss had not yet exceeded 25 percent. However, Pudgy's upper premolar started to bleed heavily when gently probed. With only a couple of twists, the tooth and its three rotten roots were easily extracted. Pudgy would feel much better with the removal of this tooth, as it most certainly had been a cause of pain and discomfort.

There are three important concepts to remember about this most common disease in dogs. First, inflamed gums hurt, and a loose tooth hurts even more. The problem may not be visible, but over time there are usually signs of a dog's discomfort.

Often dental disease is detected during a general health checkup, or when the dog has been brought in for an unrelated problem. "Have you noticed any signs of dental disease in your dog?" I'll question the owners, after I've discovered some evidence of it in the dog's mouth.

Once prompted, owners will commonly answer, "Now that you mention it, yes. I remember watching him eat, and he seemed to eat a little slower than usual." Or they'll say, "Yes, he seems to eat a little more on one side, and sometimes he seems to drop his food."

Usually the reason for changes like these in the dog's eating behavior is pain. "Seek and you shall find," I often tell my clients.

Second, the evolution of periodontal disease in a mouth may take anywhere from two to five years for significant bone loss to occur, which then causes loss of teeth. Besides the pain involved during this debilitating process, other inflammatory processes may take place in the body. All these bacteria might start to stray from bleeding gums to faraway organs involved in circulating blood – such as the heart, the liver, and the kidneys. The number one cause of endocarditis (inflammation of the thin membrane lining the heart cavities) in dogs is periodontal disease, which should impress upon dog owners the urgency to treat dental disease sooner rather than later. By the time another affected organ starts to fail, the health risk to the dog has been boosted substantially.

Third, from a clinician's perspective, helping a dog afflicted with dental disease is truly one of the most rewarding parts of veterinary medicine. How can that be? Very simple! Consider this common scenario: a dog comes in with terrible halitosis, and the owner reports that his pet must be getting old as he just lies around all day, does not want to play or go for walks, and has become very finicky with his food. The dog has lost 10 percent of its body weight. When all has been evaluated, periodontal disease appears to be the major culprit: the dog's mouth is too sore for it to eat properly, and the poor fellow starts to lose weight. Because his nutritional intake is so sparse due to the pain, the dog has little energy to do anything but lie around. His bad breath elicits grimaces of disgust from anyone who gets too close, and the dog understandably starts to feel unloved and lonely. By that point, one of the dog's major organs is likely underperforming, due to the constant attack of bacterial showers from his infected mouth. Oh, what to do?

Treatment in a case like this is simple and straightforward: comprehensive teeth cleaning, with necessary extractions, and a course of antibiotics and painkillers – with soft food for the duration, of course.

For any veterinarian, achieving the desired response to treatment is always rewarding – and happily this was the outcome in Pudgy the Pug's case. The good news was delivered at the time of our callback three days later.

"So how is Pudgy recuperating after his comprehensive dental work?" I asked.

"Very well…Pudgy seems to be another dog altogether!" Mr. Tatomir reported, sounding relieved and upbeat, "His pain is gone, his appetite is up again, he's already regained all the energy he had as a puppy, and he's back to spreading around his affection every chance he gets!"

That's exactly the kind of positive news every clinician wishes to hear. Maintaining oral health truly is about maintaining body and mental health – in dogs as well as in people.

As a dog lover, you can…

- Maintain good dental health in your dog through brushing, regular vet checkups, and teeth cleaning when required.

- Be aware of the health repercussions of poor dental hygiene for your dog.

- Take note of any change to your dog's eating behavior that could indicate dental pain.

- Act without delay in scheduling treatment of dental disease once it has been diagnosed in your dog.

CHAPTER 33

Too Young to Go Home: when is a puppy ready?

We were more than a little surprised recently when Mrs. Williamson turned up at the clinic without her tiny dog in tow. But her news was even more surprising.

"My little Sachi died yesterday," Mrs. Williamson announced gloomily, "Do you know of anyone ready to purchase any of her puppies?"

I was taken aback. How could her puppies be ready for sale already, when a Caesarian section had just been performed on Sachi three weeks ago? Sachi, a four-year-old Chihuahua had been unable to deliver any of her four puppies naturally, since one of the puppies had been stuck in the birth canal. Despite Sachi's strong contractions, the breeched puppy refused to budge, so none of the other puppies behind that one were able to move either. With no other recourse, we performed a routine and uneventful C-section that allowed all four puppies to enter the world healthy and happy.

But what had happened since then? Was Sachi dead as a result of post-operative complications from her surgery? Were the puppies being bottle-fed? Were they still thriving? At three weeks of age, they were way too young to go solo to new homes. And what about socializing them? Although Mrs. Williamson was understandably agitated and disturbed by the whole situation, she was able to clarify for me what had happened.

"It was an accident," Mrs. Williamson told me somberly, "The garage door was inadvertently lowered, and it came down on Sachi's little body. We think it probably broke her neck." Little Sachi, a registered Chihuahua barely two kilograms in body weight, had apparently wandered out of the garage just as Mr. Williamson was shutting the garage door after parking his car inside. He hadn't noticed the little dog exiting the building, nor anything else amiss.

Twenty minutes later, a horrified Mrs. Williamson found her pet's lifeless body. She had been looking for Sachi because her puppies were crying for milk. Once she'd recovered somewhat from the shock of her Chihuahua's death, Mrs. Williamson had immediately gone to the local pet store to purchase some milk replacer. Then she started the labor-intensive task of hand feeding the four puppies on demand. She soon realized she did not have the energy to handle this new maternal chore for a full month, the time needed for the puppies to reach weaning age.

You see, Mrs. Williamson was under enough tension already: she was in the process of getting a divorce from Mr. Williamson – yes, the same Mr. Williamson who had closed the garage door on little Sachi by accident – and the divorce was getting ugly. It would be a great burden for Mrs. Williamson to accommodate the puppies feeding schedule while at the same time looking for a new home and having to deal with her legal situation. But would the puppies be any better off starting their lives in new homes? Even though their eyes and ears had just fully opened, and they were finally able to do some directional belly crawling, they were still wee babies.

That was the quandary: should the pups stay with Mrs. Williamson, or should they be adopted out to new homes? In actuality, both situations really sucked. If the puppies stayed with Mrs. Williamson, they were unlikely to thrive physically, as she would probably not be able to feed them on demand. In that case, the puppies would miss meals here and there, and considering that they had little or no body fat and no blood sugar reserves, even that small margin of error in caloric intake could quickly prove to be fatal. However, if the puppies went their separate ways to new homes, one important aspect of their socialization would be lost: the discovery of how to play, so they could learn the finer points of biting and not biting. Mrs. Williamson needed to decide one way or the other soon, since her mental vigor was declining as fast as her stress level was rising, and the Sachi crisis had been yet another unexpected blow. What Mrs. Williamson needed was an answer to her question: how deleterious would it be for a puppy to be adopted at three weeks of age, instead of the traditional eight weeks of age?

In truth, such an early adoption would potentially be quite damaging. Here is why: the most crucial time for puppy socialization is during the first three months of life, during which puppyhood sociability outweighs fear. A puppy under twelve weeks of age is genetically programmed to adapt and will explore his environment with inquisitiveness instead of apprehension; during this period, he will investigate his surroundings with healthy curiosity rather than intense trepidation. If improper, incomplete, or deficient socialization occurs during this crucial window of opportunity, the ability to adapt to new people (e.g., erratically behaving young children), new situations, and other animals is significantly affected. For example, if you wish to acquire a gundog puppy – such as a Retriever – for duck hunting, gently introducing the puppy to the sound of gunshots while still under three months of age would be beneficial. Starting the gunshot lesson when the pup is two years old and on his first hunting trip would probably elicit a very different response. You would likely see indifference in the first case, and a fear reaction in the second.

The reason for such a distinction in responses? The timing of the lessons. If the Retriever puppy is habituated to gunshots in the background while still with his mother and littermates at seven weeks of age, and he sees his mother reacting calmly to the sharp cracks of gunfire, the puppy learns that gunshot sounds are of no concern. On the other paw, if a puppy reaches two years of age before being exposed for the first time to gunshot sounds, during a weekend training session in which his hunting owner makes him heel and stay while rounds of ammunition are being blasted into the sky, the young gundog is likely to react with a fear response that may be difficult to erase.

Any behavioral problems that can be eliminated or mitigated easily should be addressed as early as possible, to avoid the number one cause of death in dogs under the age of three: behavioral issues leading to abandonment and euthanasia, according to the AVSAB (American Veterinary Society of Animal Behavior). More so than at any other age, puppies should be properly handled from birth to three months of age, so they learn to accept touching and manipulation of all body parts. Until they reach three months of age, puppies should be encouraged to explore their environment in a safe manner so they can start making positive associations about objects and living beings. The primary aim during this intense period of socialization is to end all new experiences on a happy and encouraging note. At the same time, owners should avoid overwhelming the puppies with excessive experiences, especially if some fear is evident.

Socializing puppies does not imply that we should throw them in with a pack of other dogs or a bunch of screaming kids, but rather that we should carefully and safely introduce them to a wide range of experiences that they will grow to accept and not fear. Dear reader and dog lover, you are likely aware that learning is very often contextual. In other words, a dog may learn something within the specific context in which it was taught, but may not be able to apply it to another context. In our example of the gundog puppy, the pup has learned that the sharp, loud noises associated with gunshots are nothing to worry about when he is with his mother and littermates, but that is only a starting point. Our puppy in training for hunting will need plenty of positive reinforcement when exposed to gunshots in different places with different people while still in the puppyhood stage.

Returning to Mrs. Williamson's dilemma, let's look more closely at the choices for her three-week-old puppies. Should they stay with her as a group, and probably not get much social interaction or stimulation?

Or should they all be immediately dispersed to new adoptive homes? Even with the lack of sufficient data to support the stance, I would go out on a limb to say that underage (i.e., less than seven to eight weeks of age) puppies raised alone are the ones most at risk for behavioral problems later in life. An underage singleton puppy faces a significant likelihood of missing out on opportunities to learn proper canine social skills, since we humans are poor imitations of dogs and no substitute for canine littermates. (Perhaps that is a blessing!) However, we are talking about Chihuahua puppies here and not Rottweiler or Mastiff puppies; for the latter two groups, a missed opportunity to learn proper bite inhibition would create enormous risk on a totally different scale. At the very least, if Sachi's puppies were sent to adoptive homes, the best-case scenario – to ensure that they would be well adjusted – would be to send them in pairs and not solo, so the puppies could continue their apprenticeship in canine behavioral skills with a canine mate.

In the end, it was hard not to be impressed with Mrs. Williamson's decision. Considering her current hardships in life and her desire to avoid further fueling her guilty conscience after Sachi's loss, albeit by accident, she opted for the best scenario possible for her Chihuahua puppies. She hired a neighbor who worked from home to help her look after the puppies until they were eight weeks old, at which time they would be sold. Accordingly, the neighbor maintained a regular puppy formula feeding schedule for the pups, with a weaning transition to commercial puppy dog food at five weeks of age. Both Mrs. Williamson and her neighbor pitched in to provide proper socialization for the puppies – this really was the fun part of having the puppies around, and made the entire poop cleanup worthwhile.

Once all the Chihuahua puppies were placed into their new homes, Mrs. Williamson paid her neighbor from the proceeds of the puppy sales. Mrs. Williamson's dog days were over, but – just like the best kind of puppy socialization – her saga ended on a good note, without fear and without regrets.

As a dog lover, you can…

- Be aware of the importance of early socialization for puppies, especially during the first three months of life, and its impact on the animals' adult behavior.

- Be wary of breeders or pet stores that offer very young puppies for sale.

- Before acquiring a puppy, learn as much as you can about canine socialization and strategies for raising puppies to become healthy and socially well-adjusted adult dogs.

CHAPTER 34

Party Time:
the painful aftermath

Barnaby sure knew how to party. At ten months of age, with boundless energy and a wagging tail, this yellow Lab puppy was a crowd pleaser. And Barnaby had impeccable manners: he would greet guests at the door, sit when requested, and shake a paw with each one in a gesture of welcome. He would then escort guests to the hors d'oeuvres table and sit at their feet, wagging his tail from side to side in hopes of charming some snacks out of them.

"How can you resist this little sweetheart?" a guest would exclaim, popping a morsel of something into his mouth.

Then another guest would come by: "Here's a little treat for you, Barnaby!"

"Don't tell anyone," the next person would whisper with a smile, "Here's another treat for you, boy!"

This was reinforcement at its best. Barnaby merely sat by the food table, sweeping the floor with his tail, and he was rewarded with tasty treats, one after the other. Not only did Barnaby learn the lesson well, he kept busy training all the new guests that came through the door. Barnaby was no doubt pleased with himself – his "human training" technique brought him a near 100 percent success rate, since just about everyone gave him some food.

Barnaby was a bright boy, and he had developed a perfect sequence of actions followed by rewards: doorbell rings, happy dance, shake a paw, escort guest to food table, sit and sweep the floor with tail, get food reward. How many guests? Nearly fifty! How many food rewards? Nearly fifty! What was not to like about that?

But there was one shortcoming in Barnaby's brain circuitry: his synapses were connected to the here and now, so he lived only in the present moment. Tomorrow did not exist, only "now" mattered, and every food treat was pure delight. As much as Barnaby had been the life of the party, he also managed to kill it quickly with the help of nearly fifty people. By mid-evening, Barnaby, sitting by the hors d'oeuvres table, suddenly did not feel so well anymore; his tail stopped sweeping the floor, and he started to heave loudly. Within moments, all the food given to Barnaby over the last hour had found its way back onto the floor, undigested and very smelly. And there was no keeping the treats a secret any longer, since everyone staring at the large pile of vomitus could identify exactly what they had fed Barnaby. Nearly all of the fifty guests got busted: no one said a word, but their guilty looks told the tale.

Barnaby's owner quickly took the Lab pup to the laundry room to recover – a bit late, since he should have been there from the moment the first guest arrived. Barnaby was fortunate: he ended up with an upset stomach that settled quickly once removed from the party and its temptations. Many dogs do not enjoy such a happy ending.

The most sensible approach when throwing a party is to ensure that your dogs are not part of the merry making. All too commonly, the presence of dogs at parties leads to two disasters: firstly, dietary indiscretions – as in Barnaby's case; and secondly, bite wounds inflicted on a guest. Let's leave the bite wound problem for another day, and focus on the risks of party food ingestion here.

The ASPCA (American Society for the Prevention of Cruelty to Animals) nutrition experts have compiled a list of the top ten "people foods" that should not be fed to our pets. Many of the items on the list are especially relevant to party situations. Others are unconventional items, such as xylitol, that reflect our modern lifestyle.

Xylitol

In North America, the use of xylitol, a white crystalline sugar alcohol used as a sugar substitute in many products, has grown rapidly over the last few years. Xylitol is increasingly found in foods such as sugar-free gum and candy, and is also available in a granulated form for baking. This food item is popular among diabetics and those who favor low-carbohydrate diets.

People can absorb xylitol slowly, with little to no effect on blood sugar or insulin levels. However, our canine companions are not so lucky: xylitol is absorbed relatively quickly into a dog's bloodstream and strongly promotes the release of insulin, which then causes profound hypoglycemia (low blood sugar). Significant ingestion of xylitol can lead to liver failure, bleeding, and death in dogs.

In theory, we know that as little as 0.1 gram per kilogram of body weight of xylitol can cause hypoglycemia, and according to the APCC (Animal Poison Control Center), over five times that dose can lead to more serious effects, such as liver failure. The problem with xylitol is that the exact amount ingested can be difficult to evaluate, since the xylitol content is not always listed on food products such as chewing gum.

If a dog has ingested too much xylitol, the first clinical sign of toxicity is vomiting, rapidly followed by lethargy from low blood sugar. If the amount of xylitol ingested was considerable, diarrhea, collapse and seizures may occur soon after. Blood work is helpful in identifying whether acute liver failure is developing.

Can xylitol poisoning be treated? Only symptomatically. Since xylitol is absorbed rapidly, any known ingestion observed in a dog warrants an emergency visit to a veterinary hospital. Unfortunately, there is no known antidote to xylitol, so symptomatic treatment is the sole recourse in cases of xylitol toxicity. It is important to keep in mind that the onset of clinical signs may be delayed by as much as twelve hours after ingestion.

Methylxanthines

Chocolate, coffee, and caffeine certainly please our taste buds and activate our brain cells, but all are deadly to dogs. These three food products contain substances called methylxanthines, well known for their adverse effect on canines. Vomiting and diarrhea, panting and hyperactivity, excessive thirst and urination, arrhythmias, seizures and death are the signature clinical signs of methylxanthine toxicity. The worst offender is dark baking chocolate, so keep brownies away from your dog!

Alcohol

For dogs, alcohol ingestion from alcoholic beverages often causes more than a tipsy state; it can also prompt a fast ride to the emergency room. Indeed, dogs can die from alcohol toxicity. Alcoholic drinks contain significant levels of ethanol or grain alcohol, which dogs have difficulty breaking down safely in their liver. Obviously, the greater the percentage of alcohol in an alcoholic beverage, and the smaller the dog, the greater the possibility of a fatal outcome. As a reminder, beer contains approximately 3 to 5 percent ethanol, wine 9 to 12 percent, and whiskey anywhere from 40 to 90 percent.

If we read the label on a bottle, we can determine the alcohol concentration by looking for the word "proof". The proof is equal to twice the percentage concentration, so if the proof is 80, then we can assume a 40 percent alcohol content. Puppies are at higher risk of toxicity when drinking alcoholic beverages left within reach – or perhaps given intentionally – since their organs, including the liver, are immature and cannot readily process some injurious substances. For dogs, alcoholic beverages and food products containing alcohol can cause vomiting, diarrhea, decreased coordination and staggering, depression, coma and even death.

Persin (Avocados)

Persin, a substance found in the leaves, fruit, seeds and bark of avocados, can cause vomiting and diarrhea in dogs. In rare cases, ingestion of avocado products may be fatal.

Macadamia Nuts

In veterinary medicine, macadamia nuts are a puzzle. Dogs suffering from macadamia nut toxicity will have impaired coordination in the hind legs, but the exact mechanism by which such toxicity occurs is still unknown. Furthermore, researchers have not yet been able to identify the particular agents that trigger the mechanism of action causing clinical signs of poisoning. Are certain constituents of the nuts to blame? Or could the toxic source be contaminants from processing, or mycotoxins, or other unidentified components? The specifics behind macadamia nut toxicity remain a mystery. In most cases, dogs develop an inability to stand or use their hind limbs within twelve hours of ingestion. Less commonly, depression, vomiting, tremors, and hyperthermia can also be present. The prognosis in most cases is extremely good: the majority of afflicted dogs return to normal within twenty-four to forty-eight hours.

Grapes and Raisins

Juicy as they are, grapes and raisins can be killers for dogs. As with macadamia nut toxicity, the specific mechanism of action by which grapes and raisins can harm dogs is unknown. Certainly, fungi, pesticides, and heavy metals have been ruled out so far. Researchers strongly suspect that the culprit is a water-soluble toxin within the flesh of the grape or raisin, rather than in the seed, since seedless grapes can also cause toxicity. To further thicken the plot, not every dog is susceptible. In fact, many canines can tolerate large quantities of grapes or raisins without any ill effects at all.

Despite scientific uncertainty about the specific toxic agent and the minimum ingested amount that causes toxicity, we do know that some cases of grape or raisin ingestion lead to acute kidney failure. When this condition develops, the prognosis is tentative at best unless early decontamination and fluid therapy are applied.

Raw Animal Products

Raw pet food diets are the subject of Chapter 11 ("Salmonella"), but worth a further mention here given the significant health concerns related to feeding raw animal products. Besides the obvious contamination from zoonotic (transmissible from animals to humans) bacteria such as Salmonella, E. coli, and Campylobacter when dogs ingest tainted raw or undercooked animal products such as meat and eggs, deficiencies can occur in the animals. In the case of raw eggs, a biotin (Vitamin B) deficiency can result from the presence of the enzyme avidin in egg whites.

The feeding of bones is covered in Chapter 6 ("Do Smart Dogs Bury Their Bones?"), but a reiteration of certain key facts may be useful: the alimentary tract of domestic dogs has evolved very differently from that of their wolf ancestors, so processing bones is not easy for today's small breeds such as the Maltese or Poodle. Also, wolves may be better at processing bones because they simultaneously ingest a large amount of hide and fur to cushion the sharp edges. This is rarely the case with domestic dogs.

Yeast

Dogs should never have access to dough that contains yeast. Ingestion of this food item can cause the animal severe discomfort and pain, as the stomach dilates excessively from the action of the rising yeast. Since the risk diminishes after the dough is cooked (when the yeast has fully risen), pets can have small bits of bread as treats. For dogs that have an allergy to wheat, however, feeding bread is not recommended. Wheat is one of three carbohydrates that commonly cause allergies in dogs; the other two are corn and soy.

Onions, Garlic, and Chives

These three from the vegetable and herb family, if ingested in large quantities, can trigger gastrointestinal irritation in dogs. If untreated, this condition can potentially lead to red blood cell damage with ensuing anemia.

Milk

Dogs are known to be lactose intolerant, since they do not possess significant amounts of the enzyme lactase, which is necessary to break down the sugar lactose in milk and other milk-based products. Due to this intolerance, ingestion of milk often causes diarrhea in dogs.

Party treats pose a significant risk to dogs because they typically contain so many of the food ingredients that are dangerous or potentially toxic to canines. So do yourself and your dog a favor, and lock him away someplace safe whenever you decide to throw a party. You'll be glad you did. Barnaby, to your mat!

As a dog lover, you can...

- Become familiar with the list of food products that can be harmful or toxic to your dog.

- Resist the temptation to feed your dog any treats that potentially contain harmful ingredients.

- During parties or large gatherings, ensure that your dog is confined to a safe place where he cannot help himself to risky treats, and where well-meaning guests cannot feed him.

CHAPTER 35

Fatal Attraction:
to neuter or not

Two-year-old Pepper was a lucky boy: the gentle Miniature Schnauzer could still boast ownership of a pair of precious baubles, which surely made him the envy of all his canine pals at the dog park. Yes, Pepper still had two functional testicles. And to his owner's knowledge, these little charmers had not yet been put to any effective use. That, however, was about to change.

Pepper, co-owned by his breeder and Mrs. Hogan, who currently looked after him, had already won several breed championships, and his breeder had retained breeding rights on the young Schnauzer. So, depending how well Pepper did in conformation and obedience competitions, his breeder had the option of using him for stud services. Mrs. Hogan was happy to oblige, as Pepper had brought plenty of life and activity into her household. Her weekends had always been organized around his grooming sessions, training sessions, and dog shows in various cities. Wherever he went, Pepper was a guaranteed hit: he had a dynamite personality; alert eyes that tracked all nearby action; and short, cropped ears that homed in like radar antennas to any unfamiliar sounds that captured his interest.

Pepper was presented to our emergency service because he appeared seriously unwell – although he seemed to have perked up remarkably since entering our facility. According to Mrs. Hogan, Pepper had been panting incessantly, vocalizing and whining as though in severe pain, and pacing restlessly through the house. Concerned, Mrs. Hogan had taken Pepper out into her fenced backyard, but the dog had continued his erratic behavior.

Pepper's problem was not immediately apparent, so we started with some routine questions about his vital functions. "Has he been eating and drinking normally?" I asked Mrs. Hogan.

"Yes," she replied. In fact, Mrs. Hogan's answer was the same for every one of my questions. Pepper had a normal urination pattern (for an unneutered male). He had normal stools that were pickable and kickable. In fact, all his vital functions appeared stable. So what was the problem here?

We moved on to Pepper's physical exam, which was equally uneventful. And by the time the exam was over, Pepper was once again back to his usual calm, friendly, and curious self.

From a veterinary perspective, a concern always exists that animals might hide their illness when in a strange environment, especially if it is crowded with white lab coats, the smell of alcohol (not the drinkable sort!), and no doubt some lingering fear pheromones from previous dog patients floating in the air. Since Mrs. Hogan had to run some errands, we agreed to keep Pepper at the clinic for a couple of hours to monitor his state. During his stay, no treatments were prescribed, and no diagnostic work was performed: Pepper was definitely himself.

Upon his owner's return, Pepper greeted her with his customary happy dance, then hopped into the back seat of Mrs. Hogan's sedan, clearly excited to return home. Mrs. Hogan lived only five kilometers away, and that distance by car from our hospital took only nine minutes – which was exactly how long it took for Mrs. Hogan to contact our receptionist.

"It's Pepper again!" she exclaimed, "As soon as he jumped out of the car, he started to whine and pace as though he wanted to run away.

Thankfully, I still had him leashed! I thought maybe he had diarrhea and needed to have a bowel movement…but there was nothing. What should I do?" The poor woman sounded like she was at her wits' end.

Well, it was pretty obvious to us what Mrs. Hogan needed to do: she needed to either tolerate Pepper's problem for a week or so, or move to a different area for a while. The sharp and abrupt contrast between Pepper's behavior at home and his behavior at the clinic made the diagnosis very evident. But Mrs. Hogan didn't believe it, so she loaded Pepper right back into her sedan and drove once again to our facility to sit with her dog in our waiting area. In no time at all, Pepper settled right down again, sitting calmly with ears perked and eyes attentive.

Shocked, Mrs. Hogan reluctantly agreed with our earlier diagnosis – there was no doubting it any longer. Pepper had picked up the scent of a bitch in heat in his neighborhood, and it was driving him hormonally crazy. His instincts, loaded with testosterone from his intact testicles, were urging him to seek out his beloved – albeit unknown – paramour. Wherever she was, he was determined to find her.

An unspayed female dog will come into heat roughly every six months, and start to spot a small amount of blood from her vulva for about a week. Then, as the bleeding recedes during the second week, the female is considered officially in estrous, a stage in which she will accept any compatible male and form a sexual tie with him. In dog breeding, a tie is achieved when a stud mounts a receptive female with successful penetration, then turns 180 degrees so that the dogs are facing away from each other, bum to bum. A "tie" is thus formed, and both dogs might remain in such a position – facing opposite horizons – for up to half an hour in some cases. The tie is held firmly in place by the engorgement of the bulbourethral glands situated along the long axis of the male's penis. When the male dog is excited, these glands become engorged and visible.

By the time she left the clinic, Mrs. Hogan understood that until the neighborhood bitch was no longer in heat, or no longer nearby, Pepper was destined to have sex on his mind and might be difficult to control. For the duration of his one-track focus, Mrs. Hogan knew she needed to keep an eye on Pepper and a leash secured around his neck at all times. Male dogs that catch the scent of a female in heat will single-mindedly and relentlessly scale chain-linked fences, chew through walls and flooring, and run through traffic to find the source of the captivating aphrodisiac pheromone.

That was precisely what happened to Pepper. As Mrs. Hogan answered her front door one day, Pepper scooted between her legs and took off running across the street. Grabbing a leash, Mrs. Hogan quickly started after Pepper, but soon lost sight of him as he raced through neighbors' front yards and back yards, dodging trees and leaping fences. The lovestruck dog was clearly on a mission.

Then a sudden screech of brakes chilled her blood to the bones: it came from the direction into which Pepper had disappeared. With her heart in her throat, a frantic Mrs. Hogan ran toward the sound. Within moments, she came upon the dreaded scene; her stomach instantly knotted as tears sprang to her eyes. Mrs. Hogan could not believe what she was seeing: Pepper's seemingly lifeless body lay under the back wheels of a pickup truck. The driver was already out of his vehicle, bent over and trying to reach the dog's body.

Pepper was alive, but thankfully unconscious; had he been conscious, he would have been in terrible pain. The skin of his torso had split from the impact of the tire, and there was a gaping strip – some five to seven centimeters wide – on his trunk between the front and hind legs. His flesh, though barely bleeding, was fully exposed, with gravel and road dirt embedded in the raw tissue. The driver of the truck that had hit Pepper was finally able to retrieve the limp dog without fear of being bitten, and he drove the unconscious animal, with a very distraught Mrs. Hogan beside him, right back to our emergency service.

Upon the injured dog's arrival, a quick assessment revealed that Pepper was in physiological shock: his gums were pale, despite no external evidence of massive blood loss; his heart was beating very fast; and his breathing was inconsistent. Pepper had a flail (abnormal) chest: two or three ribs were cracked near where the skin had been torn off his body. On chest auscultation, wheezes and crackles were easily audible on the left side where his ribs were fractured. The dog's pupils were of different sizes (a condition called anisocoria, indicative of head trauma), but worse yet, they were totally unresponsive to light, a poor prognostic indicator.

Pepper was already hooked to an IV pump to maintain perfusion (hydration), and as the exam proceeded, we applied warm wet sterile gauzes to the exposed flesh on his trunk, surrounded his body with heating pads, and gave him pain medication intravenously. His abdomen felt fluid-filled, and a quick tap revealed frank (unmistakable) blood: likely either his spleen or liver had ruptured. We had drawn a blood sample when the IV catheter was inserted and, after a three-minute spin in the centrifuge, the sample confirmed another poor prognostic indicator: two of his liver enzymes were markedly increased suggesting significant liver damage. A firm body wrap was applied over Pepper's trunk where the skin had separated, to apply some pressure in hopes of slowing down the abdominal bleeding.

The next steps needed to proceed with urgency, once Mrs. Hogan authorized them. Pepper needed a blood transfusion, full body radiographs to further evaluate internal damage to the chest, abdomen, and skeletal system, and then prep for surgery to stop the bleeding, provided there were no further complications.

Before we had even had a chance to relay all this information to Mrs. Hogan, Pepper gently and quietly slipped away from us. There was no struggle; he simply stopped inhaling air. His EKG, which had been emitting a fast beep with the rhythm of his heart rate, was now no more than a dull continuous tone. There was nothing more we could do for the gentle Schnauzer.

Of all Pepper's injuries, the rapid abdominal bleeding was likely the factor that claimed his life. Indeed, his abdomen had further enlarged since the time of his admission. Had he not suffered from internal hemorrhages, however, Pepper would still have had no guarantee of survival. His neurological trauma had been significant, and the extent of it could not be thoroughly evaluated given the dog's unconscious state.

Furthermore, if Pepper had survived, total skin reconstruction surgery would have been necessary, involving months of pain and infection management, daily bandaging and likely supportive therapy with ongoing IV fluids – an enormous challenge and pure misery for any four-legged animal. In spite of all the sadness surrounding the loss of Pepper, the medical team was relieved that Mrs. Hogan would not be confronted with such difficult decisions in the future. She was already feeling tremendously guilty that Pepper had escaped her house and she had been unable to capture him before the accident.

"It all happened so fast!" Mrs. Hogan kept repeating. And it had. There was little she could have done once the hormone-addled dog had bolted for freedom.

At his owner's request, Pepper's body was sent for cremation. From then on, Mrs. Hogan kept her precious dog's ashes in an urn adorned with a picture of him strutting his stuff at a national dog show where he had captured "Best in Show". Mrs. Hogan's wish, as confided to us, was to have her own ashes (when her time came) mingled with Pepper's, to be dispersed together for eternity.

Upon reflection after the Miniature Schnauzer's untimely death, we might ask the question: if Pepper had been castrated (i.e., neutered), would he have been hit by a car? Likely not, as Pepper was a well-behaved show dog, and this had been the first – and only – time in his short life that he had been out of control. His escape had been totally testosterone driven, as demonstrated twice by his speedy return to a calm state once relocated beyond range of the scent of the bitch in heat (later identified as a large, friendly, brindle Mastiff, hardly a physical match for Pepper, who was only thirteen inches high).

The topic of castration in dogs used to be such a simple one. The surgery was generally advocated for four reasons: it prevented reproduction, and therefore canine overpopulation; it prevented males from roaming (true in Pepper's case); it reduced aggression; and it prevented cancers such as testicular cancer. Are all of these still true and valid arguments? And what is the appropriate age for castration? Should it still be done at six months of age? Should it be done at a later age, as some breeders advocate? Or should it be done sooner, as some shelters recommend?

Unfortunately, the topic of castration is no longer a simple one. It has become a divisive and controversial topic within the veterinary community, encompassing a wide array of medical and social engineering arguments. As an astute reader and dog lover, you are obviously seeking answers that will benefit your situation and your dog's, so you need facts and proven studies to back up the opinions you are about to formulate. With great trepidation, I anticipate that we will most likely let you down, given the dearth of epidemiological statistics on risk factors linked to disease development. This unfortunate lack of evidence is due to the absence of a critical denominator, namely the number of intact male dogs in any given population. At present, this is an elusive and unknown figure. Therefore, when we attempt to draw comparisons between neutered and non-neutered dogs in terms of disease incidence or behaviors, and a reliable count for the latter target population is unavailable, what conclusion can we possibly reach? Chances are we will simply conclude that the fly is deaf! One other important limiting factor is worth remembering here: an increased risk for disease is not the same as, or equal to, causality. In other words, exposure to a risk factor does not necessarily mean it will cause the disease.

Since we live in a practical world, however, we do have to make decisions about our companion animals. As long as we derive these decisions honestly, based on the knowledge at hand, we can rest assured that we are doing and achieving the best we can hope to do. So let's get bold and formulate some sensible statements and arguments. Here goes: intact male dogs are at increased risk of developing testicular disease and testicular cancer (this is a no-brainer), prostatic disease, and perineal hernias. Very little can be said about prostatic cancer in dogs, since incidence is low and rarely reported; castration does not appear to be protective against this cancer. According to many studies, a greater proportion of intact male dogs over five years of age suffer from BPH (Benign Prostatic Hyperplasia), or an enlarged prostate, a condition that our older male readers will certainly be familiar with. In dogs, this condition appears to be related to chronic bacterial infection of the prostate, which can remain a silent problem for years but may lead to kidney disease later in life.

On the basis of these medical facts alone, should you be convinced to remove perfectly normal body parts of male dogs? No, surely you would need more convincing! What if Pepper were brought back into the discussion? As we know, intact males are more prone to the effects of testosterone, which include a strong urge for random breeding, roaming, and in many cases, undesirable marking of fine couches and expensive carpets.

Conventional wisdom tells us that testosterone alone (or the presence of testicles) will not create aggression in dogs, as aggression is a learned behavior. If this type of behavior becomes problematic, however, retraining is more likely to be successful if the intact male loses his testicles. The added bonus of neutering an aggressive dog? The "aggressive" genes of such a dog are not passed on to the next generation!

These are some clear benefits that we can refer to when addressing the topic of neutering, but what about the disadvantages of such a medical procedure? With great reluctance, I offer to you the following quote from the American College of Theriogenologists and the Society for Theriogenology (theriogenology refers to the branch of veterinary medicine that deals with reproduction):

"On the other hand, the disadvantages of spaying or neutering may include increased risk of obesity, diabetes, osteosarcoma, hemangiosarcoma, prostatic adenocarcinoma, transitional cell carcinoma, urinary tract infections, urinary incontinence, autoimmune thyroiditis, hypothyroidism and hip dysplasia."

This quote may, of course, contain any number of deaf flies. Until well-designed, repeatable studies can be conducted on dogs, both intact and neutered, that share gene homogeneity and common environmental factors, the above findings will be difficult to verify with any certainty. For example, small-breed dogs have a very low incidence of hemangiosarcoma and osteosarcoma (bone cancer) compared to large-breed dogs. So how can neutering alone create such an effect? And how is it proposed to have such an effect?

The age at which neutering should occur is a very contentious issue that draws honest disagreement among animal scientists. From a social engineering point of view, if we are concerned about reducing the number of dogs euthanized in animal shelters every year, then we would likely support pediatric gonadectomy (gonads are the reproductive organs, and "ectomy" refers to removal), i.e., spay or neuter, performed at two months of age. Similarly, breeders who wish to prevent their dogs from entering the dark world of puppy mills are increasingly requesting gonadectomies before their breeding progeny leaves for new homes, thereby discouraging shady puppy mill owners with greedy minds and cold hearts. From an animal welfare point of view, this stance is both reasonable and admirable.

Traditionally, male dogs have been neutered at five to six months of age, an age at which the surgery can be performed relatively easily, with minimal pain to the patient (the testicles are smaller, hence a smaller incision with less bleeding) and a fast recovery. Less than two decades ago, however, such surgery was still performed with minimal post-operative analgesia.

Neutering dogs at an older age implies a slightly more invasive surgery due to larger testicles, but recovery should be equally uneventful, due to better anesthesia and modern analgesia techniques. Should we consider neutering dogs *after* puberty then, instead of before? Yes, especially if dealing with large or giant-breed dogs. The reason is that pre-puberty neutering seems to affect the growth plate closure of bones, i.e., bones grow for a longer period of time if the source of testosterone is removed before puberty. The result? A taller dog that may fail to develop the masculine, noble attributes typical of the breed. This may not matter to every dog owner, but every dog owner should at least know this. Furthermore, the delayed closure of the growth plates as a consequence of pre-puberty neutering is creating huge controversy in the veterinary world, since this factor can contribute to an increased risk of RACL (Ruptured Anterior Cruciate Ligament) of the knee joint.

There are convincing medical reasons for neutering, and others for leaving dogs intact. However, there are tremendous social reasons for neutering dogs, beyond the behavioral ones discussed here. These reasons would be undeniably compelling if we had to take a turn at operating the animal gas chambers that are still available and legal in animal shelters across the United States. Think about it: if we were forced to witness the heart-wrenching disposal of massive numbers of unwanted dogs and cats on a regular basis, could we possibly object to the neutering of male dogs?

As a dog lover, you can…

- Become familiar with both the medical and social pros and cons of neutering your male dog.

- Give serious consideration to having your dog neutered, unless you have a compelling reason not to.

- Do some research on vasectomy in dogs.

CHAPTER 36

Too Hot to Trot: heatstroke in dogs

For most people in northern latitudes, "summer" evokes images of picnics, swimming pools, sunburns, and mosquitoes. For veterinarians, as you might imagine, the word has a whole other connotation: when it isn't conjuring up delightful images of pustules and itchy skin in swimming Retrievers, ear problems in Cocker Spaniels, and eye infections in dogs that poke their heads out of moving car windows, the summer season invariably brings to mind heatstroke in dogs. This medical condition, which can result in death, is more often the result of an owner's ignorance than intentional cruelty. Most owners feel awful that they were not attuned to the clinical signs of their dog's mounting core body temperature, or that they poorly evaluated a potentially disastrous situation. Either way, dog owners who bring their afflicted pets in to the clinic are usually experiencing an extreme sense of guilt, and caring words from the medical team are in order – this is no time for lectures or reprimands.

Let's look at real-life examples of both situations, beginning with the case of Black Jack, whose owner missed the glaring warning signs of her dog's impending distress. Black Jack was a black Lab, and like all Labs, he was a pro at retrieving. Black Jack delighted everyone with his quick moves: he had a knack for spotting the flying tennis ball in the air, and could always predict the exact spot where it would first bounce. Invariably, at the right place and the right time, Black Jack would take a mighty leap and catch the ball in mid-air. Indeed, it was Black Jack's claim to fame that he could wear out any person at the game: he would retrieve endlessly, outlasting anyone throwing the ball – except on one sweltering hot summer day. There was a thick, heavy killer heat that day, so hot that people had to wear sandals when walking on the black pavement so as not to burn their feet.

That day, Black Jack had finally met his challenge in four small but indefatigable children who took turns throwing the ball to him *on the paved road.* Over and over they threw the ball, spelling each other off as the furry dog gamely raced to fetch it each time. How long could Black Jack play "retrieve the ball" on this very hot summer day, running back and forth on the tarry pavement? Not very long. Less than fifteen minutes into the game, Black Jack was panting so heavily that he finally ignored the ball as it bounced and went rolling in front of him. He stumbled forward and then collapsed, which sent the youngsters shrieking for help.

The mother of two of the children – who was also the dog's owner – immediately took Black Jack to the nearby river and immersed him in the frigid rushing currents. By the time she hauled him back out of the water, Black Jack was no better, so she promptly whisked him in to our veterinary hospital. When he arrived, moments later, he was truly in a sad state.

What could the owner have done, besides supervising the dog's activity level on such a hot day? Rather than immersing the big fellow's entire body in glacial water, she should have gotten Black Jack off the hot pavement immediately, moved him to a cooler area, such as a shady patch of grass or an air-conditioned room, and covered his body with wet, cold towels. A cooling fan, set at full speed and directed toward the dog from a meter away, would have enhanced water evaporation and cooled Black Jack much more effectively and prudently. As practical as it might seem, immersing a hyperthermic (severely overheated) dog in ice-cold water is never a good idea. Instead of cooling the animal's body, this ploy may have the adverse effect of causing vasoconstriction (constriction of blood vessels, decreasing blood flow to peripheral parts of the body), which in effect slows down the cooling of the core body temperature.

Let's step now into the medical world to better understand what actually happened to Black Jack. Upon his arrival at the clinic, the Lab's core body temperature, measured with a rectal thermometer, was 42°C (107°F). Clearly, he was in a state of extreme hyperthermia (41–43°C or 106–109.5°F), which can result in injury to body tissues. At this point, Black Jack was generating more heat than he was able to dissipate. Unless his core temperature came down quickly, he was in danger of suffering permanent and irreversible tissue injury. In fact, if his body temperature were to exceed 43.5°C (110°F) for more than just a few minutes, death would surely result.

Under normal circumstances, BJ's body temperature was kept relatively constant at 38–39°C (100–102°F) with the help of his hypothalamus, a small part of the brain that controls involuntary functions such as body temperature. As heat stress occurs, though, low blood pressure and hypovolemia (low blood volume) develop through well-known physiological processes. As a result of the decrease in circulating blood volume, heat loss through radiation and convection is also severely diminished, causing an elevation in body temperature. Heatstroke then strikes.

Although no one had noticed at the time, BJ would have shown some clear signs of heat stress. In most cases, excessive panting by the dog becomes obvious; indicators such as tachycardia (fast heart rate), and bounding pulses are also apparent. Vomiting, diarrhea, dehydration, and depression follow soon after. As heatstroke progresses, severe respiratory distress, cyanosis, and collapse would typically be observed. The previously elevated core body temperature would decrease to subnormal, as neurological signs such as seizures or coma herald an impending death. Fortunately for BJ, seizures and coma had not yet manifested. The overall prognosis for patients with heatstroke, such as BJ, depends on the length of time the animal has been hyperthermic, the amount of tissue damage that has occurred, and the animal's response to intensive supportive care. In some cases, even when the dog is fortunate enough to survive, he may recover with some lingering type of neurologic deficit.

Treatment of heatstroke depends on the condition of the dog at presentation. In BJ's case, we initiated immediate efforts to reduce core body temperature, by wrapping him with many wet, cold (not freezing, just cold) towels and setting up a fan to increase cooling by evaporation. We also inserted an IV line, and provided fluids to maintain good perfusion (blood flow to cells) and prevent tissue damage. BJ's blood parameters were monitored for twenty-four hours to evaluate possible organ damage to his brain, kidneys and liver, the primary targets of hyperthermia.

Although the black Lab remained tired and lacked a normal appetite for nearly a week after his heatstroke episode, he did recover with no lingering ill effects. Most likely, BJ survived his bout of severe heatstroke because he was young and athletic, and because he received medical assistance promptly. In heatstroke cases with unhappy endings, the dogs often fit a certain profile: they are typically old, obese, plagued with cardiovascular problems, or belonging to brachycephalic breeds, such as Bulldogs, Pugs, and Boston Terriers.

All too commonly, we see situations in which dog owners have poorly evaluated the risks of heatstroke. This unfortunate scenario is well illustrated by what happened to Felony and Perjury, two Weimaraners owned by a couple of lawyers. Felony and Perjury were travelling in the back seat of their owner's SUV on the day it happened. On her way home, Barrister Scarratt decided to make a quick detour to her favorite boutique. Since it was a hot day, she took care to park in the shade, and rolled the window down by a few centimeters before leaving the dogs alone inside. She intended to be away from the vehicle for less than five minutes.

Unfortunately, intentions do not always equate with reality. After many distractions, the dogs' owner finally returned to her vehicle thirty-five minutes later. By then, her SUV was no longer in the shade, and the dogs were clearly in distress. Both Felony and Perjury were salivating and panting heavily; they were unable to stand, and one of them had vomited bile. Their core temperature at that point was 40°C (roughly 104–105°F). Luckily for the over-heated Weimaraners, quick medical intervention to cool both dogs down – similar to the process described above – rapidly brought them back to a normal healthy state.

Sadly, heatstroke in dogs is a problem most often caused by human ignorance. As in people, the transition from simply being hot to being dangerously hyperthermic can be subtle and rapid in a dog. Quick intervention, aimed at cooling the animals down until medical help becomes available, is crucial to increasing chances of survival and decreasing permanent injury.

On hot days, prevention of heatstroke in canines calls for access to fresh water and shade, a decrease in exercise, and moving ambient air (i.e., a fan) when there is no cool breeze outdoors. By taking good care of your dog, you will ensure happy summer days for both of you.

As a dog lover, you can…

- Become familiar with the clinical signs of heatstroke in dogs.

- Prevent heatstroke in your dog by monitoring his activity level on hot days, and ensuring that he has access to fresh water and shade when outdoors.

- At the first signs of heatstroke, remove your dog from the hot area and reduce his core body temperature with wet, cold towels and a cooling fan.

- Seek prompt veterinary attention if your dog shows any clinical signs of heatstroke.

CHAPTER 37

Death by Drowning: the chilling facts

Mrs. Bradish: "Can Frenchies swim?"
Me: "Beg your pardon?"
Mrs. Bradish: "Can Frenchies swim? You know, French Bulldogs…I am told they cannot swim, correct?"

Me: "You are right, French Bulldogs cannot swim – they actually sink like a stone. If you take Peppe anywhere near water, Mrs. Bradish, he should wear a life jacket for safety, just like a young child. And he should be supervised at all times."

Mrs. Bradish: "Should he wear little water wings on his little front legs, for added safety?"

Me: "No, Peppe cannot swim because of the way he is built – he is too bulky and heavy. Only a life jacket, Mrs. Bradish, that's all. No water wings for Peppe!"

Under normal circumstances, I would have been amused by a conversation like this one, but at the time several cases of canine drowning had occurred in the area, the disturbing result of too many dogs walking on thin ice.

Just as I was getting ready to go into surgery one morning, an emergency phone call had come through: the EMS (Emergency

Medical Services) was on Highway 762, only eight minutes away from our veterinary hospital, with a large young Bouvier on board their ambulance. It was 10:30, and the dog had been spotted floundering in the frigid water of a nearby pond after he had broken through the ice about eighteen meters from shore. Since the accident happened in the countryside, the only service quickly available was the EMS. Despite the unusual request, the two qualified technicians were happy to oblige, if only to get some experience and be of service. It was their first time dealing with a canine emergency. And it was my first time dealing with a dog delivered by ambulance!

The EMS team had done well: upon arrival, they immediately provided us with the dog's TPR (Temperature, Pulse, Respiration), all in abnormal ranges. They also reported the results of their cursory physical examination: skin lacerations on both of the dog's front paws, likely from trying to claw his way out of the ice; pupils weakly responsive to light; patient in a semi-conscious state. The dog had been enveloped in heating blankets and was violently shivering, a good sign.

At that point, we did not know who the dog was; the person who first spotted him in the icy water was busy calling people in the area in an effort to locate his owner. In cases like this, our policy is to maintain life, stabilize all physiological conditions, and hold any further treatments not immediately required to sustain and maintain life until we get permission to go ahead from an owner, a guardian, or public authority.

Within minutes of the dog's arrival at Emergency, we began examining him, even as heating blankets were being transferred from the ambulance. An IV line was inserted to maintain blood pressure and perfusion (blood circulation), and to provide access for IV injections. On chest auscultation, we could hear some wheezes and crackles: he had obviously swallowed a mouthful of water into his lungs or had pulmonary edema (accumulation of fluids between tissue cells). The animal's mucous membranes were pale blue, with a sluggish capillary refill time (CRT). CRT measures the rate at which blood refills empty capillaries. This can be assessed by firmly pressing a finger over the gums until they turn white, then releasing and noting if the "return to pink" time is less than two seconds. CRT provides a quick – though imperfect – measure of peripheral perfusion.

The dog's heart rate was slow at fifty-two beats per minutes, adding to our urgency. We moved quickly to get a reading on his blood oxygen saturation level.

"Not good!" I muttered under my breath, "It's 89 – too low!" The blood saturation level, also known as SPO_2, should be closer to 95 to indicate normal levels of oxygen in circulating blood. We connected the dog to a pulse oximeter to monitor his blood pressure, all the while talking to him softly to reassure him. Poor fellow! He was in a strange environment, with people he did not know, suffering from a condition he did not understand – how frightening for him.

Would our unidentified canine patient survive? Yes, in all likelihood, he would, but he would need a little help to get through the next twenty-four hours. Before we delve into a treatment protocol for this dog, let's take a closer look at what happens to the body of a drowning victim so we can better understand how to fix it.

Drowning is defined as death from asphyxia (suffocation from a physical blockage of airways, causing oxygen deprivation) while submerged, or within twenty-four hours of submersion. Drowning can occur with or without aspiration of fluids into the lungs. All submersion victims will suffer from hypoxemia (inadequate oxygen in the blood), and some will suffer from pulmonary edema regardless of the amount of water aspirated. Drowning in salt water has a different physiological impact on the lungs than drowning in fresh water: submersion victims who have aspirated salt water end up dying slower than fresh water aspiration victims.

Two other water-related factors will influence the outcome of drowning. Can you guess what they are? Of course, the water temperature is one that has a significant impact on the survivability of submersion victims. Submersion in ice-cold water (below 5°C or 40°F), as in the case of this Bouvier, increases chances of survival, in part due to the diving reflex present in most mammals. In the diving reflex, signals sent via the nervous system cause bradycardia (slow heart rate), hypertension, and shunting or diversion of blood to the brain and heart. This mechanism helps protect these two major organs from low blood oxygen levels. Hypothermia (low body temperature) also helps to reduce the body's metabolic needs, thereby further protecting the brain.

The other important factor that influences outcome is the level of potential contamination within the water, since contaminants can reach the lungs in cases of aspiration. Fresh water lakes and ponds typically contain bacteria and protozoa, so if this dog had aspirated pond water, such contaminants might predispose him to pneumonia once he survived his initial hypoxic (low oxygen) insult. In cases of submersion in swimming pools, the contamination risk stems from another source: the chlorine may cause irritation of lung tissues, whereas suspended particulate matter is of less importance.

In cases of drowning from asphyxia, then, a state of low blood oxygen occurs due to either aspirated water or resulting pulmonary edema. Either way, the drowning victim is susceptible to heart failure and cerebral damage. Death by drowning is usually caused by a lack of oxygen to the brain and the ensuing cascading effects on other body organs, the heart in particular.

While we were still working on our patient, the receptionist interrupted with some welcome news. "His name is Jake!" she told us, "The owner is on her way, and has given permission to do whatever is needed to keep Jake alive and well!" What a relief.

Because of Jake's labored and shallow breathing, we took chest radiographs, stat: he had a diffuse light alveolar pattern in his lungs, indicating some pulmonary edema. While awaiting his blood results, we very cautiously administered a diuretic.

Just then, Mrs. Hudson – the dog's owner – walked through the door, tears streaming down her cheeks. "Will he be okay?" she asked, clearly distraught.

Leaving the team in charge of our patient, I took her aside for a quick update. "Okay, here's the preliminary assessment," I explained, "Jake is still hypothermic, but he'll likely be at a normal physiological temperature within the hour. His breathing is compromised, but should be under control within the next twenty-four hours. And his blood results will be out within the next few minutes."

Dear astute reader, you are now familiar with some of the damage that can occur to the body of a drowning victim. Had we covered all of our bases with Jake? The dog came in cold, so we started heat therapy. He had some crackling sounds in his chest, and physiological damage to his lungs – as confirmed by X-rays – so we started diuretic therapy to flush fluids out of his lung tissues. Finally, Jake seemed to be in circulatory shock, as evidenced by his pale blue gums and poor perfusion, so we started him on IV fluids.

But had we done everything possible to ensure Jake's survival? Absolutely not – we needed to get him some oxygen, and fast! The oxygen saturation level in his blood was much too low, and Jake was having obvious difficulty getting air moving through his water-infiltrated lungs. Basically, we needed to make sure that any air the dog breathed was saturated with oxygen.

When the blood results came in, we saw that Jake's blood cell counts and blood chemistry were within normal ranges, but his blood gas analysis indicated a mild metabolic acidosis that was already being corrected through his IV fluids with electrolytes and bicarbonates. No signs of infection yet on the blood work, thank goodness. But since he likely aspirated dirty pond water, we decided to take the added precaution of starting Jake on IV antibiotics that would cover both Gram-positive and Gram-negative bacterial infections. (Gram staining of bacteria is used to differentiate between two types of bacteria, based on the physical and chemical properties of their cell walls.)

With the help of an intranasal tube, Jake was kept on oxygen for just over an hour; due to his semi-comatose state, he had accepted intubation without objection. Thankfully, his oxygen saturation reading climbed to a level almost within normal ranges during that hour, as the diuretic was also taking effect. When he regained consciousness, Jake vehemently protested the nasal tube; he did not like the sensation of the tube through his nostrils, and pawed at it vigorously to let us know. Clearly, he was feeling better!

We continued monitoring Jake over the next twenty-four hours, a process that became increasingly difficult as his frustration grew. He repeatedly tried to chew his IV line off, and managed to get the line twisted around his body and limbs several times while doing 360s in his kennel, trying to find the perfect restful position. The following morning, Jake was declared fit to go home, a huge relief to all of us who had worked to save his life.

Once he was freed from the constricting tangle of tubes, the Bouvier's joy and enthusiasm knew no bounds. He engulfed his breakfast so fast that he immediately regurgitated it – only to re-ingest it again before we could get to him. This time, though, the food stayed in his stomach. Jake was indeed a happy Bouvier: his little stumpy tail was wagging with so much energy that his entire rear end swayed back and forth with the frantic rhythm of it. Obviously, he had suffered no neurological deficits from his submersion in the icy pond water. But Jake had been lucky: he survived only because a neighbor saw him struggling and flailing about in the water. A few more minutes, and the big friendly Bouvier would have drowned, no question.

Later that same week, Mrs. Redmond called to put us on alert that her three Bernese Mountain dogs were on the loose. Her property was well fenced to contain her dogs, but on that fateful morning her child had forgotten to close and latch the gate properly. The door of their pen was found open, so we can only speculate on what happened to entice them away. The three dogs – Willow, Aspen, and Cedar – probably caught a whiff of the scent of a deer, and went on a merry chase.

Two hours later, Mrs. Redmond began getting worried. Her dogs had escaped before, but they had never stayed away for so long. As we told her when she called, there had been no news or reports of them at our hospital. Very concerned by now, Mrs. Redmond decided to drive around to see if she could spot them on any of the nearby acreages.

An hour later, we learned the sad truth: Mrs. Redmond's three dogs had been found dead less than one kilometer from home. All three dogs had ventured out on a large icy pond and had broken through the ice. This was November and it was freezing outside; the thermometer that day had dipped down to -23°C (roughly -10°F). To make matters worse, each dog weighed nearly 45 kilograms and had a thick fur coat ready for winter. As soon as the dogs broke through the ice, their heavy, wet fur likely dragged them down. Very soon, they would have become numb from the bitterly cold water, further deterring their efforts to clamber out of the water.

Local firefighters were called in to retrieve the three large bodies from the icy pond; they went about their ghastly task in somber silence, with disbelief on their faces. All three dogs were cremated, and their ashes were buried the following spring on Mrs. Redmond's land where they had so happily spent their lives. In homage to their respective names, three trees – a willow, an aspen, and a cedar – were planted on the gravesite of Mrs. Redmond's beloved pets.

Most dogs, obviously, can swim. But very few are able to survive in the adverse conditions encountered by Mrs. Hudson's lucky Bouvier and Mrs. Redmond's unlucky Bernese Mountain dogs. In fact, some dogs – like Bulldogs – are likely to sink even in the saltiest water with increased buoyancy, such as the Dead Sea. The most common victims of drowning or near-drowning are dogs that fall through ice into frigid water, dogs afflicted with arthritis that swim in very cold water, and dogs that swim in rivers with strong currents .

So, while we assume that most dogs are able to swim, the reality is that they are relatively safe from drowning only if they are in top physical condition and swimming in "normal" bodies of water – not frigid, not contaminated, not tangled with weeds, not rife with currents or ice. In any circumstances other than normal, fatal submersion is a very real possibility.

As a dog lover, you can…

- Be aware that even healthy dogs that are strong swimmers can easily drown in adverse conditions.

- Monitor your dog closely when near frozen bodies of water or rushing river currents.

CHAPTER 38

Medical Errors:
how do they happen?

L ess than ten years into my practice, I faced the possibility of being sued for malpractice. Actually, I was being set up, though I was unaware of it at the time. For a full understanding of the context, we need to travel back to the 1990s, when the ostrich business was a fledging industry in North America. These giant flightless birds were purchased from farms in Africa, quarantined somewhere in Europe (often the Netherlands), and relocated to their new homes on Canadian farms usually in the middle of the winter. Freshly arrived, they were raised by farmers who had never seen such birds, and cared for by veterinarians who had never touched such birds. From an outside perspective, the birds and farmers seemed to be on an inevitable collision course, destined for disaster. Indeed, the ostrich industry did implode before the end of the century, not because of poor husbandry techniques or inadequate medical care, but due mainly to the absence of secondary market development. Overall, the transition from expensive breeding birds to affordable meat birds was unsuccessful, and sadly many entrepreneurial people lost both money and their farms.

Just how expensive were imported adult ostriches? In Canada, a trio of the birds (a male and two females of reproductive age) fetched $75,000, and babies were sold for $1000 per month of age (i.e., a ten month-old ostrich sold for $10,000) until reproductive age at two or three years old. Based on this formula, an adult would cost $25,000 at two years of age. Simple math for simple facts: the birds were expensive, not every bird was covered by insurance for various reasons, and an ostrich veterinarian could definitely not afford to practice without malpractice liability insurance. In those days, insurance coverage of $1 million was considered safe!

Ostriches had a deadly habit: they ingested everything in sight. How could anyone blame them? They had been plucked from a desert environment and flown to farms teeming with interesting objects, such as pens in people's pockets, tuques and mitts on children's heads and hands, shiny unlocked padlocks, ladies' necklaces and earrings, and entire boxes of nails left on the ground for fencing. Most of these foreign objects, if left in an ostrich digestive tract, led to the bird's premature death from impaction and obstruction, perforation and starvation.

Mr. Green had witnessed his "star" laying ostrich ingest a measuring tape and a screwdriver right in front of his eyes. He moved just in time to prevent her from swallowing a hammer. How did this happen? Mr. Green had been doing some repairs to the ostrich pen and inadvertently left his tool box open. It was an expensive mistake, but not a fatal one for Bonnie the ostrich. Unfortunately, Mr. Green had not bothered to take out any insurance on his birds, and surgery to remove the two foreign bodies from her stomach (proventriculus) was going to cost him over $1000. As I was soon to discover, Mr. Green was having second thoughts about ostrich farming: the sale price of ostriches was starting to drop along with demand, and Mr. Green was hoping to recoup the cost of this $25,000 hen.

Just as Bonnie the ostrich was being chemically sedated and prepared to surgery, Mr. Green pulled me aside. "So if Bonnie dies in surgery, can I sue you and get my money back on her?" he casually inquired.

Totally focused on Bonnie, I replied calmly, "If Bonnie dies in surgery, you can sue me – but you will have to prove negligence on my part, and that will not happen." As it turned out, Bonnie did well in surgery, the screwdriver and measuring tape recovered from her stomach were surrendered to her owner, and Mr. Green was subsequently fired as a client.

Dear dog lover, I realize you may not be an ostrich buff, but the story above illustrates all too well the world of medicine your beloved pets are about to enter, if they have not already. This is the world of "defensive" medicine. Yes, dogs die in the hands of professional health teams just as humans do. According to the *Journal of the American Medical Association* (JAMA), medical error is the third leading cause of human death in the US.[4]

Such data does not exist for our companion animals, since statistics are not compiled and reported consistently. In veterinary medicine, however, strong parallels can be drawn from the well-documented litigious world of human medicine. Consider the study from MSU (Michigan State University) performed by Dr. E. James Potchen[5] on human radiologist errors: a similar study done on animal-certified radiologists would likely yield comparable results. Dear dog lover, please indulge me in the following thread, as this information is crucial to understanding the evolution of defensive medicine, human failings, and the fact that radiologists may have too much imagination. In the MSU study, a series of sixty chest X-rays (or films), including some duplicates, were read by more than 100 certified radiologists. Several interesting and worrisome findings emerged from the study. The most fascinating finding was that if a radiologist looked at an X-ray for too long, the chances of hurting the patient increased. Indeed, after about thirty-eight seconds, many radiologists started to see things that were not really there. Creative

---

[4]Starfield, B. (2000). Is US health care really the best in the world? *JAMA, 284*(4), 483–485

[5]Potchen, E. J. (2006). Measuring observer performance on chest radiology: Some experiences. *Journal of the American College of Radiology, 3*(6), 423–432

diagnosing potentially leads to grave mistakes!

Another intriguing finding pointed to the significant variability in the ability to read X-rays. There was "inter-observer variability", in which radiologists disagreed among themselves an average of 20 percent of the time when asked if the film was normal. There was also "intra-observer" variability: when radiologists re-read the *same* series of chest X-rays at a later date, they contradicted their own earlier findings 5 to 10 percent of the time.

One X-ray in the series had been taken of a patient who was missing his left clavicle (collar bone). Surprisingly, 60 percent of the radiologists failed to notice the missing clavicle, which emphasizes the natural human tendency to focus on positive data and ignore negative data. This translates to our natural ability to see what is wrong with a picture in terms of what does not belong, as opposed to what is rightly missing from the picture. In the study, over sixty certified radiologists examined the patient's X-ray, and dismissed it as normal even though a significant bone was missing. Furthermore, when offered the clue that the chest X-rays were part of a series of studies to detect cancer, 17 percent of the radiologists *still* failed to identify the missing bone. We can conclude here that a specific clue can significantly improve performance, but to err is fatally human!

Understanding the subtleties of making a mistake is difficult not only for health professionals but also for the public at large. Let's not forget that health professionals have sworn an oath to practice medicine at a high standard, not at a level of perfection; the difference here is significant. Mistakes, negligence, and malpractice are three very distinct terms, with malpractice alone carrying a serious implication of legal action. A mistake is just that, a blunder. Negligence is carelessness, but not as grave as "gross negligence". Gross negligence implies seriously careless conduct that poses an unreasonably high degree of risk to others, whereas malpractice refers to unskilful and faulty medical or surgical treatment. For a plaintiff to be successful in a veterinary malpractice case, he must demonstrate to a court that the veterinarian had a duty to be careful and that the veterinarian failed in that duty, giving rise to damages.

In order for a health professional to dodge a malpractice lawsuit, justified or not, three elements must be present: competence, communication, and compassion. In some cases, a fourth element should be added: that the stars align properly for success. Some lawyers see the field of companion animal care as a huge financial goldmine, ripe for exploitation. In fact, several law schools, including Harvard University, have incorporated animal law into their curriculum to cater to this growing litigious aspect of the world. Consider the increasingly popular dog custody battles in divorce settlements, for example, or the push for change of pet ownership to "guardianship", the lobby to create a new animal property law category called "sentient property", and court cases creating precedents for emotional distress damages for the loss of a pet. Inevitably, these new trends affect the way veterinary practitioners handle animals under their care: an emerging need for defensive medicine translates into increasingly expensive treatment options to cover the soaring costs of malpractice insurance and the administration of a medical paper trail.

Despite changing trends in medicine, holding animal doctors accountable to the same standards as human doctors is difficult to imagine, for a couple of reasons. To better understand some of the differences between animal and human medicine, and their implications, let's follow Missy's footsteps into treatment.

Missy, a giant-breed Newfoundland weighing over fifty-five kilograms, came to us as a dog with glowing credentials: in the past, she had delivered three litters of purebred Newfoundland puppies, several of which had won championships. Missy was brought in for a clinic exam because she was feeling mildly lethargic, had a diminished appetite, and was leaking a green discharge from her vulva. In all likelihood, Missy was developing pyometra (pus in the uterus), a condition that often becomes fatal unless the pus-filled uterus is surgically removed. Confirming such a diagnosis calls for a complete blood panel and urine analysis and, at the very least, abdominal radiographs to evaluate the shape of the uterus and eliminate the possibility of other potential problems.

If Missy had been a person, she would have been sent to a laboratory for blood collection by a technician, and her blood panel analysis would be done by a pathologist. Then Missy would have gone to a radiology department to have films taken by a certified technologist and read by a radiologist. Once her diagnosis was confirmed, Missy the person would have been referred to a gynecologist for a preliminary evaluation and preparation for surgery. Before entering the surgery room, Missy the person would have had an IV line inserted to start fluid therapy, and an anesthesiologist would prepare and review her case. Once in surgery, Missy the person would be surrounded by computerized equipment that would provide both the gynecologist and anesthesiologist with complementary and essential data that could not be easily computed otherwise. A medical recovery team would have assisted Missy the person during her return to consciousness and kept her relatively pain free without any dire complications.

Now let's go back to Missy the dog. First of all, Missy's owner declared that she was low on money since she was completing some house renovations, so she simply could not afford all the diagnostic work for Missy. She agreed that the blood work was important, however, so she approved that step but declined any radiology study. Missy's owner viewed the use of an IV line with supporting fluids during surgery as an extraneous expense, so she decided against approving that as well.

"Missy is a tough dog, you know," her owner said proudly, "So I think we could also skip the painkillers and anti-inflammatories." Just like that, another treatment aspect was nixed! To save additional expense, the ailing Newfoundland's owner decided she would take Missy home as soon as she woke up, regardless of whether or not her vital functions had returned to normal. Missy's owner told us, with apparent pride, that she was an animal midwife and therefore felt confident that she could handle any possible emergencies that might arise. And besides, the plumber would be coming by to install her new ceramic sink before lunch.

By that point, it became abundantly clear that a perfect medical storm was brewing. The owner was dictating her dog's medical treatment based on her own personal convenience and willingness or capability to meet her veterinary financial obligations, *not* with

Missy's best interests in mind. Our Newfoundland patient's owner had already told us several times in the past that Missy, as the foundation bitch of her breeding program, was a star: she had produced a total of twenty-six registered puppies, which certainly enhanced her kennel's excellent reputation. Indeed, Missy's owner would have continued to breed her star bitch if not for this unexpected case of suspected pyometra.

Clearly, if the medical team proceeded with all the restrictions imposed on the dog's treatment plan, and anything went wrong with Missy, there would be serious grounds for malpractice, including performing major abdominal surgery without IV fluid therapy and adequate pain protocol – and all this based on a presumptive diagnosis. Furthermore, in the event of an unfavorable outcome, all the responsibility would fall to only one person – the veterinarian who took on so many roles. The veterinarian would be the one that took the blood sample and analyzed it. The veterinarian would be the one that helped take radiographs of Missy's abdomen, and then read the radiographic images. The veterinarian would also be the one that prepared the anesthetic protocol, implemented it via an IV catheter and endotracheal intubation (putting a tube in the trachea for air passage) to allow passage of anesthetic gases to keep Missy asleep, reviewed all surgical monitoring equipment, started surgery while at the same time monitoring the anesthetic and IV line, and then assisted Missy in her recovery after surgery, and implemented a pain and infection control protocol. Whew.

Although the veterinarian certainly would have benefited from the assistance of experienced staff, the monitoring of medical staff is yet another added function on the veterinarian's list of duties. If a member of the staff makes a mistake, the veterinarian takes the blow. If the veterinarian proceeds with the owner's imposed limitations, and harm comes to Missy, the veterinarian is fully exposed to a malpractice lawsuit. This is where defensive medicine takes a front row. Defensive medicine is about providing the best possible treatment in circumstances that may not be ideal, and obtaining the owner's consent to proceed. Not just any consent, but "informed" consent. This implies that a client should be provided with sufficient information so that a reasonable person in the client's position could make an intelligent and voluntary decision about whether to proceed with the proposed treatment plan. Informed consent is a simple concept but when applied clinically, complexities and ambiguities often arise regarding the content of the consent, as well as its process. In terms of the content, was there "full disclosure," and were all appropriate facts explained? In terms of the process, multiple variables come into play: did the practitioner's communication skills influence the process of informed consent? Did the maturity and intelligence of the owner affect the process? What about the interactions specific to the dog owner and the practitioner that day? For instance, was one of them hurried, or frazzled, or distracted?

If informed consent constitutes the first step of defensive medicine, the second step is the documentation of the consent and all ensuing aspects of the treatment plan – including client communication regarding the approved treatment plan. Not just any documentation, but "proper" documentation. The owner's signature and initials are required on several documents, to either permit or decline specific aspects of the treatment plan, including a DNR (Do Not Resuscitate) order. In the case of Missy the dog, her owner would have confirmed with her initials that IV supportive fluid therapy, radiographic surveys, adequate pain management protocol, and proper recovery procedure were all declined.

In the face of such owner demands, the practitioner then has two choices: to either proceed with a treatment plan that does not meet a minimum standard of care and remain optimistic that all will be well, or not. If the clinician opts to proceed, and any adverse consequences were to befall Missy (for example, an anesthetic death that could have been prevented if IV fluids were given), her owner could decide to take legal action for improper treatment. Then, rightly or not, the practitioner would have to spend a huge amount of time, energy and money to defend the position taken. On the other hand, the practitioner could decline to proceed with the abbreviated treatment plan based on the strong likelihood of a perfect storm and potential legal headaches, and refer Missy's owner elsewhere in hopes that she would hear the same treatment plan from another practitioner and finally acknowledge its importance to her animal's health.

The third component of defensive medicine, as highlighted through the dog owner's option of legal action if Missy were to suffer any harm, is adequate malpractice and liability insurance. Ideally, the insurance policy ensures that legal expenses are sufficiently covered (albeit not always and not necessarily the case); however, the practitioner's time and energy required for a lawsuit are not. Some insurance company guidelines invoke that no admission of guilt be expressed in the form of an apology to the injured party, for fear of endangering the outcome of future litigation. This is the rub! Not being able to say, "I am sorry I screwed up, and I will fix my mistake," when it needs to be said makes all the wheels squeak loudly in protest.

The unfortunate fallout of the increase in animal litigation is the escalation of medical costs for animal care. The time involved in obtaining and documenting informed consent, exceeding – or at least meeting – the minimum standard of care, and arranging ever more expensive malpractice insurance coverage leads directly to higher veterinary fees, which in turn make medical care less and less affordable for a larger portion of society. Due to the increase in litigation processes, veterinarians are becoming more reluctant to practice medicine at a "less than minimal" standard of care (even more so when financial pressures are applied), for fear of providing inadequate care and increasing potential harmful health consequences to their animal patients.

Dear reader, if you are a legal beagle, you have probably already raised two very important points of contention in our discussion so far, and I congratulate you for that. The first one is, of course, the question of animal ownership: who is legally defined as the owner? In Missy's case, for example, the husband may have brought Missy in for treatment and fully approved the treatment plan. But the wife could later declare that she was the dog's owner, not her husband, and refuse to pay for the full treatment. Similarly, if any untoward complications arose during Missy's recovery, the wife could take legal action on the grounds that, as the dog's real owner, she had not granted permission.

The second – and very sensitive – point of contention is the definition of minimum standard of care: what exactly does it mean? Currently, the standard is ill defined, the subject of variable regional regulations, and a fast moving target. It may not be a stretch to suggest that, in the not-too-distant future, omitting the recommendation of an MRI (Magnetic Resonance Imaging) as a diagnostic tool for animals could well be viewed as malpractice in diagnosing certain medical conditions.

We have tracked Missy's footsteps through a hypothetical treatment scenario to determine if animal doctors could and should be held accountable to the same degree as human doctors. The answer is no, for two obvious reasons among many: the higher *standard* of medical care for humans, and the higher *cost* of medical care for humans. You can certainly understand why surgeons and anesthesiologists would never consider proceeding with surgery on human patients without proper diagnostic work (e.g., blood analysis) beforehand. And to perform abdominal surgery without the basic support of IV fluid therapy would be condemned as heresy, if not total lunacy. These very essential components in human medicine are deemed by some animal owners to be less important in veterinary medicine. Such steps can be omitted for the sake of saving money, of course, but not without consequence: the omission may very well jeopardize a successful outcome for the animal patient. Since the minimum standard of care in human medicine is much higher than that in animal medicine, the cost of medical and surgical procedures in animals can be as little as one-tenth the cost of comparable procedures in humans. Some human physicians carry malpractice insurance coverage to the tune of six-digit figures. Needless to say, their incomes reflect that, and they are able to absorb that expenditure both financially and emotionally.

Such costly insurance is hardly feasible for veterinarians, however, since it would necessitate an incredibly sharp rise in the price of animal care, likely beyond the financial reach of the vast majority of the animal-owning population. This calls for the question: should pets be considered a luxury that only wealthy people can afford? What do *you* think?

As a dog lover, you can...

- Take full responsibility for your dog's health care, including any financial outlay necessary for maintaining his health.

- Realize that cutting corners in your dog's treatment can have dire consequences for the animal; avoid placing unnecessary restrictions on a vet-recommended treatment plan.

- Be aware that health practitioners are only human, and that even the most experienced and competent among them can make inadvertent errors.

- Understand the causal link between animal owners launching malpractice suits and the rising costs of animal care.

CHAPTER 39

The Tale of Liberty and the Dog Factory

Puppy mills do not exist. As a practicing clinician who sees puppies every week for health checks, I can tell you in all honesty: puppy mills do not exist. If they did exist, then every new puppy owner I have interacted with in the last decade has inadvertently lied to me. How could that be?

In my practice, every new puppy exam starts with the same question: "How long have you had your puppy, and where did it come from?" The reason I ask is to get some background on the mental and emotional, as well as the physical, health of the puppy. Naturally, a puppy found emaciated and comatose on the side of the road, or in a dumpster, will have a different start in life than a purebred puppy with papers in tow from a reputable breeder to attest to the genetic health of the parents. As you might imagine, the "dumped" puppy is very likely to have a gut crowded with undesirable worms, and minimal socialization. When I ask about the origin of a puppy, not once has an owner ever said, "From a puppy mill, what do you think?" The answers typically include "from an advert online," "from a pet store," "from a friend who has a farm," "from a rescue group," or even "from a guy selling them out of the back of his pickup in the mall parking lot." Not once has anyone uttered, with either pride or shame, "From a puppy mill in Missouri!"

If puppy mills actually exist, then where are all the puppies they produce? In truth, those puppies could be anywhere; they can potentially be found anytime a new owner acquires a puppy without having seen the breeding facility or the puppy's parents, especially the lactating bitch. Where does *your* puppy come from? Most dog owners who have adopted a puppy never suspect that their adorable new pet might have originated from a puppy mill. The reason for this is disturbingly simple: most prospective puppy owners have taken no precautions, and done little or no research, to ensure that the puppy they are about to purchase did not come from a dog factory farm or puppy mill (these terms are used interchangeably).

What exactly is a "puppy mill"? Simply put, a puppy mill (or dog factory) is an economic entity that specializes in dog breeding to produce and sell dogs for profit. As for any business venture, greater profit is realized when less money is spent on producing the goods (in this case, maintaining breeding stock and puppies). The focal point for widespread public outrage over puppy mills is the substandard care provided to factory dogs, especially the breeding stock that will never leave the farm (unlike the puppies, which are intended to be sold off), in order to create a greater profit for the owner. With monetary gain as the sole goal, business parameters set out for producing puppies reflect "the lowest cost possible" mindset in all production guidelines: food (cheapest versus most nutritious), health care (absence of disease prevention via vaccines and dewormers, lack of genetic testing, etc.), housing (small kennel areas, with minimal flooring and roofing), grooming (absence of), and socialization of puppies (absence of). A profit can be generated more quickly and easily when dog factories provide only the minimum requirements to keep dogs alive and able to breed.

If you wish to learn more about the short and miserable lives of dogs in puppy mills, a quick Google search for "puppy mill" will reveal plenty of information. But if you are faint-hearted or sensitive, beware: do not do a thorough search, and skip the photos.

Dog factories do exist, absolutely, but no one – including pet store owners – will admit that they are in possession of puppies originating from these mass-production facilities.

What, you might ask, is the harm in acquiring a puppy from a factory farm? After all, those puppies need good homes too, don't they? To find out, let's follow Liberty and her beleaguered, nameless mother (we'll call her "no name mother" or NNM) on their life journeys. Originally, NNM was a bouncy Pug, and like all Pugs, she endeavored to distribute as many face-washes as she could with her curled-up tongue to any human that came close to her. She came from a reputable breeder, who unknowingly sold her, at two months of age, to a broker with plans to ship the little Pug to a puppy mill in Quebec, Canada. Upon arrival at the mill, NNM started her new life in a cage barely one-and-a-quarter meters square. She received none of the lavish attention that most new puppies get from a loving family, nor was she ever taken for walks, let out for playtime, or allowed more than minimal interactions with humans or other dogs. The only physical contact she had with a warm body was at mealtimes, when food was deposited in her kennel, and during kennel cleanings, when an attendant came in briefly to swab the floor.

NNM started her professional life early: at six months of age, when she came into heat, she was placed into a larger kennel for four days with a stud Pug, to be impregnated. Her "teenage" pregnancy, two months in duration, went by uneventfully back in her one-and-a-quarter meter-square kennel, and ended with the birth of four tiny puppies, one of which was found dead in the kennel. Given how cramped her small kennel was after the arrival of her litter, it is likely that she accidentally rolled over the puppy and suffocated it.

Liberty was one of the three remaining live puppies, and at six weeks of age, barely weaned, she and her littermates were taken away from NNM. The little pups were packed into a shipping kennel along with many others from the dog factory farm, and loaded onto a truck to be shipped across the country. They had just been sold to a broker, who in turn would unload the puppies at different points of sale, always where the dog breeder and breeding stocks were conveniently nowhere to be seen. This alone – the absence of the dog breeder and, more importantly, the bitch – should send up an instant and very serious red flag for anyone looking for a puppy. Pugs are considered a "hot" breed and easily sell for over $1000 apiece. Up to this point, everyone had gained financially and encountered few, if any, challenges along the way. The money was changing hands as fast as Liberty and her littermates did – from the initial breeder who unknowingly sold NNM to a broker, to the factory farm breeder who then sold her three tiny puppies to another broker, to the broker who quickly unloaded the three puppies to a pet store and, finally, to the pet store owner who promptly sold all three puppies to unsuspecting buyers, along with dog food, bowls, leashes, collars, grooming kits, dog coats, house-training pads, and a series of puppy obedience classes.

Was Liberty a sound puppy to purchase as a pet? That depends entirely on your criteria. NNM had not received any preventive medical care, so Liberty came loaded with Coccidia, protozoan parasites that inhabit the gut and cause profuse liquid diarrhea. So guess who made money next? The veterinarian did! He did so by performing several fecal analyses, by transferring isotonic fluids to Liberty's little body because, at seven weeks of age, runny diarrhea is cause for rapid dehydration and, finally, by writing Liberty's new owner a prescription to eradicate the Coccidia parasites.

In hindsight, the protocol Liberty's adopter should have followed was to call the puppy's breeder to inquire if there were any problems with her littermates, and learn from that. Unfortunately, there was no identified breeder to call; that trail had already gone cold. With puppy mill puppies, cash in the bank means an end to all prior interactions – and an absence of any medical history that could benefit new puppy owners.

Who was the next one to make money from Liberty? Turns out it was the veterinarian again, as the little Pug was now losing fur, becoming bald around her paws and face. A few skin scrapings confirmed that Liberty was infested with Demodex mites, microscopic, cigar-shaped parasites embedded in her skin. She came to her new home with those crawling visitors already clinging to her small body. Demodex mites are normally transferred from mother to offspring through physical contact in the first few days of life. Most dogs grow up unaffected by the mites, and never show any of the clinical signs of their presence, such as baldness, bleeding or irritation of the skin. However, if the puppy becomes immunosuppressed (whereby its immune system becomes deficient) due to some physiological stress – such as the presence of other diseases or poor nutrition – or genetic weakness, the mites will proliferate and cause serious inflammation of the skin.

Since the presence of these mites often suggests a deficiency of the immune system, it is not at all surprising that the young Pug was infected, considering her first rough six weeks of life. In all likelihood, her littermates that had gone to other homes were also experiencing the same health problems as Liberty. Demodex is not an easy parasite to eradicate, and Liberty, despite appropriate medical treatment, was destined to host them for an entire year. This certainly made her less huggable, even though the mites do not spread to humans. Poor Liberty was half-bald by then, and nobody thought she was "cute" anymore. Due to Liberty's tender age and her previous bout of Coccidia diarrhea, as well as her obvious infection with Demodex, no vaccines were present in her system to ward off viral invaders. Unfortunately for the small Pug, that was exactly what prompted the next very expensive visit to the emergency animal hospital late one evening.

Prior to that visit, Liberty had been taken to the dog park at the edge of town, where coyotes roam. This was definitely not a prudent decision on the part of her owner, to take an unvaccinated dog to an area frequented by many canines. Little Liberty showed up at the emergency hospital totally listless and unable to lift her head, with profuse smelly, bloody diarrhea oozing from her anus. Needless to say, there was no tail wagging from the distressed puppy. Liberty had contracted parvovirus, for which there is no specific treatment, only supportive therapy necessary to sustain life. Parvovirus was barely known before the 1970s, when it became a major and catastrophic cause of death in dogs. Currently, vaccinations against the parvovirus are very effective and protective against the disease in young dogs. Prevention is, of course, much preferable to dealing with a disease for which there is no specific cure. In the experience of many clinicians who have treated such afflicted animals, if a parvovirus-infected puppy does not improve by the fourth day of supportive therapy, chances of survival are slim.

Fortunately for Liberty, she was back on her paws within four days, although her owner was another $1500 poorer. With life finally showing signs of stabilizing for Liberty and her owner, the Pug was banned from the dog park until her vaccine series was completed. This was done to protect Liberty from contagious diseases, such as the parvovirus she had just survived, and to prevent her from spreading the virus to other dogs through her excrement. At six months of age, Liberty was spayed; by then she was sporting a full coat of hair, and her Demodex days seemed behind her.

Then something unusual happened. Liberty met another small dog on one of her walks, and although it was all fun and games initially, she suddenly turned vicious, attacking the other dog despite his non-threatening demeanor and proper social greeting. Obviously, Liberty had misunderstood the dog's body language, probably due to the chaotic nature of her early socialization. Subsequently, she went on to attack other dogs under different circumstances.

Dear astute reader and dog lover, I suspect you can guess who next made a profit from our little Liberty. Indeed, it was the dog trainer whom Liberty tried to bite during the application of a firm correction after an unprovoked growling episode. Liberty's frustrated owners were at their wits' end with their misbehaving puppy and, this being a society of disposable pets, finally surrendered her to the local shelter due to her aggression. Liberty then underwent some behavioral testing by a trainer at the shelter, and he deemed her too aggressive to be adopted. After only three days at the shelter, Liberty was given a lethal injection that ended her short and difficult life. Sadly for the little Pug, this particular shelter had a low-kill – rather than a no-kill – policy.

You may wonder what happened to Liberty's mother, NNM, but

that story is even more disturbing. She went on to live her miserable little life in her miserably cramped kennel without any significant contact with humans. The only contact she had with other dogs was restricted to stud dogs every time she came into heat, about every two to six months after weaning a litter, and then her offspring for a brief time. Her puppies were routinely taken away from her at five to six weeks of age, to promote a prompt return to another productive estrous (heat) cycle. As it happened, NNM missed getting pregnant on two subsequent heat cycles, which had dire consequences for her: in business terms, it meant she had been fed for an entire year without any puppies to sell. NNM was no longer profitable, and certainly the cost of investigating her "sterility" was not affordable in the context of a factory farm. The only way to make money from her at that point was to send her to an auction, which is exactly what happened. This is where it pays for a puppy mill owner to be wise and choose the right type of auction, if his aim is to recoup as much money as possible from unwanted dogs.

There are several different types of dog auctions, albeit with some overlap in function and purpose. Generally speaking, the following is what a buyer can expect if in search of factory dogs. A complete kennel dispersal auction is held when a kennel is going out of business and selling off all equipment and dogs. A kennel reduction auction is self-explanatory: the business is downsizing. A complete breed dispersal auction indicates that a kennel operation is disposing of one or more of the breeds that the owner no longer wishes to carry. And a consignment sale is a venue for breeders from all over to rid themselves of unwanted breeding dogs. These dogs are usually the culls or "duds" of a kennel, and are sold to the highest bidder. This type of auction would appear to be a fit for NNM. Finally, there is the "Best of the Best" sale, for which there are restrictions in terms of the health and age of dogs; prices are relatively high in this type of auction, given that top quality breeding stocks are available. For a puppy mill owner, a complete kennel dispersal sale would be the most desirable place to buy dogs at a good price. Sure, there would be some culls in the bunch, but there would likely be some good quality animals too, given that someone is just going out of business.

Consignment sales, such as the one for which NNM was listed, are truly the bottom of the barrel, and avoided by most commercial breeders. The quality of dogs at these sales is definitely inferior, and even the most savvy "buyer beware" purchaser will likely make some disastrous acquisitions. However, these are precisely the auctions where most dogs in need of rescue will be found. This becomes the contentious point: should you attend these auctions and, in the name of humane charity, purchase some of these dogs that have suffered enough? Or, by doing so, are you now cleaning up the mess left by commercial breeders who will continue to thrive? Remember, dear dog lover, that these dogs have had minimal socialization and no house training. In all likelihood, many of them would require major dentistry work, as their teeth would be a mess due to longtime neglect and poor nutrition. The rehabilitation of these dogs would likely require solid financial backing, as well as the patience of an angel. From what we know, factory farm-produced dogs have had a difficult start in life: their early experiences, so critical to a normal development, may disrupt any chance of emotional stability later in life – as was possibly the case with Liberty. When a puppy such as Liberty is taken from her mother and littermates early in life, to be available for display at a pet store at her "cutest" stage, the consequences for the unsuspecting puppy adopter can be emotionally deleterious: such cases often end with either the surrender of the dog to a shelter or euthanasia.

Dear reader, if you have already done a cursory search on the web for puppy mills and dog auctions, you are no doubt aghast at what you have discovered. You may be wondering how it is possible for puppy mills, factory farms for dogs, and commercial breeding operations to thrive in our well-informed and compassionate society. After all, animal cruelty is animal cruelty, and who among us would willingly tolerate such cold-hearted disregard for the health of vulnerable animals?

First of all, the term "puppy mill" is a label that every dog breeder and every pet store owner vehemently denies; none will admit that it applies to them. Second, most prospective dog owners are ignorant to the fact they are about to purchase a dog from a mill. And third, animal shelters and government-run county pounds seem to be the only ones in the loop, since they bear the costs for the care and euthanasia of numerous unwanted dogs, many of which likely originate from puppy mills.

Puppy mills are allowed to thrive because current laws to restrict their activities are inadequate and ineffectual. Compare these laws to animal welfare regulations governing other agricultural enterprises raising animals, and the gap becomes evident. A farmer raising pigs to slaughter, for instance, will see his pigs slaughtered at a hundred and eighty days of age; chickens will be slaughtered at forty days of age for their meat; calves are slaughtered at a hundred days for their pale and anemic muscles, which are considered a restaurant delicacy; and lambs are slaughtered at a hundred and fifty days as spring lamb. Puppies raised on factory farms, like other livestock, would normally be destined to live twelve to fifteen years, but these can be miserable years due to either shoddy care or genetic diseases that have not been screened out of the breeding stock. These puppies, unlike livestock destined for a slaughterhouse, are in for the long haul. If lobbyists and politicians with questionable agendas did not interfere, stricter regulations aimed at enhancing the well-being of the dogs could be implemented, and would markedly reduce the profit margin of puppy mills.

For any business transaction to be completed, a product must be produced, and then said product must be sold. In the case of factory farms, the second half of the equation puts responsibility squarely on the buyers of mass-produced puppies. Often, such a transaction is completed because the prospective owner is simply not aware of the origin of the puppy. As mentioned earlier, one way this can be remedied is for the buyer to insist on negotiating with the breeder – not the broker – *and* visiting the breeding facility to see the lactating bitch with her puppies. Of course, we cannot be so naive as to think that this alone will solve the whole problem. The unsuspecting breeder who initially sold NNM to a broker honestly thought that NNM was going to a good home, where she would receive a name of her own and the love she deserved. He was later appalled and saddened to find out what had actually become of NNM. Many well-informed breeders address this problem by selling puppies at two months of age, already spayed or neutered.

Currently in our society, we allow and facilitate the unlimited breeding of dogs on factory farms, where they are raised in substandard conditions and then sold to brokers or outlets (such as pet stores) instead of directly to the final owner. By not speaking out against puppy mills, we tolerate the dismal lack of decent attempts to socialize breeding stock and puppies, and accept the continued absence of regulations for animal welfare that already exist in other livestock industries.

Why do we, as a society, need to mass-produce dogs, when millions are euthanized every year because there are not enough homes and hearts open to them? Imagine a world where every animal born is wanted, and has a home ready for it, where pets are not abandoned, neglected or mistreated. Imagine a world where dogs and cats are not routinely killed because they are "surplus." I ask you, as animal lovers: is that not a world worth striving for?

As a dog lover, you can…

- When adopting a dog, always ask questions about where the dog came from; if you have any doubts or concerns, ask to speak directly to the original owner or breeder, and be wary if there is no paper trail.

- When adopting a purebred, be sure to visit the breeding facility to see the dog's dam and littermates.

- Avoid purchasing puppies that have come – or may have come – from puppy mills (commercial breeders), so beware of internet and pet store buying .

- Speak out against puppy mills, and demand more effective and stringent animal welfare regulations to restrict their operation.

Epilogue

Dogs are entirely our invention. Through centuries of selective breeding, a full spectrum of dog variations has been created, for better and for worse. Historically, breeds of dogs emerged out of the purposeful intent of humans. Dogs were needed for specific jobs, and made significant contributions that enabled their human counterparts to live better and easier lives. Herding livestock, hunting down prey, keeping predators away, and exterminating pests such as rats were some of the skills that dogs of a bygone era could have slipped onto their resumes. However, most dogs shown today at official dog shows have been bred for their conformance to desired standards, and not for their inherent ability to perform certain jobs. Sure, retrievers still have an instinct to retrieve, if they can concentrate long enough and not be distracted by the temptation of food on the side. And yes, guard dogs still have an instinct to guard, if they do not become crippled with bone diseases. Likewise, herding dogs still have an instinctual drive to herd, but they have become somewhat less selective about what needs to be herded; some, tragically, have been known to run into fatal head-on collisions while attempting to "herd" fast-moving vehicles.

However, many dogs meet an untimely death because we, as their creators and caregivers, have gone a little awry in our intent. Too many breeders think they are being progressive in their practice of line breeding, i.e., breeding mother and son, or father and daughter, in incestuous couplings that nature never favors. In so doing, such breeders produce countless numbers of physically or mentally inept dogs. For instance, flat-coated retrievers evolved as a breed from very limited foundation stock and repeated line breeding; should we then be perplexed that such genetic homogeneity often produces fatal diseases, such as histiocytic sarcomas, in these retrievers before they reach middle age?

And what about dogs with strong instinctual performance remnants that suffer cruelly when used for unusual and unnatural purposes? Tragically, their demise becomes inevitable when their owners get frustrated because the dogs fail to fulfill an impossible mandate. As one example, how can a 59 kilogram Great Pyrenees dog, genetically programmed to patrol and guard, possibly adapt to condo living without a yard?

Since humans created dogs through selective breeding, it becomes our moral responsibility to take action and clean up the mess that fellow human beings have created for these innocent creatures. The 39 chapters of this book have revealed how ignorance can be cruel, negligence unkind, malice sometimes unintentional, and deliberate brutality always evil. The fact that gas chambers are still used to destroy unwanted companion dogs in many animal shelters in the United States is a chilling testament to our intentional blindness. We are all aware that dog factory farms, or puppy mills, not only exist but produce millions of puppies. Yet we remain blithely oblivious to the fact that our animal shelters destroy a surplus of four to six million pets per year in the USA alone.

Norm, a gentle and affable dog, was just one of the millions of casualties. Norm had been one of my patients for over five years when, unbeknownst to me, he was surrendered to a local shelter. The family was moving away, so Norm quickly became excess baggage. This lovable animal was a brown Coonhound mix with droopy eyes and lips, the former oozing love and the latter generous with wet kisses. But Norm had the misfortune of being dropped off at the shelter at the worst possible time: the place was severely overcrowded, and unwanted dogs had to be destroyed at a faster pace than usual to make room for the newcomers. In fact, Norm occupied the kennel of a previously abandoned dog that had been disposed of that very morning. Like his predecessor, Norm had exactly three days to find a human whose heart was filled with enough compassion to adopt an elderly dog (Norm was nine years old) afflicted with arthritis. Sadly, like so many other gentle and affable dogs, Norm ran out of time. He was "humanely" destroyed.

Is it not peculiar how intentional blindness transpires to shield us from reality? Perhaps it happens through the word play of semantics. We use terms such as "animal shelters," when in fact they also double as death row facilities. Shelter descriptors such as "low kill" and "no kill" are pronounced so quickly that an untrained ear can barely decipher the difference between them. And why should it matter, since no-kill shelters can only exist because there are low-kill shelters? We prefer to hear that four to six million pets are "euthanized" – rather than killed – every year in the USA, but the word "euthanized" implies a merciful end, performed with dignity and caring. Is that truly the case for every one of the millions of dogs that undergo batch killings, either by lethal injection or in gas chambers? The word "destroy" is likely more accurate, but so much more repulsive.

Current wisdom tells us that, of all the animals the medical profession treats, one third will likely recover by themselves and another third will heal despite our medical efforts, while the final third is the lucky group on which we make a real impact in improving their lives. In terms of numbers, the entire life's work of a single veterinary practitioner – about 40,000 animals – is wiped out in fewer than five days by low-kill shelters in the USA! Staggering as it is, this simple calculation should not be cause for despair, nor should it be an impediment to pursuing practical, simple and reasonable measures that can enhance the well being of our companion animals; rather, it should steer us to rethink issues that we may have thought were already resolved.

One of these issues is the termination of life, either unexpected or willful, as demonstrated through the many cautionary tales you have read in this book, and it is one of the greater paradoxes that dog lovers face. Although the decision of euthanasia for a beloved companion dog is emotionally difficult for most owners, it is much too easy for others. The intensity of the bond between a dog and his owner, and the compassionate aptitude of the owner – which can be fluid over time – are two major factors involved in making the critical decision for euthanasia. At a deeper level, how can an owner be brought to tears over having to euthanize a lifelong companion when he has no remorse about adopting a new puppy that originated in a puppy mill where animals live in constant distress? How is it that the same tearful owner who suffers emotional agony over the loss of his canine friend gives no thought to the millions of chickens and cattle raised on inhumane factory farms and brutally slaughtered every year? And how is it that this same tearful owner can cheerfully attend Greyhound races where racing dogs live almost exclusively in small cages, and healthy "surplus dogs" are disposed of in untold ways?

Why is it that our circle of compassion is so limited? Is it self-preservation that creates the intentional blindness at the core of our daily choices? Why is it so difficult for us to follow in the footsteps of the great humanitarian, Albert Schweitzer, who wrote, *"Compassion, in which all ethics must take root, can only attain its full breadth and depth if it embraces all living creatures and does not limit itself to mankind."* or alternately expressed, *"Until he extends his circle of compassion to include all living things, man will not himself find peace."*

In the context of the veterinary profession, I have earned the right and privilege of a license to kill. I am among the lucky ones: I can use this license on my own terms more than a hundred times a year. In larger animal shelters, that same number of dogs would be executed in a few days, in the most effectual and affordable way. It takes special people to do this janitorial work. Almost all of the cases in which I assist truly revolve around quality of life issues, which can be defined in terms of two main factors: physical well being or suffering, and the ability to have joy and meaning in life. Most of us equate pain with suffering, but that may be overly simplistic and not reflective of reality. We all know people who suffer great physical pain but lead purposeful lives within the confines or possibilities of their handicap. It is no different for dogs.

There is also a clear distinction between pain and discomfort as it impacts the joy of living. Let me explain: a dog suffering from severe hip arthritis may have learned to cope by altering its gait to inflict as little pressure as possible on its sore joints. The animal will walk with lameness, but with the aid of anti-inflammatory medication, will still experience joy in following its owners around and performing its daily routine, albeit at a slower pace. There is still meaning and joy in the life of this lame dog. The transition from discomfort to pain may be too subtle for human senses to easily detect, but other signs of the shift will be more apparent; most notably, the joy of living, i.e., accomplishing daily tasks beyond the survival basics such as eating, will dim significantly. We must be attuned to this change when it happens; we must also refrain from judging or blaming people whose perceptions of quality of life differ from what others regard as acceptable or appropriate.

A license to kill carries with it the responsibility to help people recognize the reality at hand and the options available. Inherent in such a responsibility is the implicit understanding that an animal's death will occur with dignity, caring and respect; anything less is likely to resonate with emotional discord at the core of our being.

Despite the sorrow in my soul when gently inducing death after a life not well lived, my being is also filled with warmth and hope in the realization that, once all the unnecessary issues of our contemporary lives are stripped away, there is much humanity in a human heart. Dogs, as our companion animals, have fully grasped the true essence of grace, which is to simply live life with all of its mysteries, placidly accept its uncertainties, and greet the present moment as it evolves before us. We, as animal lovers, have much to learn from them.

Acknowledgements

To be entrusted with the medical and surgical care of another being is truly an honor and a privilege. It is in all humility that I express my gratitude to all the animal owners and care-givers that have done so over my twenty years of practice. Every patient be it a dog, cat, horse, ostrich or tiger has taught me patience, love, and compassion especially in the last moments they have graced this earth.

The many and diverse topics covered in this book are based on my professional experience and I wish to thank profusely Dr. Daphne Barnes, Dr. Susanne Imorde, Susan Tompkins, Lori Rogers, and Judy Setrakov for their insights and suggestions to broaden my perspective. Mona Jorgensen and Cindy Brown have accompanied many animal patients to their last moments by my side and I thank them for their gentleness toward all involved. I am most grateful to Patricia Conrad who tirelessly edited this manuscript with incredible professionalism and enthusiasm and to Sue Impey who has contributed immensely as graphic designer *extraordinaire*.

To all of you that will take the time to read these non-fictional stories I wish to thank you. Perhaps together we can alleviate some suffering and slowly allow our circle of compassion to embrace all living beings.

Finally, I feel most fortunate that my husband Kim and my son Erik have shared my passion for veterinary medicine for so long and have untiringly accompanied me on so many late night emergencies and taken the time to listen to all my frustrations and satisfactions related to this professional venture. The reward truly is in the journey, and the company of such fine individuals makes it a delight.

If any errors have slipped in this book, I take full responsibility for them.

Note to Readers: *If you wish to help further...*

There are too many unwanted dogs gracing our planet. Dr. Judith Samson-French is leading the internationally-recognized **Dogs With No Names** *project to address this problem.*

Please purchase a copy of **Dogs With No Names : In Pursuit of Courage, Hope and Purpose.** *All profits are donated to Dogs With No Names.*

www.dogswithnonames.com

www.facebook.com/DogsWithNoNames

About the Author

An experienced veterinary clinician and surgeon with over 20 years of experience, Dr. Judith Samson-French owns and operates a veterinary hospital in the heart of the beautiful Rocky Mountain foothills. Dr. Samson-French acquired a BSc from McGill University and a MSc from the University of Alberta by completing a thesis on lungworm pneumonia in bighorn sheep. She received her doctorate in veterinary medicine from the Ontario Veterinary College.

Dr. Samson-French's experience with animals is multi-layered and diverse: she has worked at both the Calgary Zoo and the Honolulu Zoo, she has worked as an emergency veterinarian as well as a general practitioner, she has invested several years of her career to pursuing medicine and surgery for ratites (ostriches, emus, and rheas) in North America and Europe, and has pursued education in aquatic veterinary medicine, studying at the Woods Hole Oceanographic Institute and Bamfield Marine Station in western Canada.

She is currently leading an internationally-renowned project that involves implanting contraceptives in unwanted dogs on First Nations land to prevent the potential births of 100,000s dogs with no names.

She lives in Bragg Creek with her husband Kimberley Samson-French, her son Erik, three dogs and six donkeys. They have no cats.